The Utopian Vision
of H.G. Wells

The Utopian Vision of H.G. Wells

JUSTIN E.A. BUSCH

McFarland & Company, Inc., Publishers
Jefferson, North Carolina, and London

LIBRARY OF CONGRESS CATALOGUING-IN-PUBLICATION DATA

Busch, Justin E. A.
    The utopian vision of H.G. Wells / Justin E.A. Busch.
      p.   cm.
    Includes bibliographical references and index.

    ISBN 978-0-7864-4605-6
    softcover : 50# alkaline paper ♾

    1. Wells, H. G. (Herbert George), 1866–1946 — Criticism and interpretation.   2. Utopias in literature.   3. Future in literature.   I. Title.
PR5777.B76   2010
823'.912 — dc22   2009040805

British Library cataloguing data are available

©2009 Justin E. A. Busch. All rights reserved

No part of this book may be reproduced or transmitted in any form or by any means, electronic or mechanical, including photocopying or recording, or by any information storage and retrieval system, without permission in writing from the publisher.

On the cover: H.G. Wells, 1943 (photograph by Yousuf Karsh); background illustration ©2009 Bertrand Benoit

Manufactured in the United States of America

McFarland & Company, Inc., Publishers
   Box 611, Jefferson, North Carolina 28640
   www.mcfarlandpub.com

To the memory of my parents,

who had faith in me even when I lost faith in myself,
but who did not live to see that faith so rewarded:

Jeanne S. Busch (1930–1999), who introduced me to H.G. Wells, and
Norbert A. Busch (1930–2005), who nurtured my love of freedom.

My upbringing was not perfect, but it was utopian.
I shall be grateful always.

"This here Progress," said Mr Tom Smallways, "it keeps on."
"You'd hardly think it *could* keep on," said Mr Tom Smallways.*

"What is the *good* of it? Will there be any *finality* in your success?"
None whatever, is the answer. Why should there be?†

---

*H.G. Wells, *The War in the Air* *(Harmondsworth: Penguin, 1967), p. 9.*
†*H.G. Wells,* You Can't Be Too Careful *(New York City, G.P. Putnam's Sons, 1942), p. 298.*

Table of Contents

Introduction   1

1. The Individual   19
2. The Role of the Novel   42
3. The State   91
4. Freedom and Social Patterns   130
5. The Problem of Death   156

Chapter Notes   173
Bibliography   195
Index   201

Introduction

Coming at, and as, the climax of a century of geological and biological research, speculation, and writing, Darwinian evolutionary science altered radically the place of human beings within the natural world. The picture presented, of a set of blindly opportunistic insensate forces moving from extinction to extinction across sufferings and deaths untold toward an end in which the only certainty is utter dissolution, offered no vestige of a meaning, no prospect of amelioration. Suffering had long been known, of course, and even versions of the idea of evolution itself, yet never before had a single account explained them so comprehensively, so elegantly, or so starkly.

As the evidence in support of Darwin's theory mounted, thinkers and writers wrestled with its implications for human history and society. Some ignored the theory, or derided it as irrelevant[1]; others saw in it a justification for their own particular theories[2]; still others attempted to graft on a melioristic teleology of one sort or another.[3] Each of these efforts, to a greater or lesser degree, failed to recognize the most serious implication of the new science: in an evolutionary universe, any definition of what counted as human could be only arbitrary and provisional, since any basis for the definition was itself subject to change, to modification, and eventually to disappearance altogether. Nothing existed forever, and nothing came to rest, save only in extinction. The burden of proof rested with those who would claim some special dispensation from the cosmos for humanity. *Sub specie aeternitas* took on an entirely new meaning.

Some of those who discussed Darwinian theory confronted its consequences directly. One such person was T.H. Huxley, Darwin's staunch friend and advocate[4]; another was Huxley's most famous pupil, H.G. Wells. One of the earliest and most important works to explore in evocative detail the outcome of the process of evolution was Wells's novel *The Time Machine*, written in 1895.[5] Bound by the best science of his day, Wells projected his vision a much shorter distance into the future than would now be required, but its message remains untouched: humanity is subject to the same laws of decay and dissolution as the rest of the universe; there is no escaping the destiny of decadence and extinction. The Time Traveller finds our descendants, in the year 802,701, to be two vastly different, and by his standards sub-human, species, the Eloi and the Morlocks, the former serving as food for the latter. Escaping this nightmare, he leaps into what, in 1895, was the farthest plausible future:

> So I travelled, stopping ever and again, in great strides of a thousand years or more, drawn on by the mystery of the earth's fate, watching with a strange fascination the sun grow larger and duller in the westward sky, and the life of the old earth ebb away. At last, more than thirty million years hence, the huge red-hot dome of the sun had come to obscure nearly a tenth part of the darkling heavens.... The darkness grew apace; a cold wind began to blow in fresheninggusts from the east, and the showering white flakes in the air increased in number. From the edge of the sea came a ripple and a whisper. Beyond these lifeless sounds the world was silent. Silent? It would be hard to convey the stillness of it. All the sounds of man, the bleating of sheep, the cries of birds, the hum of insects, the stir that makes the background of our lives — all that was over. As the darkness thickened, the eddying flakes grew more abundant, dancing before my eyes; and the cold of the air more intense. At last, one by one, swiftly, one after the other, the white peaks of the distant hills vanished into blackness. The breeze rose to a moaning wind. I saw the black central shadow of the eclipse sweeping towards me. In another moment the pale stars alone were visible. All else was rayless obscurity. The sky was absolutely black.[6]

No comparable vision had been offered before. Not the death of an individual, or of a city, or even of a country is depicted here, but the end of life itself, an end guaranteed by the emotionless unconscious mechanistic forces operant throughout the universe and the laws of nature.

Wells's narrator found the vista unveiled by the Time Traveller unpalatable. "I, for my own part," he says, "cannot think that these latter days of weak experiment, fragmentary theory, and mutual discord are indeed man's culminating time." Although, as the narrator admits, the Time Traveller "saw in the growing pile of civilization only a foolish heaping that must inevitably fall back upon and destroy its makers in the end," the narrator, speaking with the voice which we now describe as Wellsian, insists that "If that is so, it remains for us to live as though it were not so."[7]

The question is how so to live.

This book is an examination of a Wellsian (although not necessarily Wells's own) answer to this conundrum. The Darwinian universe does not, perhaps, eradicate deity altogether, but it assuredly removes it from any daily concern with the affairs of humanity.[8] Meaning is not given, although whether it may be discovered or created remains at issue. Likewise purpose. For Wells, meaning must be created, but allowing for this requires the purposeful prior creation of a setting within which the individual can then act freely: a utopia. The term has a particular resonance for Wells, and it is important in reading what follows to keep in mind the distinction between three common types of imaginings about the future. A utopia is an idealized vision of a society which represents in some significant ways a major improvement over that of at least the writer and the intended readers. A dystopia would be a fictional account of a future state worse than that known to the author and first readers; an anti-utopia would be a fictional account intended to suggest that the idea of genuine future improvement of more than a marginal amount is either meaningless or impossible, whether because of "human nature" or the impossibility of defining "improvement," or what have you. I do not propose to enter into a debate over the proper classification of any particular work along these lines, but only to suggest that the categories themselves are both plausible and helpful. In either of the latter cases, though, the purpose of the author is presumably to suggest that some specific sort of approach to the future of humanity should be avoided, even if that approach is the utopian mentality itself; in this sense, that is to say the sense of having an eye on the best interests of humanity, even anti-utopians are interested in the same things as the utopians. Wells wrote both utopias and dystopias. He and I are mainly concerned with the former.

Any sort of pluralistic politics does not, and cannot, rest upon any metaphysical certainty; the political actions of humans rest, in the end, only upon the grounds which can be provided by the individual within a community, whether for or against it. Another of the questions stemming from the initial question — "What Are We to Do With Our Lives?" (itself the title of one of Wells's books) — has to do with the possibility of establishing those grounds without metaphysical justification yet in a manner public enough to warrant consideration and supportive action on the part of others. Such grounds needs must be social and flexible: the former in order to guarantee the possibility of genuine intersubjective understanding, and the latter in order to avoid stagnation and decay at both the personal and the political levels. The creation of a utopia, then, is a foundational moral act in the form of an answer to questions scarcely asked by most and completely unimagined by many. Such answers are widely variegated; a Wellsian one involves a form of idealized, or utopian, political theory which takes a combination of human freedom, compassion, and creativity as its foundation and goal. The focus of Wellsian utopian schemes is upon the individual, but in order to allow the individual the greatest range of hopes and action the whole apparatus of the utopian state, in fact of an indefinite number of sequential utopian states, is needed. As Wells insisted, "The fertilising conflict of individualities is the ultimate meaning of the personal life, and all our Utopias no more than schemes for bettering that interplay."[9] Accordingly, Wells offers depictions both of the sorts of individuals involved in the transition to utopia and as utopian inhabitants, and of the sorts of structures and organizations necessary to approach, and to maintain, the many states within which these individuals of the future are presumed to live. What follows will explore the grounds for these states, major aspects of the kinds of people who will create them, and of others who will inhabit them, and the components necessary for something to be truly utopian in a Wellsian sense. The topic is complex, and informed by many different strands of thought; a major portion of the book will be devoted to pulling together those strands and demonstrating their connection to a Wellsian vision. I say "*a* Wellsian vision" because, given Wells's exploration of a wide range of social and political ideas, both in fiction and nonfiction, over the course of more than fifty years of writing, it would be possible, by arbitrarily choosing to examine only one text, or a small group of texts closely connected chronologically, to arrive at an entirely different, yet quite Wellsian, utopian vision. Any fully coherent version of a large scale body of intellectual work produced over many years must inevitably leave out, gloss over, or reinterpret much. My task here is not to harmonize all of Wells's apparent contradictions, but rather to assemble and present a coherent Wellsian utopia which takes into account as much of his writing as possible. Many of those contradictions, nonetheless, I will show either to be not contradictions at all, or to be necessary for motivating yet another step along an infinite road. At the same time, since that vision is of a process, and not a finished product, I will attempt to demonstrate the impossibility of arriving at any such thing as a fixed utopia. Utopia recedes as we approach; this, in fact, is what gives it its value for Wells.

    My discussion of this theory, or set of theories, concerning utopia will be developed in two ways. One is a straightforward critical explication, development, and discussion of Wells's ideas as drawn from his texts and from the implications of those texts. Wells himself was no systematizer; nowhere does he develop in a linear explicatory fashion the whole of his utopian vision. Nor, indeed, could he have done so and remained true to the underlying nature of the vision itself. The body of his work provides, as in miniature did his novel

A Modern Utopia, "neither the set drama of the work of fiction you are accustomed to read, nor the set lecturing of the essay you are accustomed to evade, but a hybrid of these two."[10] The nature of the hybrid, it will turn out, is fundamentally related to the purpose and nature of the Wellsian utopia. Utopia is neither strictly linear in its development nor fixed in its goals; Wells's own work reflects, echoes, and expands upon this characteristic; this essay reflects, echoes, and expands upon Wells. In developing this side of the discussion, I will also at times recur to previous utopian thinkers, in particular Plato, as a means of opening up the utopian conversation. No utopian thinker is more profound than Plato, and his influence on Wells was quite extensive, yet in many cases Wells's utopia stands in opposition to Plato's and, by extension, those later utopians who trod in his metaphysical footprints. Since Platonic thought, veiled or open, lies behind much that is utopian in later thinkers, and much that is taken for granted in later philosophy, religion, and politics, the comparison of Wells and Plato will often serve usefully as a hermeneutic device for better understanding what it is that makes the Wellsian utopia so striking. But I shall leave out many details as regards Plato's thought. Since I am using Plato for dialogically illustrative points, and as this is not an examination of Plato or the utopian tradition as a whole, I will neither endeavor to present the whole of Plato's utopian vision nor to explicate the succeeding tradition in any depth, save where necessary to highlight Wells's efforts and achievements within, and against, the work of his predecessors. In referring to Plato I am referring to an old and influential tradition, full-scale explications of which are easily found, and I will make no attempt to add to them. Plato stands for, and in many ways sums up, a particular approach to utopia, one so powerful that it is often erroneously taken to sum up the possibilities of the genre; Utopian critic Ralf Dahrendorf, for example, asserts baldly but quite inaccurately that "all utopias from Plato's Republic to George Orwell's brave new world of 1984 have had one element of construction in common: they are all societies from which change is absent."[11] He has been misled by a misunderstanding of Plato's appeal to underlying metaphysical realities, and misapplied what other teleological utopians have asserted regarding their own visions. His error is understandable; Plato does claim flatly that the philosopher, who is expected to rule the ideal society, contemplates "fixed and immutable realities ... to which he assimilates himself as far as he can."[12] Similarly, Raphael Hythloday, the narrator of More's *Utopia*, concludes his tale with an encomium upon the quality, and presumed stability, of the Utopian commonwealth: "The Utopian way of life provides not only the happiest basis for a civilized community, but also one which, in all human probability, will last for ever."[13] Yet this sort of approach is, as I shall demonstrate, at odds with, and often diametrically opposed to, that of Wells, whose vision is indeed radically distinct.

The second approach, although linked to the first, remains distinct. It involves an attempt to go beyond the admittedly vague formal outlines of the Wellsian approach and achievement and to indicate, in the attempt, the open-ended character of the sort of vision offered by Wells. This book is designedly and avowedly an essay, as befits a discussion of a vision which itself disavows finality. Thus my claim is, and my project is to demonstrate, that Wells offers a utopian vision which is both stable and self-transcending—one which, if adopted seriously as a means of thinking about the future of humanity, requires radical revisions in both our modes of thought and our manners of action. This is never easy, and it grows more difficult the more closely we challenge the conventions of power within which we live. Further, the vision proffered returns the responsibility for 'achieving' genuine utopia to the ordinary individual, in whatever time or (reasonably secure) social setting. I do not claim that all individuals, or even most, at any specific time and social setting are capable of acting so as to further the creation of utopia; given the horrendous realities of life for millions of individuals such an assertion would be a vicious joke at best. What I am claiming, though, is linked to this: that anyone who lives in a society wherein the possibility of recognizing such a distinction as I have just drawn exists has already a utopian responsibility, and that ignoring or remaining apathetic to that responsibility is itself a moral action. Not only is utopianizing, both in thought and deed, whether on a large scale or a small one, a moral action, it is closely linked with the grounds for all other moral actions, grounds which are themselves continually changing shape and location. In part, my purpose here is, as writers of fiction (and therefore of utopias) are continually admonished to do, to *show*, rather than to *tell*, the most important matters. The function of utopia, properly understood, is to act as a means for recontextualizing our moral selves; this essay is an attempt to contribute to that process even while discussing it. Part of the utopian process is an endless dialogue among its adherents and inhabitants. I hope to provide, as Wells did through his dialogue novels, a sense of a variegated set of resonances and corrections overlapping with the central discussion. Accordingly, I have used a multiplicity of quotations as a means of including voices from a variety of sources neither directly relevant nor completely irrelevant, in order to further emphasize the open-ended nature of the subject and any discussion thereof. There is a deliberate degree of repetition of ideas here, for every idea touched upon herein forms a part of a mosaic whole, but no single idea represents the entirety of the utopian, or even of the Wellsian, project and approach thereto, and therefore each idea needs to be understood within a variety of contexts, some implicit and some explicit.

In the course of developing these ideas, I shall veritably barrage the reader with subsidiary notes. Many of these are there simply to provide the bibliographic information necessary for an evaluation of my claims: whether the authors I am quoting say what I say they say, and whether I am setting their words within a reasonable context. Many others, though, are quite deliberately discursive. Think of each of these as a crossroad; one sign (the main text) points in one direction, while another apparently sends you off in a different direction entirely. Just as side roads frequently arrive at the same place as the main highway, though with more varied scenery, so too these footnotes are meant to encourage the reader to take a different view and to suggest ways of doing this. I will, at least to a degree, have failed if you finish this book and say, "Yes, I agree completely." There are undoubtedly matters I have discussed only tangentially which others might see as vital, and matters I have discussed at length which others might see as tangential. What counts is the utopian project itself, the striving toward the betterment of the situation of humanity. This will never be done by one person acting alone, but only through cooperation and collaboration. The footnotes are one way among others of encouraging a discussion even in the absence of a physical interlocutor.[14] Encouraging but not demanding, which would be contrary to the utopian spirit; the reader is always free to ignore the footnotes, or read them later.

The experienced world is only partly linear, but an account of it, whatever its outward form, is necessarily so. In presenting this discussion and vision, therefore, I must needs take some time before arriving at its heart, lest that heart have no body in which to circulate the blood. Accordingly, in the first chapter I shall provide an explication of a Wellsian view of personality; it is at the level of the individual person that any hope for initiating a genuinely utopian process must begin, and it is here that the central problems of realizing utopia in any sense at all reside. Until we have a specific idea of what sorts of persons utopian writers are addressing, and what sorts of resistances are likely to be encountered therein, any utopian speculation is at best a pleasant fantasy or pious hope. With such an understanding, even if incomplete or partially flawed, the evolution of utopia can at last begin.

Whether such an evolution *does* begin is another matter; there must be some means of igniting the necessary fervor within each individual, or again what remains is merely a vague sense of dissatisfaction with life as lived. The second chapter takes up this question, and examines and expands upon Wells's account of the role of the novel in relation to the utopian process. Herein lies the heart of the essay. For Wells, unlike almost any prior utopian thinker, speculative narrative literature, and specifically fiction, is the focal point of utopian yearnings and possibilities. I shall explore a variety of his ruminations on the subject, expanding and developing them as needed. Fiction is commonly taken as standing in contrast with critical philosophy; I shall discuss this presumed difference and indicate why it is imaginative literature, as opposed to critical analysis, which must blaze the trail into utopia. Philosophy, at least as it is now constituted, relies upon arguments. There can be no arguments as regards first principles, for those arguments would themselves require shared underlying principles in order to be convincing, and if successful would therefore demonstrate that it was not the foundations which were being examined but some element of the superstructure. This allows, or perhaps even compels, us to see another approach to attaining foundational changes in our outlook, that of imaginative literature. Literature has the capacity to reshape our understanding of self and society, indeed to restructure our very consciousness, and to awaken us to hitherto unrecognized possibilities at a fundamental level not immediately available to analysis and argument. What was impossible, or unacceptable, in the light of one set of first principles may well become not merely possible or acceptable but eminently desirable in the light of another, and it is the ability of literature to provoke this shift which renders it vital to the utopian process — whether that of Wells or of anyone else, as we shall see.

As the tone of the preceding might suggest, Wells's attitude to the forces underlying the process he envisioned might be, and at times was, even by him, characterized as religious; in exploring the role of the imagination I shall therefore examine also the place of religion, as well as the necessary redefinition thereof, in reconstructing individual attitudes and efforts toward utopia. From imaginative literature, the means, and religion, the motive, I will turn to education, which provides the initial opportunity of transforming individuals and social structures. It is safe to say that no utopian thinker since Plato spent as much energy, both in and out of their utopian writings, as did Wells in considering the structure and demands of education in relation to both the individual and the State, or the needs of the individual in relation to education. Many of these proposals remain interesting today, and I shall discuss some of the most important, and the intentions underlying them, relating them in turn to the overall project of which they form an important, but not definitive, portion.

Utopian beginnings must lead somewhere if they are to have any meaning; the third and fourth chapters take up the complex, and often controversial, topic of the State. Most utopian visions depict, or assume, an ideal state.

Not so that of Wells, rather, each and every such state is, and can be, only a way station along an infinite pathway. I shall examine several stages of this process as seen by Wells, exploring the ways in which each is flawed, both designedly and accidentally, in such a way as to elicit from within itself the next stage in the indefinite series. Both chapters will include elements regarding ordinary life under utopian conditions, but the emphasis will be different in each. Chapter three will be concerned primarily with practical matters involving the political organization of the initial stages of the utopian process, with things which underlie considerations of the state as a political entity in general. Chapter four will examine a few of the specific theoretical considerations foundational to the general considerations adumbrated in the preceding chapter, especially those regarding the vital role of freedom. While I will not discuss every aspect of the many stages of the utopian process, I will consider several in some depth. Imagination requires something upon which to work. If a given utopia is to have more than purely hortatory force, there must be some sense that what in imagination is envisioned can in fact be attained. Wells, like all significant utopian thinkers, has provided much detail about his proffered societies, details worth examining not only in themselves, but in relation to the foundational needs of the utopian process. This chapter, therefore, will examine some of the practical matters involved in creating and sustaining the utopian process; I will offer strong, if perhaps not conclusive, reasons for supposing that the evolutionary utopian challenges to *a priori* oppositions based on claims about the supposed fixity of human nature and human relations are valid.

The final chapter contemplates the spectre of death, at the level of the person and at the level of the human species. In the face of extinction, of what avail is utopia? Here I can provide no specific answers, as these must come from within the individual her or himself, but I can at least consider the problem from within the Wellsian evolutionary utopian world view, and offer suggestions which may perhaps serve in some small measure to advance that view as well. Here it will turn out that the very attitudes which are necessary for the initiation of the utopian process itself become the starting point for a transformation in our attitudes toward both our own death, which is certain, and that of life itself as we know it, which is almost equally certain.

The reader may ask, "Why Wells?" After all, Wells himself, as can quite accurately be pointed out, disavowed being a philosopher or original thinker, utopian or otherwise[15]; surely, then, he and his writings can be of little significance beyond the bounds of intellectual history (and perhaps not even there). Furthermore, it will be averred, utopianism, like the modernism of which it is such an important, if often unacknowledged, part, is dead, slain by its own contradictions and failures. "For most of its history," claims Zygmunt Bauman, "modernity lived in and through self deception." It is time, he says, for modernity to acknowledge its flaws and give in to postmodernity, which "is modernity coming to terms with its own impossibility; a self-monitoring modernity, one that consciously discards what it was once unconsciously doing."[16] It would appear that utopianism is futile, of interest only to gravediggers and satirists, and that examining Wells is anachronistic, a project of marginal literary or philosophical importance.

I claim otherwise. Nor I am alone in so claiming. George Orwell, even while attacking Wells quite harshly, doubted "whether anyone who was writing books between 1900 and 1920, at any rate in the English language, influenced the young so much."[17] As recently as 2004 the Wells scholar W. Warren Wagar maintained his opinion that Wells was "one of the most significant minds at work in the twentieth century, and one of the few whose world view remains fresh and imperative today."[18] The choice of Wells is further impelled by several considerations. Some of the reasons are grounded in what it is he has to say, and will emerge as the essay develops, but a few others may be limned here. For one, Wells himself proudly, and at times not a little belligerently, donned the mantle of utopianism; what he wrote of his project in *A Modern Utopia* applies equally well to much of his output: "Our business here is to be Utopian, to make vivid and credible, if we can, first this facet and then that, of an imaginary whole and happy world."[19] Here the imagined planet is named Utopia, and the same is true in *Men Like Gods*, a novel otherwise unrelated. In his autobiography and elsewhere, Wells consistently refers to himself as a utopian (or utopist), and few have seen fit to deny the claim, even if they simultaneously reject the messages. Among others, we may count Lewis Mumford, writing in 1922, who described *A Modern Utopia* as "the quintessential utopia." Henry Newbolt said of Wells that "where the old Utopists built like children with a box of wooden bricks, he has been experimenting like an electrician, with eternal and immeasurable forces." The anonymous author of Wells's obituary in 1946 for *The Times Literary Supplement* refers to his "fatal utopian positivism." More recently, Krishan Kumar has described Wells as "the greatest of the modern utopists — his own preferred term — even though he never wrote a proper utopia, in the strict sense." The examples could be multiplied; there are few to the contrary, of which George Kateb (see below) is perhaps the most prominent.[20]

Another reason, which I have already mentioned, is that Wells was strongly influenced by Plato, undeniably the greatest of utopian writers, but with the addition of other influences which predisposed him to take a significantly different path than did his erstwhile mentor, influences and expressions of which open quite distinct vistas for contemplation. Wells first encountered *Republic* while still a young boy; he found it "a very releasing book indeed for my mind."[21] He commented that Plato, "as I got to the mighty intention behind his (to me) sometimes very tedious and occasionally incomprehensible characters, was like the hand of a strong brother taking hold of me and raising me up, to lead me out of a prison of social acceptance and submission."[22] What Wells took from Plato was not, in general, what most Plato scholars, concerned with fine-tuning interpretations rather than changing society, would recognize. "Here," he said perhaps fifty years after his first encounter, he found "the amazing and heartening suggestion that the whole fabric of law, custom and worship, which seemed so invincibly established, might be cast into the melting pot and made anew." Similarly, in *The Outline of History*, Wells describes *Republic* as "the first of all Utopian books," and as "a landmark in this history; it is a new thing in the development of mankind, this appearance of the idea of wilfully and completely recasting human conditions."[23] Plato's vision encouraged the nascent socialism of the young Wells. "All my thoughts leapt up now in open affirmation to the novel ideas he opened out to me," Wells recalled; "Chief of these was the conception of a society in which economic individualism was overruled entirely in the common interest." It was his "first encounter with the Communist idea."[24] It was exhilarating; "by way of Plato, I got my vision of the Age of Reason that was just about to begin. Never did anyone believe more firmly in the promptitude of progress than I." This wasn't all; the adolescent Wells also took something of more immediate personal relevance from his reading: "In the free lives and free loves of the guardians of the *Republic* I found the encouragement I needed to give my [burgeoning sexual] wishes a systematic form."[25] In this sense, at least, Wells remained something of a Platonist for the rest of his life.

The faith in the promptitude of progress (dubiously Platonic in any case) soon vanished, but the interest in change (likewise dubiously Platonic, to be sure) remained. Wells rejects much of that upon which Plato rests his state's structure, providing an alternative which is both connected to the primary utopian tradition and a fresh departure. In so doing Wells revisits many of Plato's concerns, including extensive examinations of the nature of the person, the necessity for power and its control, and the character of life in a vastly different society. Wells's knowledge of previous utopian writings was extensive and well used; his works are thus by no means isolated eccentricities. Rather, what we see here is an enormous, and enormously complex, conversation between supremely able representatives of two fundamentally opposed, yet equally vital, views of the nature and prospects of humanity The philosophical concerns which motivated Plato are basic to utopian thought; even where they are not explicitly developed they remain present in Wells, yet within a context little explored by any previous utopian writer.

One reason for this fresh approach is that Wells cross-fertilized the Platonic philosophical influences on him with those of a thinker almost diametrically opposed: Heraclitus, "the most fragmentary of philosophers."[26] Exactly what Wells knew of the Heraclitean fragments is unclear, but he found enough in what he did read to consider Heraclitus a major influence; "There are moments now," Wells wrote in 1906, "when I more than half suspect that all the thinking I shall ever do will simply serve to illuminate my understanding of him...."[27] The putatively Heraclitean phrase "Panta rei" appears as the motto for the novel *The World of William Clissold*, and Heraclitean fire[28] plays a major role in Wellsian imagery, from *The Time Machine* on. Wells explicitly set the two Greeks against each other; immediately after dismissing the Platonic "ideals," Wells comments that "Heraclitus, that lost and misinterpreted giant, may perhaps be coming to his own...."[29] From Heraclitus, Wells took the idea that nothing is permanent, that all is subject to change, and that therefore anything, including any social structure, can, and indeed must eventually, be reshaped, whether by conscious choice or not. While it is certainly the case that by modern scholarly standards Wells's understandings of Heraclitus and Plato would not hold up under scrutiny, this is irrelevant. Wells never pretended to be a Plato scholar, and indeed would have scoffed at the idea that being one would constitute a good use of his time. What he would insist upon as important here is the catalytic impact of his understanding of these ideas, and of the possibilities inherent in similar understandings of his own works and similar utopian efforts. The question, he would say, is not whether one has gotten Plato right, but whether one has used Plato effectively as an element in envisioning improvements in human life and society. Most scholars would disagree with this approach, but Wells is avowedly no scholar, and any study which uses him ought at least to attempt to approach the ideas under consideration along his path, even if only to turn away later on.

A third influence, one not philosophical but of even greater importance than either Heraclitus or Plato, has already been mentioned. The mere fact of endless change is not enough on which to found a social philosophy. There must be some sort of explanatory mechanism undergirding, and explaining the nature of, that change. Wells early on discovered, and began to fly the banner of, Darwinian evolution. He studied, briefly, under Darwin's foremost English champion T.H. Huxley,[30] and remained ever after a Darwinian evolutionary thinker. "Darwin and Huxley," he wrote, "in their place and measure, belong to the same aristocracy as Plato and Aristotle and Galileo, and they will ultimately dominate the priestly and orthodox mind as surely, because there is a response, however reluctant, masked and stifled, in every human soul to rightness and a firmly stated truth."[31] The Darwinian vision of organic evolution melded with the Heraclitean vision of universal flux to convince Wells of the impossibility of discovering fixed forms, or maintaining fixed realities, especially at the level of the human species and its constant parade of passing individual representatives.[32] The scientific proof of evolution provided, for Wells, the key which unlocked the possibilities of directed change; it also provided a grim reminder of the probable results of undirected change. Wells thus became, as a matter of historical accident, the first utopian author (though hardly the first author) to explore in an extensive manner the idea that human society has no teleological basis, and that utopianism must become an evolutionary process without foreseeable end. In this, if in nothing else, he can be distinguished from his predecessors. It is worth stressing this point: there is no evidence that Wells saw evolution as guided or as automatically leading to a situation ever better for human beings. Indeed, he is one of the few utopians to recognize explicitly that the natural working of the universe is such as to lead inevitably to the extinction of everything like life as we know it, and most probably to the eventual dissipation and disappearance of everything even remotely connected to life at all. Not only this, but he recognized that the slow course of evolution removes many of the traditional grounds for postulating any kind of moral guarantees within the structure of the universe and humanity's place within it. For most of the planet's history the rule has been one of uninterrupted slaughter, pain, death, and extinction. There is little reason to believe that the workings of nature have been suspended for the benefit of humanity; if we are to avoid desuetude or extinction, we had better do the work ourselves. Wells is quite explicit on this matter:

> The utopia of a modern dreamer must needs differ in one fundamental aspect from the Nowheres and Utopias men planned before Darwin quickened the thought of the world. Those were all perfect and static States, a balance of happiness won for ever against the forces of unrest and disorder that inhere in things.... Change and development were dammed back by invincible dams for ever. But the Modern Utopia must

> be not static but kinetic, must shape not as a permanent state but as a hopeful stage, leading to a long ascent of stages.[33]

In a teleological utopia, someone comes along and sets it up for the inhabitants; in an evolutionary utopia each inhabitant is responsible for her or his own place and involvement. This emphasis on individual responsibility alone would distinguish Wells from Plato, More, and virtually any other utopian in the teleological vein.

Grounded in Darwinian biology, Wells offers an unusual example of a writer who produced a number of distinct utopias. In part this stems from his views as to the nature of utopia, and in part from his own changing views, but in any case it allows for examining a wider range of the intellectual and emotional possibilities, or lack thereof, inherent in a significant writer's approach to utopia than would otherwise be the case; Wells allows for the investigation of several approaches to utopia under the aegis of one writer. Wells provides points of significant contrast with prior utopias: those in the mainstream tradition founded by Plato are teleological, theistic, and foundational; Wells's are evolutionary, non-teleological, atheistic, and at least largely anti-essentialist.

Finally, it is my contention that what I am calling the Wellsian approach to utopia allows for both a revision of the ostensible attitude of modernity and a way out of the relativistic political sterility of postmodernity; I say "ostensible" because I am not convinced that the common postmodern diagnosis of the problems of modernity is either accurate or fair to the fundamental principles of a very large number of thinkers commonly yclept modern, from Francis Bacon onward. I will not here attempt to justify this view; rather, I will for the moment accept the postmodern stance as regards modernity, in order to more vividly highlight Wells's contribution, which offers a way out of a dilemma many writers have identified, whether or not that dilemma is objectively "real" or not. The Wellsian utopian approach is neither so structurally rigid as its predecessors nor so vacuous as the common 'free market' attitude, the root of postmodernism, in which all ways of thinking and acting are of equal value intellectually and morally (if not necessarily practically), and therefore of no real value at all. While it is undoubtedly true that the so-called modern attitude can, in its rigidity and often inappropriate essentialism, lead to political and moral catastrophes (e.g., the Holocaust and the Gulag), it is equally true that any response to such horrors which is itself relativistic merely solves (dis-solves) the problem by denying it. Relativism has no answers to moral problems, and can have none; it is this reason which underlies the difficulty even staunch relativists have in living up to their own claims. While it is no disproof of relativism that no one ever manages to hold it consistently (even relativists complain when treated non-relativistically, as if somehow their relativism was a view which ought to entail some particular form of action on the part of others), it does suggest that, where the topic is the structuring of political relations so as to insure, at the least, against chaos and social self-destruction, relativism in its pure form need not be given more than a passing nod. If the moral foundations of modernity are weak, then the proper course of action is to replace them with something stronger. It is this which, I contend, Wellsian utopianism does. Further development of this point will have to await further development of the discussion, but for now it may be noted as a premise to be explored.

Even the most detailed, careful, and plausible explanation of the means by which some approach to utopia can be made is of little value if the reader is left uninterested in the conditions of life therein. One need not expect to live in the utopia oneself, but one will not be inspired to think about it, much less work toward it, unless one has an idea of what daily life for the utopian citizen will be, and finds that life on the whole attractive, or at least understands why it is better than what one has now. Wells, who had the benefit of an extensive knowledge of his forerunners, took cognizance of this fact, and explained why so few utopias are genuinely attractive as visions of places in which actual people might truly live. "There must always be a certain effect of hardness and thinness about utopian speculations," he wrote. "Their common fault is to be comprehensively jejune."[34] It is something of a paradox that the more care the author has taken with her or his creation of an imaginary world, utopian or otherwise, the less likely that creation is to feel comfortable to the reader. This fact is taken full advantage of by such superb science fiction writers as C.J. Cherryh, whose detailed creations work precisely because they feel so alien to the contemporary reader. Much of the best science fiction is in fact counter-utopian, however splendid a future it may portray, precisely because it (usually deliberately) offers a vision intended to leave the reader feeling as if they have been plunged into a genuinely alien world, one disconnected from their own experiences. This is an inescapable corollary of any imaginary social structure or practice; the further from ordinary practice it is, the less it will accord with the reader's experience. Imagined institutions are forever at a signal disadvantage in regard to those they would replace.

> Whatever institution has existed or exists, however irrational, however preposterous, has, by virtue of its contact with individualities, an effect of realness and rightness no untried thing may share. It has ripened, it has been christened with blood, it has been stained and mellowed by handling, it has been rounded and dented to the softened contours that we

associate with life; it has been salted, maybe, in a brine of tears. But the thing that is merely proposed, the thing that is merely suggested, however rational, however necessary, seems strange and inhuman in its clear, hard, uncompromising lines, its unqualified angles and surfaces.[35]

The imagined structure, or institution, or even state suffers by the very fact of the clarity with which it has been foreseen; what no author can fully imagine is the way in which social intercourse will have worn down the practices and policies under invention. Hence the slightly embalmed quality of even the best utopias, not to mention the positively repulsive quality of others. Even Wells's greatest predecessors fail in this regard; "I doubt if anyone has ever been warmed to desire himself a citizen in the Republic of Plato," Wells notes; "I doubt if anyone could stand a month of the relentless publicity of virtue planned by More."[36] This explains why the writing of successful dystopias is so much more easily done than writing successful utopias: all one need do for the former is exaggerate certain societal tendencies or structures people already dislike (and allow their dislike to fill in the gaps in one's imagination), whereas in the latter one needs to invent whole new tendencies or structures and then overcome the resistance to the new found in so many people. Hence Wells's choice, already adumbrated above, to make a virtue of necessity, and allow the stagnant quality of any single utopian portrayal to suggest the need for moving to another level.

Some sense of the method I will use here should have become apparent already, but a few more details may be helpful in orienting the reader. This book is philosophical in its intentions, yet those intentions themselves bring into question certain restrictive attitudes toward the character of philosophical discourse. The presentational style, as well as the nature of the discussions offered, reflects this. Martha Nussbaum, herself a renowned philosopher, points out that "any style makes, itself, a statement: that an abstract theoretical style makes, like any other style, a statement about what is important and what is not, about what faculties of the reader are important and what are not." She comments further on "the conventional style of Anglo-American philosophical prose," which she describes, I think on the whole accurately, as "a style correct, scientific, abstract, hygienically pallid, a style that seemed to be regarded as a kind of all-purpose solvent in which philosophical issues of any kind at all could be efficiently disentangled, any and all conclusions neatly disengaged."[37] It seems to me that, while certain formal proprieties must be observed, there should, in any essay on imagined futures for humanity, be room for exactly the kind of discursive and even at times pointillistic style the Wellsian utopian literature adopts. The entire purpose of the Wellsian approach is the disavowal of fixed moral and even human realities against which any belief or action, under whatever conditions or in whatever times, can be measured. Stephen Wilbeck, protagonist of *Apropos of Dolores*, speaking in a Wellsian voice, refers to "a false assumption that holds its own against us, a Proteus so flexible and persistent that maybe it will defeat us altogether." He expands upon the point:

> This tenacious false assumption is the belief in Perfection. It changes its shape, it is here, it is there; it is always the same. Few people get the full significance of the biological science we talk about so glibly. They do not realize that it disposes of delusions about perfect forms and perfect health. Underdeveloped minds cling to those — "*ideals*," shall we call them? The realization that life is and must be for ever a struggling maladjustment, is too difficult, discouraging, uncomfortable and frightening for them. They refuse to believe that that is how they are made; they think there must be a perfect way somewhere, a fatuous shiny *rightness*, so that, once found, they will thereafter be able to go through life in a state of eupeptic invulnerability. Only you see people have put them wrong about it and so they have missed this natural perfection.[38]

The evolutionary perspective writ large, which is the point and manner of a Wellsian utopia, not only leads to a degree of vagueness, it *requires* it. Certain concepts can be indicated but not delineated in every detail; certain methods can be suggested but not demanded; certain goals can be invoked but not defined. Rigidity in discussing such a program as offered by Wells would be not merely unfair, it would be contrary to the spirit in which he writes and the situation within which life exists.

This does not mean, however, that no clarity is possible or desirable. In what follows, I shall make every effort to distinguish between clear understandings of the means to be used in discussing the ideas and the innate indistinctness of the ideas themselves. There are quite valid reasons for insisting that some ideas cannot be fixed and chiseled out once and for all time, but those reasons themselves can be made amply evident. That the goal of a Wellsian utopia is something which can never be known in its entirety is not a reason for ignoring the landmarks along the infinite road thereto; indeed, a major portion of this essay is devoted precisely to mapping out a number of the more important among them. Nonetheless, the further ends of even the trail which can be projected become misty in inverse proportion to the efforts to discern them, and any pretense to the contrary would betray the purpose of the journey.

Where the ends change as we approach them, the means themselves must be flexible. The latter can be known only in relation to the former, and in part help to determine its features; any choice of means to be examined is already implying a choice regarding the ends to be attained. As I shall show, the conflict is unavoidable and potentially useful, but I would ask the reader to remember that it *is* a conflict, and that the efforts to mitigate it themselves entail further conflicts between certain expectations and their traditional realizations.

1

The Individual

Any utopian political theory must rest on at least two conceptions of the human individual: one involving those to whom the theory appeals directly, and another involving those, probably as yet unborn, who would live under and sustain the envisioned society. The two may overlap to a very large degree, but they cannot be entirely the same, or the utopian state would already exist; even if the difference is found only in the nature of what is desired in the future, it must be present in some form.

That the creator of a utopia must have a particular conception of the individuals addressed follows from the nature of the utopian project. Creating a utopia requires communicating, from within one set of moral and political beliefs and practices, the need for, and desirability of, a different set of moral and political beliefs and practices. In order to appeal to anyone's sense of what would be better than the present, one must have an idea of what their sense of the good is, and/or what the good should be. Further, if the utopian scheme presented is to be practicable at all, the various roles to be played by this or that individual or group must have been thought out, and in order to be thought out the character of the individuals involved, whether as individuals or as members of groups, must have been recognized and delineated. It does no good to preach to an audience of plutocrats that they ought to give all their money to the poor unless one has a theory regarding the mentality of plutocrats which makes one's appeal appear likely to succeed, or in which the failure of one's appeal itself inflames ardor for change on the part of others. One must have an idea of the motivating forces operant upon one's audience in order to apply those forces, or at least to appear to do so. Such an idea need not be either completely clear or completely accurate (and in fact, as I shall claim, the Wellsian approach denies the possibility of both criteria) to be effective, but there must be some similarity between what the author offers and what the readers expect and can grasp, or there is little purpose to the exercise. Where there are no similarities at all, there can be no communication.

Likewise, any utopian scheme presupposes some difference between those living now (the "now" of the author and initial readers, at the very least) and those living in the imaginary then ("then" being the period wherein the specific ideals being advocated have been attained). What this difference is will vary widely, depending on the presumed nature of the individuals addressed and the final state envisioned, among other things. "Final state envisioned" means, for evolutionary utopians such as Wells, merely the last point reached in the given set of imaginative speculations; it does not imply any claims to perfection, ultimate knowledge, or stability. The specific character of the utopia concerned, and the intentions of its creator and recipients, will determine whether its construction is seen as final or merely as one stage among many. That state may be something as simple as a change in desires, or a better regulation of those desires, but it may be something as radical as a change in species characteristics. This is not so uncommon as one might guess; examples from authors with otherwise widely differing standpoints include Marge Piercy's *Woman on the Edge of Time*, where, among other things, the necessary genetic engineering has been done to allow men to breast feed, and Frederik Pohl's short story "The Man of the Year Million," in which massive colossal physiological and psychological changes are described, and the reader told outright not to be so dismissive of their superiority or even acceptability. In fact, Wells's *Men Like Gods* contains references to a kind of telepathy, although this is a primarily decorative element with metaphorical significance rather than a serious positing of a necessary step in the evolution of humanity toward utopia. Nonetheless, the sorts of persons living in the utopia must be described in such a way as to make the reader aware that hitherto unavailable options (whether cognitive, behavioral, physical, political, or emotional) are not unimaginable, and that once imagined they may be seen to be superior to the present situation. This presents problems for the writer: too radical a change and readers will be alienated; not radical enough a change and readers will see no compelling reason to desire the different state of existence over that which they already experience. No utopia, if it is to be successful as a means of stimulating action on the part of its readers, can ignore the likely character of those readers, even if part of its success stems from an ability to transcend its own immediate conditions of creation. However far into the future the utopian writer projects her or his speculations, they must in the end be grounded on contemporary reality. As Wells acknowledged, "Whatever sort of community you dream of you realize that it has to be made of the sort of people you meet every day or of the children growing up under their influence."[1] One of the measures of great utopias is the degree to which they have overcome this hurdle.

An initial task for utopian authors is one of classification. The way in which this task is carried out will in itself determine much of the character of the utopia which results, and the attitude underlying the classification will in turn color the suggestions for attaining the envisioned utopia. For a teleological utopian such as Plato, the telos determines, justifies, and sustains the means; for an evolutionary, or non-teleological, utopian, for whom the ends are continually changing, the means become entirely provisional; although still justified by the ends, such justification vanishes directly upon the end in question having been reached. In either case, the ends must justify the means. The gravamen here is that, unless the telos is both knowable by all and permanent, there will be some class which is expected to apply the means to people who cannot understand their justification, and who therefore cannot tell the difference between necessary means and means the maintenance of which has become an end in itself (e.g., most modern bureaucracies). Where the ends are shifting in response to the changing lives of individuals, and where the structure of society is such as to allow those individuals both to contemplate the ends and determine the means, such dangers are at least minimized, if not altogether eradicated. The difference rests in the distinctions. Where classifications can be firm and precise, so can the social structures which rest thereon; where they cannot be, the social structures will, if they are to bear any relation to their foundations, necessarily be looser and less constricting.

The traditional metaphysical and religious classifications of life and nature involve essences, presumed characteristics which are irreducible and from which everything else follows. As with so much in philosophy and religion, these ideas are given their first fully worked-out analysis by Plato, and it is worth examining his conceptions briefly as a contrasting background to much of what will follow. Plato's conception of the individual is grounded on a metaphysical theory of fundamental distinctions, distinctions which can be recognized and understood; "what fully *is* is fully knowable, what in no way *is* is entirely unknowable."[2] The purpose of dialectic, of philosophical investigation, is to arrive at this knowledge, to "systematically to determine what each thing essentially is in itself."[3] Plato thus sees one of the tasks of philosophy as understanding the proper classifications of things; to do so, it must delve beneath the realm of appearances and ordinary life. When this is done, the analysis will reach an understanding that some sort of essence must exist, an essence toward which the individual examples are tending to a greater or lesser degree. As Plato says, when discussing things, "we always postulate in each case a single form for each set of particular things, to which we apply the same name."[4] He gives the example of beds and tables, saying that, while there are many particular examples of each, "there are only two forms, one of bed and one of table,"[5] and it is those forms which the maker has in mind, however unclearly, when constructing the individual bed or table. The forms appear to be a distillation of similarities, since Plato says that if god, who created the "bed-in-itself in nature," had created two such beds, "another would emerge whose form the other two shared, and it, not the other two, would be the real bed-in-itself."[6] There is some essence which makes any bed a bed, but that essence is not a thing which can be constructed by a given bed maker.

The same applies to the classification of human individuals, although the classificatory process is, as one might expect, more complex. Plato sees the individual as comprised of a hierarchical tripartite soul[7] (reason, spirit, and appetite), with the three parts corresponding to the classes of citizenry found in the just city. The highest part is reason; within the individual, "reason ought to rule, having the wisdom and foresight to act for the whole, and the spirit ought to obey and support it."[8] The two together, if in proper harmony, "must be put in charge of appetite, which forms the greater part of each man's make-up and is naturally insatiable."[9] Left untended, appetite can gain complete control and wreck the life of the individual by demanding too much in the way of physical pleasures. The ideal life corresponds to that of the philosopher, although the exigencies of statecraft require that the philosophers not be allowed to lead their ideal lives for a sizable portion of their existence.

This vision of the human character has important repercussions. Plato divides his society into three types of individuals: "businessmen, Auxiliaries, and Guardians."[10] A person falls naturally into one of the three types based on which element of the soul dominates, and the hierarchy of the social structure rests on a mutual recognition and acceptance of this fact. Plato allows for the possibility that a person born of parents belonging to one class might actually be naturally a member of another class, but this is a matter of innate qualities rather than education. As Socrates indicates, "no two of us are born exactly alike. We have different natural aptitudes, which fit us for different jobs."[11] What education does to a large extent is refine and develop the qualities already given at birth. While it may be true that without education no one could do anything at all, it is also true that the purpose of education is to see to it that each person is most productive of things needed by society which she or he can most fully contribute by nature; "Quantity and quality are therefore more easily produced when a man specializes appropriately on a single job for which he is naturally fitted, and neglects all others."[12] Indeed, one of the necessary functions of education is to inculcate in the whole population an acceptance of this idea. Since the class memberships of individuals are fixed by internal qualities, the relations within the society comprised of those individuals are similarly fixed. There is no evidence that Plato saw education of any sort as being able to move individuals from one class to another. Instead, it is clear that he sees individuals as capable, under appropriate guidance, of strengthening and focusing their particular natural abilities.

This, in short, represents a view which held, and for many continues to hold, tremendous explanatory and hortatory power. It is difficult, though not utterly impossible, to reconcile with any scientific evolutionary view, and its political implications are quite distinct from those worked out by Wells. For Wells there are no true fully determinable overarching classes, whether logically, sociologically, or physically. He develops this idea with chairs, rather than beds or tables.

> Take the word Chair. When one says chair, one thinks vaguely of an average chair. But collect individual instances, think of arm-chairs and reading-chairs and dining-room chairs, and kitchen chairs, chairs that pass into benches, chairs that cross the boundary and become settees, dentist's chairs, thrones, opera stalls, seats of all sorts, those miraculous fungoid growths that cumber the floor of the Arts and Crafts Exhibition, and you will perceive what a lax bundle in fact is this simple straightforward term. In co-operation with an intelligent joiner I would undertake to defeat any definition of chair or chairishness that you gave me.[13]

What holds true for chairs holds true for all other physical things, for concepts, and ultimately for human beings; "only in the subjective world, and in theory and the imagination, do we deal with identically similar units ... the uniqueness of individuals is the objective truth." As Wells points out, "In the more modern conceptions of logic, it is recognised that there are no identically similar objective experiences; the disposition is to regard all real objective being as individual and unique."[14] It may be argued that this sort of definition rests on something of a play with words, and that Wells himself recognizes the very distinctions he pretends, perhaps for rhetorical purposes, to deny. Max Black has shown why this objection won't work as forcefully as it might at first appear. "Wells is here conflating two distinct features of the meaning of *chair*," he writes.

> The first, in its *variety of application* to such things as dentist's chairs, thrones, and opera stalls, might be met, where the context demanded it, by further specification. The second, which here engages our interest, is less easily removable: specify as you please, by heaping up adjectives or switching to specialized words, the term you obtain will still admit of possible *borderline cases*, with respect to which it will be impossible in principle to decide whether or not the term applies.[15]

One could perhaps imagine Wells magnanimously, and a bit sarcastically, granting Plato his forms as unique entities, but he would deny that those forms had any relevance to anything outside themselves; each individual at a given moment is its own form, and no point in the continuum of the individual's history takes precedence over any other, save by an act of definition, either external or internal, imposed or chosen. Seen thus, it is consciousness which gives the world its structure, rather than the structure of the world which gives focus to consciousness.[16] This applies to everything; even objects found in nature have significance only in relation to some sort of consciousness and intention. For a starving person a blueberry patch means food (but even here only within the mental structure which recognizes blueberries as edible); for a well-fed aesthete a blueberry patch may be instead an occasion for poetic rhapsodizing (one can imagine a city-born and bred aesthete who first sees a beautiful blueberry patch and admires its color scheme without having the faintest idea that the berries are edible). At one point tomatoes were thought of as poisonous; a person holding that belief strongly enough could presumably starve to death in a field of plenty. Although Wells is not about to not deny external physical reality, he considers it to have meaning, purpose, and value only in relation to a given set of intentions and mental structures found concentrated within particular individuals, and within the congeries of intentions of individuals acting collectively. Reality in the raw is a collection of unconnected facts awaiting interpretation and evaluation; it is in the mutual discovery of our overlapping assessments that we begin to form social purpose. As Gemini Twain explains it, "The one and sole *reality* in human life is mental." In writing this Wells does not mean to take up an idealist position; rather, it is that "our selves are mental assemblages of our activities."[17] What gives our activities meaning can come only from within us, not from the activities themselves.

Yet even individuals, speaking strictly, are not unique unitary entities; they are themselves comprised of distinct elements with their own characteristics. This suggests that an individual person as a fixed being does not in fact exist; "the integrality of the individuals in the higher metazoa up to and including man, is a biologically convenient delusion ... a multitude of loosely linked series of behaviour systems which take control of the body and participate in a common delusion of being one single self."[18] Plato gave great attention to the three divisions of the soul—the appetitive, the courageous, and the rational—and these divisions find an echo here, but for Wells there is an indefinite number of these behavior systems, and it is largely a matter of temporary social convenience which one is taken to be primary. This is grounded in our evolutionary past.

> Self-consciousness and a conception of other individuals as consistent persons are necessary to social behaviour. The self-conscious human organism, *whatever it does and however much it does it*, will ascribe its behaviour as an individual to Self, and whatever stimulus may turn its mind to another phase of behaviour it will succumb to the delusion that it is the same Self, still in continuous operation.[19]

Certain acts, such as murder, are taken by a majority, or even a vociferous minority, within society to allow for the defining of the individual thereby; one is known, and treated, as a "murderer," regardless of other qualities one may have, however dominant they may normally be.[20] Other acts, under the right circumstances, are taken by the individual as self-defining, again regardless of the actual portion of their existence connected to, or even conscious of, those acts; a person who once violated their own strongest moral beliefs may come to think of themselves as being essentially an immoral person due to the mental weight attaching to one, perhaps even minor, act. Thus, for Wells, a complex of different physical and mental states operates continuously within one corporeal body (although this, too, changes over time, the changes are, on the whole, less important for Wells than those within the mind). If the range of reactions and processes is comparatively narrow the body is externally, and usually even internally, experienced as a unity by the foremost element within the personality; a dominant line of memory defines the person. "What is a personality but a memory?" asks Sarnac in *The Dream*.[21] Although Wells does acknowledge that "it is the body that holds the mind together and not the mind the body," the answer to Sarnac's question clearly is, not much.[22] But the stream of memory, of memories, can diverge, can restructure the whole of the person involved, the whole of their actions, reactions, and thought processes. If those reactions and processes are too wide-ranging the person is deemed difficult, manic, or even to have a split personality; "If the systems vary widely, you call [the person] a moody or inconstant man, and if they vary still more widely you may have such contradiction that at last you have a "double personality."[23] This in turn will have varying social ramifications; in some societies or groups this mental instability leads to restraints being placed upon the individual, while in others it leads to those individuals being credited with unusual powers or abilities. They are seen as abnormal, but the boundaries and consequences of that abnormality are extremely fluid. Each of these states of being, during its tenure in control, takes itself and at least most of those states it remembers to be a part of an overall unity, to be a single person. "But in fact," Wells claims, "they are a collection of mutually replaceable individual systems held together in a common habitation. One ascends; another fades before it."[24] Wells rejects any sort of parapsychological transference of self-identity from one body to the other, but he also rejects any sort of *absolute* unity of self-identity based merely upon a bodily continuity. Self-identity grows in strength through the reinforcement of certain memory and behavior patterns over time. No one element within those patterns is necessarily the ground for self-identity, but as one set of patterns becomes stronger certain elements which conflict with it are compressed in their range and diminished in their influence. The result is a more fully focused and forceful individual. The focus, though, is by no means always clear. Different aspects of our personalities lurk always about, awaiting their opportunity to regain control of our thoughts and actions. An obvious example of this is the struggle faced by alcoholics in their fight against their disease; even a single drink can empower the addicted element of their composite personality and lead to consequences unwanted, and actively opposed, by other aspects of that person's self-consciousness.

Human beings appear to be unique in the extent of their correlative self-consciousness, although this is in part a function of their being members of a gregarious species.[25] These two elements — individualism and gregariousness — create a tension within each of the variegated consciousnesses. Certain general tendencies may be identified, but these are tendencies only, and not to be taken as implying a fixed and quantifiable human nature. A human being, Wells writes, referring to human beings as presently constituted, not to human beings as permanently defined, "wants to stand out, but not too far out, and, on the contrary, he wants to merge himself with a group, with some larger body, but not altogether."[26] Standing midway between isolation and dissolution, between being cut off altogether from human contact and losing one's identity altogether within a larger group (as was the goal of fascist indoctrination, e.g.), a human being is subject to strong temptations to become fixated on one sort of definition or another, either of self or of others. Individuals confront forces, internal and external, which make self-definition difficult or confusing; many look to groups to (re)gain definition, and then reify the group with which they have chosen to affiliate themselves; having joined a loosely affiliated collection of individuals, the person uses some imagined universal characteristic as a means of identifying the true believers both inside and outside the often arbitrarily defined membership. The group, any group, is unavoidably defined by the individual's own understanding, an understanding which leads toward a further contradiction: for the individual to identify with any given group, the individual must exclude elements of themselves from their own self-understanding. The individual must attempt to define her or himself through the expectations of others; as those expectations stem in turn from a complex set of relations, internal and external, the individual's attempt to conform completely is foredoomed. No group can possibly overlap completely, in its character as a group of disparate individuals identifying themselves as members of the group by virtue of specific aspects of their own interests, with the full range of mental characteristics of any one member of that group. One can take on the label of "communist," for example, but it is impossible that every aspect of one's self will be accounted for by membership in that group, unless one defines "communist" in such a way as to correspond with the totality of one's mental states. This, however, is a manifest repudiation of the very character of a group. In affirming the self through identification with a group, the affirming self denies itself. Any intentional membership in a group thus creates a tension within the individual, since portions of that individual's being are denied, even as other portions are developed.

The converse is true as well; any imposed definition based upon presumed membership in a given group also denies many, and indeed probably the majority, of the characteristics of the person subsumed under the definition. This is the hallmark of bigotry: the denial of full humanity through an emphasis on some stereotypical characteristic presumed to be present in all members of the hated group. One need merely think of the peculiar racial classifications practiced in Nazi Germany, apartheid South Africa, and the post-bellum southern United States to recognize this problem.

A self, for Wells, is a process of developing interrelated elements, out of which, at any given moment, one element, or a small group of closely related elements, is taken to stand for the whole. This he sees as necessary;

> Our minds need this fixity to function; a human mind has to hold a thing still for a moment before it can think it. It arrests the present moment for its struggle as Joshua stopped the sun. It cannot contemplate things continuously and so it has to resort as it were to a series of static snapshots. It has to kill motion in order to study it as a naturalist kills and pins out a butterfly in order to study life.[27]

We each engage with the contradictions surrounding us, and even in overcoming them we develop new ones. As individuals we cannot escape this bind, for it is within our relation to the world, and thereby is felt in all of our relations with other human beings. We ourselves are a process of evolution and revolution, since what we are is only partially determinative of what we will be. In defining ourselves at any given moment (which we nonetheless must do in order to function), we must leave out an enormous range of elements, elements which may in fact prove to be far more important than what we took as primary in the initial act of definition. Further, we define ourselves differently depending upon the circumstances under which the definition is demanded, such that a single person can quite honestly think of her or himself in ways which are really quite contradictory at different, but closely linked, times. The changes from one state of being to another can be slow or rapid, noticed or unnoticed; if they are too drastic, or if the consequences for society are seen as too damaging by those with power, the individual suffers.

The result of this interplay of influences is that persons take on a set of characteristics which comes to predominate; they develop a personality from which it becomes increasingly harder to imagine escaping, or even wanting to escape. Our redefinitions require a continual thoughtful self-examination (one thinks here of Socrates), but "no man's intelligence is continually dominant; fatigue him or surprise him, and habits and emotions take control."[28] That is, since any given set of behavior patterns contains elements which overlap with any other set within all but the most dissociated personalities, any given personality may, despite being nominally in control, succumb to patterns of behavior connected with another set of thoughts. This is recognized in popular parlance when we say, "I wasn't myself when I did x." Of course we can never not be ourself (who, then, would we be?), but we can act in a manner not commonly associated with the self-identity most often in charge. As a given self-identity (set of behaviors and memories, etc.) becomes reinforced, it tends to become identified as something solid and unchanging, both internally and externally. We take the accidents of our influences for the essence of our being, and come to see ourselves as necessarily embodying a particular character. We then connect ourselves, through our actions and associations (e.g., membership in clubs and political parties), with others whose behaviors suggest similar outlooks; this in turn reinforces the experience of ourselves as being fixed and stable. Even the very way in which we exchange thoughts and ideas is strongly effected by this self-concept; when one person communicates with another, "the thought, *so far as it finds corresponding ideas and suitable words in your mind*, is reflected in your mind."[29] This whole network of relations continues to ramify throughout our conscious lives, and has a tremendous effect upon the ways we are prone to classify others, both those with whom we are in regular contact and those with whom we are not.

Therefore, while it is true that in order to function in the world we must classify, we must acknowledge that "the presumption which biological science brings one is that the senses and mind will work as well as the survival of the species may require, but that they will not work so very much better." It is clear that Wells accepts the idea that an external reality exists, but insists that our understanding of that reality is itself limited by the "tools" (including our own senses) available to us. As he says, "The forceps of our mind are clumsy forceps and crush the truth a little in taking hold of it...."[30] In other words, whatever definition we reach is definite only in virtue of deliberate exclusions based on decisions made in advance, whether knowingly or unknowingly. In regard to the physical world such decisions, while still retaining moral colorings, are largely unilateral; in regard to the world of persons such decisions demand multilaterality. This, though, complicates definitional questions immeasurably.

It is this conflict between the need for, and the difficulty of, classificatory understanding, especially as applied to the self and its relation with others, which drives humans toward utopia, and which undergirds the social side of Wells's vision. Human beings seek to overcome the conflicts between self and society (that is, between the experienced complexity of their own lives as lived and the external forces, recognizably grounded in the wills and attitudes of others, which seek to restrict them within artificial, and often extremely arbitrary, boundaries); since many of those conflicts are grounded in definitional questions (e.g., who defines what appropriate behavior is, and on what grounds, or who gets to define what individuals must do to be seen as productive members of society, and, again, on what grounds), a condition of social and individual being in which those conflicts are lessened is seen as desirable. Where the means of minimizing the conflicts takes into account in a compassionate manner the situation of others, one of the conditions for utopian thought is present. So while some sort of provisional classification is necessary if we are to make any social changes at all, such a classification is best based not on "accidental categories" (such as the division "into labour and capital, the landed interest, the liquor trade, and the like,") but on "temperaments,"[31] which is to say the patterns of thought as revealed in behavior over time.

Stemming from the foregoing considerations, Wells proposes a loose four part division of the human types within present society,

> called respectively, the Poietic, the Kinetic, the Dull, and the Base.... They are not hereditary classes, nor is there any attempt to develop any class by special breeding, simply because the intricate interplay of heredity is untraceable and incalculable. They are classes to which people drift of their own accord.[32]

Wells, as has been remarked before, was no philosopher, and his use of the term "classes" should not be understood as having the same sort of definitional rigidity it does for, at the very least, analytic philosophers[33]; as he notes, "in actual experience these qualities mingle and vary in every possible way. It is not a classification for Truth, but a classification to an end."[34] Wells does not see these types as fixed, but he does see them as corresponding roughly to the present state of human affairs now and for some time ahead. For the most part people are carried along by thought and behavior patterns into these groups, but there is no deterministic aspect to this; under the appropriate circumstance, and given the necessary motivation and willpower, one can move about considerably. Unlike Plato's, Wells's classifications are transitory, of use presently but sooner or later likely to be superseded by something else.

In Wells's case, the end at which the classification aims is "to determine the broad lines of political organisation." He recognizes that the classification is "a rough one…; it was so far unscientific that many individuals fall between or within two or even three of its classes." This has the expected effect upon the consequent political organization; the looseness of definition is "met by giving the correlated organisation a compensatory looseness of play."[35] The bureaucracy (and here it must be reiterated that this term, together with the classifications to which it is responding, refers only to the character and organization of human beings at a particular point not so very far removed in time from us, not to some essentially human way of being) is shaped by the variegated nature of its constituents, not the other way around. In later chapters, I will develop different portions of this relationship as it unfolds over the course of utopian history.

The classifications themselves are redolent of Plato, though with certain significant differences. The foremost is the Poietic, the "creative class." It includes a great many types, "but they agree in possessing imaginations that range beyond the known and accepted, and that involve the desire to bring the discoveries made in such excursions, into knowledge and recognition." Where the individual is primarily concerned with creating or discovering beauty, they fall under the rubric "artistic"; where the person is more concerned with discovering things within the natural world she or he is of the "scientific" type. The two approaches can overlap, and at their best do so "in the universal reference of the true philosopher."[36] The scientific type, on Wells's account, is akin to the Platonic philosopher. The artistic type is likewise akin to Plato's artists, but Wells ranks the type far higher than does Plato. It is from the Poietic type that most creative changes in human existence have stemmed; "the forms of the human future must come also through men[37] of this same type, and it is a primary essential to our modern idea of an abundant secular progress that these activities should be unhampered and stimulated."[38] Thus education must do its best to expand the number of these individuals, society and the state (suchever as they may be) must allow them the fullest opportunities to explore, discover, and create. This topic overlaps with other considerations to be explored later; for the moment the descriptive point may merely be noted.

The Kinetic type includes most of the people "our earthly anthropologists have in mind when they speak of the "Normal" human being."[39] The type as a whole is mainly "distinguished by a more restricted range of imagination.... They are often very clever and capable people, but they do not do, and they do not desire to do, new things. The more vigorous individuals of this class are the most teachable people in the world,"[40] and the class as a whole is in fact more likely to be morally trustworthy than the Poietic class, the members of whom are constantly experimenting with the forms of living. Energetic and intellectual members of the Kinetic class provide the bulk of the administrative and judicial functionaries; otherwise the individual concerned is likely to be "an uninventive, laborious, common mathematician, or common scholar, or common scientific man." Less intellectual members will be successful actors, preachers, and politicians, and, operating at somewhat lower levels of mental energy, is found "a long and wide region of varieties, into which one would put most of the people who form the reputable workmen, the men of substance, the trustworthy men and women, the pillars of society on earth."[41] It should be evident that Wells is not in the least deprecating these individuals; rather, he recognizes that the energy for initiating progressive change is unlikely to initiate with them, however much they may support the process by which such change unfolds. In many ways, though, these are the people who will benefit the most from utopian developments on a large scale, as it they who are most repressed emotionally, intellectually, and politically.

The third group of types of intellect is the Dull. These "are persons of altogether inadequate imagination, the people who never seem to learn thoroughly, or hear distinctly, or think clearly.... They are the stupid people, the incompetent people, the formal, imitative people, [who] count neither for work nor direction in the State."[42] The Dull are the people to whom, in our present society, life merely happens; they are people who have been beaten down by circumstance and self-surrender into a quiet complicity in their own defeat. Wells by no means sees this as either a hereditary class or one whose size is more or less a matter of statistical regularity; were everyone "carefully educated they [that is, the Dull] would be considerably in the minority in the world."[43] While members of this class will not be encouraged to reproduce, their children will be treated exactly as would any others in the state, and would be given the same opportunities as any others. It cannot be stressed too much that Wells, in these classifications, is portraying individuals as they reveal themselves to be over the course of their own development, not as they are presumed to be through some accident of deterministic heredity.

While it is true that Wells wants an improved society, and to whatever degree possible improved human beings, he is not willing to pay any price to obtain either it or them, and it is worth considering this fact in some detail. A careless reader might be forgiven for presuming a more forceful, or even violent, approach on Wells's part, when confronted with such passages as the rant of the artilleryman about the people needed for the future underground resistance to the Martians in *The War of the Worlds*: "We can't have any weak or silly. Life is real again, and the useless and cumbersome and mischievous have to die. They ought to die. They ought to be willing to die. It's a sort of disloyalty, after all, to live and taint the race."[44] Similarly, (and, oddly enough, also in the context of a presumed Martian invasion of Earth, though a much subtler one) the outburst of Professor Ernest Keppel regarding ordinary folk might well raise some eyebrows. "That is where my hate goes," he says. "I hate common humanity. This oafish crowd which tramples the ground whence my cloud-capped pinnacles might rise. I am tired of humanity — beyond measure. Take it away. This gaping, stinking, bombing, shooting, throat-slitting, cringing brawl of gawky, under-nourished riff-raff. Clear the earth of them!"[45]

Within the context of the respective novels themselves these diatribes take on a different meaning altogether. In the former case, the artilleryman is swiftly revealed as a self-inflated windbag; in the latter, Keppel's speech comes as the climax of a series of frustrated comments about contemporary social conditions, and refers to no plan of action. What is being expressed in each is a dissatisfaction with things as they are at the given moment in the narrative, not a program for changing them; indeed, the artilleryman's grandiose proposals are merely the prelude to what is discovered very soon after: that the Martians have succumbed to earthly disease microbes, had been "slain, after all man's devices had failed, by the *humblest* things that God, in his wisdom, has put upon this earth."[46] While the apparent implication of theistic design is an artifact of the literary structure, and reflects no specific religious commitments on Wells's part, the insistence on the importance of even the smallest part of nature is intentional, and will find echoes of various sorts in many of his writings. It is well in this context to remember also Wells's comments on the common person in *Mankind in the Making*: Reformers, he says, "are all too apt to raise this bitter cry of popular stupidity, of the sheep-like quality of common men. An unjustifiable persuasion of moral and intellectual superiority is one of the last infirmities of innovating minds."[47]

No life is necessarily without value, although some lives may be such as to require careful observation, or even action, by the state (or its descendants, in the later stages of utopia). In line with what Wells has posited as the discursive character of the personality, he posits likewise a broad and humane justice system. First offenders and youths (under twenty-five) will receive "cautionary and remedial treatment." The choice between "the wide world of humanity" and "this evil trend in you" will be presented to them, and they will be allowed to return to society. Only afterwards, when they again demonstrate the true nature of their choice by reoffending, will they be removed from society, quietly but quickly. The action will be neither dramatic nor hidden. "The thing must be just public enough to obviate secret tyrannies, and that is all."[48]

Removal from society does not mean death, however; "There would be no killing, no lethal chambers." The justification for this lies in the connection of the state (or, in the early stages of the utopian process, the State) with the community; "Crime and bad lives are the measure of a State's failure, all crime in the end is the crime of the community."[49] This suggests already the equation Wells will draw between the citizenry and the means of governance, an equation to be examined in detail later. He has broached an important point: where there is too great a gap between the powers of enforcement and those most likely to be effected by them there is already the seed of another social disjunction; where social disjunctions exist exist also the possibilities of dissatisfaction, unrest, and revolt.

Nor will there be prisons as we now understand the term; "All modern prisons are places of torture by restraint, and the habitual criminal plays the part of a damaged mouse at the mercy of the cat of our law."[50] Prisons represent a reaction upon the entire person for the crime committed by but one portion of his or her being; they punish the whole for a transgression of the part. Wells recognizes that the dominant element in a person's make-up may indeed be such as to be defined as criminal, but sees no need to go beyond that fact to the isolated incarceration of the whole human being. Prisons warp the prisoner further, and achieve only a worsening of the person who presumably is at some point to be released. Prisons also require prison guards, and warp them as well. "No men are quite wise enough, good enough and cheap enough to staff jails as a jail ought to be staffed." Wells's suggestion is famous, though perhaps not as he would have wished. He recommended using isolated islands; "to these the State will send its exiles, most of them thanking Heaven, no doubt, to be quit of a world of prigs."[51] Nor are these islands merely the equivalent of Alcatraz writ large; the residents will be given "just as full a liberty as they can have.... I do not see," Wells comments, "why such an island should not build and order for itself and manufacture and trade."[52]

Only the production of weaponry and means of flying or floating away would be forbidden.

One gap in Wells's account may already have been caught by the careful reader. He is quite clear on what will be done with first offenders and the young, and just as clear on what should be done with hardened criminals and malcontents. What, though, of those who reoffend once or twice over a long period? What of those who commit different sorts of crimes? (It is to be assumed here that both Wells and I mean serious crimes such as rape or murder, not traffic offenses such as speeding, or the breaking of trivial ordinances somehow still on the books). One answer is implicit in the foregoing, though Wells does not develop it. Given the Wellsian view of personality, where a person commits two offenses of a clearly different character each offense would have to be treated as a first offense. One of the businesses of the initial utopian bureaucracy would be to develop a classification of offenses against society (which, in the end, any offense worth creating legislation about must be), perhaps along the line of the classification of individual types. This would ensure that an offender's counseling would include education about possible offenses, different as acts but similar as social harms, to be avoided. Once this approach was in place, second offenses of a serious nature could be taken as genuine recidivism, and treated accordingly.

A second answer would stem from the first. The law already recognizes levels of culpability; it would be no great leap to include, after much debate (and subject always to revision), a comprehensive ranking of types of criminal action by their social seriousness. Certain islands could be set aside for temporary inhabitants; if the conditions, both on the islands and in the world outside, were similar to what Wells described, the loss of freedom would be a strong disincentive, but the exile not so harsh as to produce embitterment, especially as the other residents on the island would be likewise temporary, with no incentive, therefore, to do anything which would extend their isolation.

Aldous Huxley derived much amusement from caricaturing the idea of island exile in *Brave New World*, and others have mentioned it merely to dismiss it as ludicrous, but Wells had already foreseen the challenge. "This sounds more fantastic than it is," he wrote. "But what else is there to do, unless you kill?"[53] Of course, modern technology allows, or shortly will allow, for such things as total personality reconstruction, as foreshadowed factually in the uses of brainwashing and lobotomies and fictionally in such works as Alfred Bester's *The Demolished Man*. The results, however, are just as unpalatable as killing, just as subject to errors in judgment, and just as irreversible. Humane exile seems far more likely to result in a balanced society than executions or personality destruction It also avoids the two great problems any advocate of the death penalty must always accept. The first is that no system of justice is perfect, and therefore some innocent persons are almost certain to be swept into the executioner's purview and killed. One can revoke an exile; one cannot revoke a death. Secondly, the Wellsian program disavows the creation of a bureaucracy of death, one requiring some citizens to kill others. Any killing will have its effect on the killer; where it does not, we recognize the incipient sociopath. It makes no sense, then, to institutionalize killing, for this merely ratifies the attitude of the sociopath at a higher level, surrounding it with rituals intended to assuage those who do the killing and those who demand it. All killing comes from weakness; "Utopia will have the strength that begets mercy."[54] The choice, then, seems clear: either we accept the old manner of retributive punishment, with all its room for deadly errors and frightening, but equally deadly, technological devices being used to subjugate human beings; or we find some means of handling purported criminals which neither destroys or corrupts. It is not enough simply to dismiss such suggestions as Wells's; either their inferiority to the present system of mass incarceration must be shown or something better must be developed. Either option would be perfectly palatable to Wells, though he would naturally prefer the latter. No matter what the alternative proposed, though, Wells would demand, I think quite rightly, that it be at least a demonstrable improvement over that against which it is being measured.

These proposals, it should be noted, presume a general lessening of crime under the impact of the improvement of material welfare and the increasing quality and comprehensiveness of education. In *The Shape of Things to Come*, for example, "all these crimes, which filled the jails, arising out of the scramble for money and property in an age of insufficiency, have almost completely vanished." The crime statistics for 2104 show only "715 cases of stealing for the whole world."[55] Perfection has by no means yet been attained; as the author of the history being transcribed notes, sexual offenses, particularly those occasioned by jealousy, and acts of "annoyance, destruction, assault and so forth," still exist, revealing all too clearly "that this world is still not a Paradise for every type of individual." Nonetheless, the overall outlook is positive; the total of offenses of all sorts (including 71 murders) across the world "is just three quarters of a million in a world of 2500 million people," which gives "a quantitative measure of human progress in two brief centuries that justifies a very stalwart confidence in the human outlook."[56] The point is not whether Wells's specific numbers will come true; rather, it is to understand that he foresees a decided downturn in the number of crimes of all sorts under changed conditions. As society becomes freer of present material and personal imbalances, the specific results of those imbalances will vanish.

Potentially more serious as a challenge to Wells, especially in light of history after the bulk of his writings were published, is the matter of eugenics. Death as a punishment refers to an individual already formed, takes away that which already exists; eugenics is at once a form of pre-emptive transgression upon the individual (the person who may be sterilized, or who may undergo a variety of treatments intended to reshape the fetus within her) and a purely social concern: that society not be burdened with individuals unwanted or perceived as drains upon putatively limited resources. Eugenic proposals are common in utopian writings. Plato offers a clear defense of eugenic procedures. In Campanella's *The City of the Sun*, for example, in order "to moderate all the excesses," the state requires that "large and beautiful women are mated only with large and aggressive men, fat ones with lean men, and lean ones with fat men ... wise men are mated with women who are naturally vivacious, vigorous and shapely. Similarly, keen-minded, quick, lively, and, as it were, passionate men are mated with the fatter and gentler women."[57] And so on; Campanella presumably considered himself a wise man, and expected to be treated accordingly. Wells has at times been taken as similarly advocating eugenics of the most mechanistic sort; one such charge, more vehement than most but not altogether atypical, is found in a fairly recent book-length attack on Wells:

> He injected permissibility into political eugenics [what exactly this phrase means is unclear], varnished murderous ideas with respect and reputation. At its most simplistic level the belief of the social engineers was that by exterminating or incarcerating perhaps one half of the world's population the remaining half would enjoy unparalleled benefits. Wells not only went along with this, he encouraged it.[58]

Wells's early hero Plato certainly did advocate eugenics of one sort or another, although the degree to which he did so can be argued. For a brief period, probably under the influence of Plato, Wells took eugenics as both possible and desirable; this, though, changed fairly rapidly. In *Anticipations*, written in 1900, Wells took a rather thoughtless supportive stance regarding eugenics; within less than four years, he reversed his view on the topic, adopting the critical stance he would retain ever after. He admitted the shift in attitude; "It seemed to me then," Wells wrote in 1904 of those early reflections on the topic,

> that to prevent the multiplication of people below a certain standard, and to encourage the multiplication of exceptionally superior people, was the only real and permanent way of mending the ills of the world. I think

that still. In that way man has risen from the beasts, and in that way men will rise to be over-men. In those days I asked in amazement why this thing was not done, and talked *the usual nonsense* about the obduracy and stupidity of the world.[59]

Problems with human eugenics arise immediately, and it was these which led Wells to change his mind. While the theory of eugenics might appear sensible, Wells notes, it is in practice impossible to figure out exactly what it is one is supposed to be doing. The theorists ignore the fact that we are "not a bit clear what point to breed for and what points to breed out."[60] This problem will remain a consistent element in all of Wells's discussions of eugenics; the analogies with animal breeders break down precisely as they shift from, say, cattle to humans. A breeder of cows wants a particular quality, and can ignore everything else. "A young calf with an incipient sense of humour, with a bright and inquiring disposition, with a gift for athleticism or a quaintly-marked hide, has no sort of chance with him at all on that account. He can throw these proffered gifts of nature aside without hesitation." But not so the would-be breeder of superior humans; homogeneity is not what is desired, but variety. What is needed in humanity, according to Wells, is "a rich interplay of free, strong, and varied personalities."[61] That is to say that, by recognizing human beings as complex entities in their own right, we reach the conclusion that any particular program of eugenic mating is quite unlikely to attain any predictable result whatsoever, especially given its initial premises. Wells draws the vital distinction very clearly: "We breed dogs and horses for uniformity, for certain very limited specified *points*— speed, scent, and the like. But human beings we should have to breed for variety: we cannot specify any particular *points* we want." He goes on to mention a number of the different types of person we might want, and points out that "the qualities of one would be the weaknesses of another." As he says immediately afterward, "We do not know what we want nor do we know how to get it." It should be clear that these concerns stem directly from his conception of the nature of individuals.[62]

There is no ambiguity here. The Wellsian position is the opposite of that usually associated with eugenicist schemes grounded in some ideal of human physiological perfection, and this fact was recognized as soon as Wells took up the opposition he never thereafter abandoned. G.K. Chesterton, often opposed to Wells's views on political and religious grounds, praised his opposition to eugenics in no uncertain terms: "He once held, I believe, the opinion which some singular sociologists still hold, that human creatures could successfully be paired and bred after the manner of dogs and horses. He no longer holds that view. Not only does he no longer hold that view, but he has written about it in *Mankind in the Making* with such smashing sense and humour, that I find it difficult to believe that anybody else can hold it either."[63] Where one has a concept of the ideal human being then one needs only an understanding of the mechanics of heredity, and a means of controlling those who will reproduce, to create human beings to specification. Nor is there any plausible objection to so doing, *on those assumptions*. I stress, though no doubt in vain, that the point here is not a defense of eugenics *per se*, but an altogether different point about the relation between technique and purpose. *IF* one wants to do x, and if one knows how to do x, then any objection to doing x must come from outside the justification of the original intention. This is precisely the problem with eugenics; no amount of knowledge about what we *can* do will ever, by itself, allow us to determine what we *ought* to do. This is also Wells's point, which should be clear even on a cursory reading of his more carefully considered opinions on the topic, opinions held consistently for over forty years after his first fumbling acceptance of the contrary idea. To reject eugenics where the best is both knowable and obtainable is to deliberately choose the less good, which is probably reprehensible and perhaps even malevolent. I say "probably" to avoid irrelevant arguments; nonetheless, on traditional foundationalist ethical viewpoints doing less than the best one can do is invariably reprehensible. The problem is determining just what it is that is the best that one can do. Wells's response to this conundrum will develop as I proceed, but it clearly does not involve eugenics in the forceful sense described above. The specific concern raised by would-be eugenicists is that in any society where the "best" and the "lesser" come into contact, to choose not to breed the best is to condemn one's offspring to servitude of one sort or another; they or their descendants would sooner or later likely be unable to hold their own against the superior individuals, and would eventually have to submit to them in one way or another. That is, and this is the vital point, if one accepts the ideals of perfection in the first place. *Wells does not*.

On Wells's view, this approach is not only unnecessary, it is in itself doomed to failure. Suppose, he says, we were to try to breed for beauty. We would quickly discover that beauty is merely "a term applied to a miscellany of synthetic results compounded of diverse elements in diverse proportions." As Wells says, "One can no more generalize about it in relation to inheritance with any hope of effective application than one can generalize about, say, "lumpy substances" in relation to chemical combination."[64] The same would hold true for other ostensibly desirable qualities, such as health, strength, or "energy" (one of genuine eugenicist Francis Galton's terms). Wells picks holes in each of these ideas at length, but the message remains the same: positive eugenics cannot, given the diffuse character of human beings, and the effect of social definitions on the reception of the various supposedly desirable qualities, achieve its end. This is not at all to say that Wells denies the importance or effects of heredity; indeed, he goes so far as to say the science of heredity is "ten times more important to humanity than all the chemistry and physics, all the technical and industrial science that ever has been or ever will be discovered"; although his phrasing displays his era's ignorance of the delicate interplay of electro-chemical forces within the human organism, as well as of the technological advances which have so helped to develop the study of the human genetic structure, the underlying point remains worth considering very carefully. Presumably Wells would think that, where we had genuine knowledge which would free people from debilitating birth defects and congenital illnesses we should use that knowledge. But that is a far cry from breeding humans for specific purposes.[65]

Negative eugenics — the prevention of certain people from reproducing — provides a somewhat grayer area, and Wells's response is correspondingly less clear and more open to criticism. Some of these criticisms stem fairly from his own position, with which he is at times carelessly inconsistent. Such a one, for example, is his comment, apropos a "deaf and dumb wedding" reported in a contemporary newspaper, that the progressive thinker "would certainly try to discourage this sort of thing."[66] As he has just spent a good deal of time arguing that the evidence for the transmission of *diseases*, let alone communicative impairments, is by no means strong enough to warrant state action, this petulant little outburst needs no more than a brisk dismissal as both untrue to his argument and ungrounded in his facts.

Many of the same concerns apply to the idea of involuntary sterilization, though with the added complexity that the individual being sterilized is most likely a person on virtually any philosophical grounds. In this context, it may be noted that Wells made a rather half-hearted endorsement of "the segregation and sterilization of mental defectives."[67] He passes on quickly to the claim that certain unspecified congenital defects are heritable and that there is no reason to avert this. "Nor," he adds, "is there any sound objection to the sterilization of criminals convicted of brutish violence." He also refers to the idea of "temporary" sterilization, but does not explore it. In any case, the entire section on eugenics where these comments are found is treated by him as but a prelude to the claim that "it is to better education, and to better education alone, therefore, that we must look for any hope of ameliorating substantially the confusions and distresses of our present life."[68] Despite this, if Wells's understanding of the flexibility of social policy is taken into the equation, it seems unlikely that even the eugenic programs he endorsed in such a lukewarm fashion would be permanent fixtures of utopian society. Wells himself would be the first not only to acknowledge, but to insist, that expanded understandings require adjusted policies, and that greater comprehensions of human complexity necessarily supplant earlier, more simplistic, positions. Thus any given thoughtful criticism of Wells's supposed eugenicist attitude may well be valid and persuasive, but only so long as that criticism includes a recognition of the entirely provisional nature of Wells's position on the topic. Otherwise, Wells is being held to account for a far more rigid position than can be justified by reference to his writings on the subject, which is to say that he is being criticized for something in which he did not believe. Eugenics occupies but a minuscule portion of Wells's social thought, but has acquired a notoriety out of all proportion. Wells's approaches to it, though by no means always as clear or consistent as one might wish, are worth considering both as a corrective to certain misunderstandings and as a means of recognizing some of the limits he sees both on individual freedoms and on state power and authority.

Wells's hopes, and most of his plans, rest on the first three of his social classes, which are more or less distinct within a continuum. Those hopes and, especially, plans are challenged by the fourth class, the Base, one which can overlap with any of the others. It is the only class which is directly hostile to the utopian project, because it is the only class the members of which actively working for anti-utopian ends. "The Base," writes Wells, "have a narrower and more persistent egoistic reference than the common run of humanity,"[69] and a greater capacity for, and tendency to, arrogance, dishonesty, and cruelty. In their self-absorption, and especially in the demands they will accordingly make on the resources and energy of others, "they count as an antagonism to the State organisation."[70] Wells was not especially interested in the Base individuals, and they need little further attention here, save to note that the term, the class, and the opprobrium by no means apply exclusively, or even especially, to any existing socio-economic, intellectual, ethnic, or racial group. A well-educated and highly paid economist of international renown serving enthusiastically as the advisor to a murderous dictator is as much as a Base individual as is one of the dictator's jackbooted killers, and perhaps, given the economist's initial advantages, even more so. The Base are vile by choice and, like all whose careers are grounded in destruction, will face distinct social controls on their ability to act upon their hatreds, though controls rather more humane than their own actions.

With this we reach the beginnings of the boundary between the individual qua individual and the individual in relation to the community. Having begun to develop an understanding of the individual, it is necessary next to consider how that individual may best be enticed into a broad concern for their community and the world within which it exists. We know ourselves, or think we do; to reach beyond those selves requires reaching beyond knowledge. This requires the awakening and expansion of the individual imagination, which awakening is the task of artists, and in particular novelists, to whose work we now turn.

2

The Role of the Novel

Imaginative literature is at the very core of Wells's utopian ideals. Scientific speculation is all very well, and indeed of tremendous importance, but its construction rests on an explicit exclusion of the human element. Without that element, however, any speculation is morally worthless, as it has no reference point whence to derive value at all. Without creativity, all learning is without meaning or purpose, a mere dry accumulation of trivia; the gravest charge against Dr. Winkles in *The Food of the Gods*, for example, is that "he is utterly devoid of imagination and, as a consequence, incapable of knowledge."[1] Imagination justifies knowledge, because it is only within a synthetic, which is to say imaginative, setting that knowledge is knowledge at all. Otherwise it remains at the mere level of belief: that which has been, and is felt to have been, imposed from outside.[2]

The idea of a utopia, of creating through words a different world, a world meant somehow at once to be fictional and to be truer than the world in which it is encountered, is a peculiar one. The envisioning of better political conditions would appear to be the job of politicians; they do it every day, and often with a much stronger grounding than the speculative writer in the particular facts concerning the present situation (whether military, budgetary, or purely political). What is wanted, it might be argued, is practical experience, not theoretical constructs. Surely something like this attitude is behind the claims of philosophers as distinct as A.J. Ayer and Richard Rorty, for example, that philosophy has nothing to say to politicians, and that philosophers, *qua* philosophers, should therefore say nothing. Proper philosophers, according to Ayer and the many who agree with him, believe "that the only way to discover what the world is like is to form hypotheses and test them by observation, which is in fact the method of science...."[3] On what grounds the initial hypotheses are to be formed is unclear, since these would require acts of imagination which are, at least in the eyes of such philosophers, themselves not scientific (it should perhaps be noted here that few scientists, at least of the first rank, are as dogmatically opposed to the role of speculation and the imagination as are their philosophical counterparts).

The problems with this emphasis on practicality as regards the betterment of humanity manifest themselves immediately. Since any political choice includes a moral component, and since moral demands are not subject to empirical testing, no justification of a moral theory from within a practical structure is possible. Thus, for example, the proposition that we *ought* to act so as to minimize human suffering, since it cannot be tested factually, is meaningless philosophically, though by no means necessarily as a personal commitment. Ayer, as is well known, adhered to a form of ethical emotivism, in which ethical statements are merely assertions about the internal mental state of the individual making them, and carry no objective weight. "Holocaust, boo; Association Football, hurrah," Ayer might say, but he can say nothing more to the Nazi who inverts the claim.[4] Likewise, the practical politician, whose worldly experience is indubitable, has no more grounds for insisting upon the necessity of a particular moral goal than does any other citizen, for the moral goal is not itself a matter of experience. Here we see the force of Wells's claims for the writer, self-consciously utopian or otherwise: the imaginative writer transcends science and philosophy; she or he encourages us to recognize that reason and argumentation can go only so far in persuading people to step outside of their individual interests and develop a sense of human commonalty, yet that if such a sense is to be nurtured and strengthened in more than a temporary manner the means must be such as to sustain extensive examination. The writer challenges the status quo, both socially and individually. This has always been part of the role of storytellers, of "fiction — pointing a way to achievement — and the august, prophetic procession of tales."[5] Fiction is a way of controlling the world without yet crossing a barrier behind which, once passed, retreats cannot be made. Fiction allows, indeed encourages, each reader, each listener, to imagine themselves in the situation, and to imagine the problems they would face therein, and the hopes they would achieve. There is no limit to the power of fiction, because there is no limit to the power of the awakened human imagination. "And that first glimmering of speculation," Wells writes of an imagined primal storyteller eons in the past,

> that first story of achievement, that story-teller, brighteyed and flushed under his matted hair, gesticulating to his gaping, incredulous listener, gripping his wrist to keep him attentive, was the most marvellous beginning this world has ever seen. It doomed the mammoths, and it began the setting of the snare that shall catch the sun.[6]

The storyteller is free of the constraints which encircle the scientist, the politician, the philosopher. The storyteller is free to take from each of these others such elements as are necessary for the invention of a new world, and to place such elements of humanity as are desired into conflict, or cooperation, with that world. The reader then is free to decide as to the plausibility and desirability of what is portrayed. Our moral stances are shaped by the world of our experiences; storytelling (in whatever form) is a way of reshaping that world, and thus at least potentially reshaping our moral stances, without changing anything physical at all. We become who we are in part because we have been led to imagine ourselves differently. We then act so as to change the now less satisfactory "real" world.

The distinction between imaginative literature and philosophy is more often assumed than demonstrated. Although defining philosophy is at best a tendentious exercise, it is necessary to indicate, as a common starting point, one particular broad and certainly widely accepted definition thereof. Certain characteristics may, and for our purposes here must, be singled out. The Anglo-American academic context under the shadow of which most utopias have been written emphasizes critical conceptual analysis; "the strictly philosophical questions ask what is logically presupposed and logically implied by various kinds of discourse and whether these presuppositions are or are not logically compatible with one another."[7] Most philosophers within the dominant tradition and many of its antecedent traditions would agree with this (recall Ayer's comments above). A position is taken, and evidence and arguments intended to convince the reader or listener of the truth of the position are presented. Objections are considered and rejected, and every step is subject to detailed critical analysis. The result is, or is supposed to be, that a truth visible to all who take the same steps in the same order is attained. Reason is dominant; as Plato demanded, "Reason ought to rule, having the wisdom and foresight to act for the whole, and the spirit ought to obey and support it."[8] Philosophy is, if not always the discovery of truth, at least the unveiling of error through the exercise of analysis and critical reason. Philosophy, and by extension its practitioners, cannot be concerned with the individual, but only with general statements (although perhaps derived from the situations of individuals). Philosophy can be passionate, but it cannot be compassionate, because compassion requires the surrender of the general view to the needs of the specific personal situation. Philosophers, as such, are interested in intellectual and theoretical relations to a far greater degree than they are interested in human lives as lived. The foregoing is true of other analytic disciplines as well; the scientists working on the atomic bomb, for example, were largely concerned with a series of factual problems, not with the human results of the intended use of the bomb, though this began to change as they contemplated what they had wrought. Literary critics have on the whole no interest in the reactions of readers (or the impact of their criticisms on authors), save inasmuch as these confirm or deny some larger theory. There are exceptions to this, but many of them are regarded with skepticism by their academic colleagues. None of this is to say that individual critics or scientists cannot personally be compassionate, but only that such compassion is regarded as an irrelevancy in the practice of their discipline. As Richard Kostelanetz, for example, has noted regarding philosophy,

> Most philosophy in our time is primarily about the intellectual enterprise bearing that name and secondarily about Life; for each new work of philosophy (even social philosophy) is designed to comment initially upon issues in that intellectual field. New philosophical research is, like a new painting, valued primarily for its contributions to a conscious tradition of concern and only incidentally for its relevance to common knowledge.[9]

While it may be objected that this distinction is too sharp, one need merely dip into virtually any widely respected philosophical journal to see the process at work. A minor industry is concerned with producing articles purporting to show nothing more than that this or that philosopher has failed to analyze this or that concept clearly enough, or to provide enough evidence to support this or that claim. Emotional responses are ruled out as evidence, even to essays purporting to show that logic and reason are mere constructs of a particular culture or discipline. It is virtually impossible to imagine a contemporary philosophical treatise which consisted of rhetorical gestures, no matter how powerfully written, against even a strict post modernist, if such a phrase is not already an oxymoron, or emotivist position in ethics being accepted as legitimate by the faculty at any philosophy department in North America, even by faculty who describe themselves as post modernists or emotivists. Yet if these positions are true (or perhaps one should write, "true"), then anything purely rhetorical which served to achieve the desired ends would have to be just as valid a response as any carefully crafted, logically sound, and well documented argument. That the former is unacceptable, while the latter is not, is a function, and indication, of the boundaries which delineate professional academic philosophy.

The above distinction is long-standing, which may explain a peculiar fact: since Plato, no utopia has been written by someone widely respected as a philosopher (with the partial and, within the bounds of the teaching of the history of philosophy, dubious exception of Francis Bacon, in 1624, well before current academic specializations were even a glimmer on the intellectual horizon). Philosophy, at least until recently supposed by many of its practitioners to be the summit of human interests and understandings, has nothing to contribute to the utopian urge and project. Writing about the future is inherently vague, and by nature difficult to constrain within the bounds of empirical or analytic rigor.

Literature, on the other hand, is generally less concerned with argumentation, analysis, or indeed even 'truth' in the sense of a correspondence with logical proprieties. As Whitehead remarked, "You don't go through Shakespeare or a detective story and at the end of each sentence say: True or False?"[10] It is the overall set of impressions derived from a literary work which add up to an experiential whole; if the impressions are too variegated, the experience may prove unpleasant or incomprehensible, but it takes many false steps to lead the reader into a true dead end. The opposite is generally true of critical philosophy, where one false step in the syllogistic procession can vitiate an entire book. Peter Caws has described the distinction admirably:

> Writers as such do not argue for the propositions they assert, they simply assert them; they do not attempt to convince, but count on a general plausibility — of the world described, or, in the limit, of their own literary enterprise — to carry the reader without protest. It would be ungracious on the reader's part to quibble with an assertion about the writer's world on the grounds that it was not true of the real world, although a critic (i.e., a careful and articulate reader) might complain of the work as a whole that it was too improbable and without other virtues, or that, while within the limits of verisimilitude, it contained internal inconsistencies or infelicities of other kinds. Philosophers come in both varieties — writers and critics — but by and large they are not expected to take creative liberties with the world; it has also come to be expected, at least in English-speaking circles, that the philosophical writer will at the same time be a critic, not putting anything forward in the first capacity that would not survive scrutiny in the second and furthermore being explicit about the critical principles involved.[11]

There are exceptions to this general distinction, most of them European in origin (one thinks of Nietzsche's *Also Sprach Zarathustra*, for example), yet by and large it holds.[12] It follows, therefore, that literature is free to do things which philosophy is not; as the Canadian novelist Timothy Findley has written, what imaginative writers have done is "create an imagined setting for truths, where they could be seen in ways that life did not present them."[13] Such freedom is vital in the creation of utopias; what utopian authors in particular have done is create imagined settings for the whole of humanity, where we can see life in ways reality has not yet presented. Imagination is what allows us to transcend empirical fact (the idea of an empirical statement about the future, which does not yet exist to be present to our senses, is already a contradiction). Yet imagination, stemming as it necessarily does from what is already present to us, can never cut itself off from fact completely; it therefore serves as a bridge between experience and desire, across which intentions may cross. Herbert Marcuse has reminded us well of this dual nature and function of art:

> The world intended in art is never and nowhere merely the given world of everyday reality, but neither is it a world of mere fantasy, illusion, and so on. It contains nothing that does not also exist in the given reality, the actions, thoughts, feelings, and dreams of men and women, their potentialities and those of nature. Nevertheless the world of a work of art is "unreal" in the ordinary sense of this word: it is a fictional reality. But it is "unreal" not because it is less, but because it is more as well as qualitatively "other" than the established reality. As fictitious world, as illusion, it contains more truth than does everyday reality. For the latter is mystified in its institutions and relationships, which make necessity into choice, and alienation into self-realization. Only in the "illusory world" do things appear as what they are and what they can be. By virtue of this truth (which art alone can express in sensuous representation) the world is inverted — it is the given reality, the ordinary world which now appears as untrue, as false, as deceptive reality.[14]

In the conflict between things as they are and things as they could be, the portrayal of the latter has an advantage: it can respond to the needs of the person rather than requiring that the needs of the person respond to it. The utopian writer confronts us with our own dissatisfactions, and offers the possibility of using those dissatisfactions as fuses whereby to ignite practical change. The utopian imagination is free to an extent that the empirical experience of social and political "fact" is not. Experience in itself is always grounded in the present; an imaginative act, although likewise experienced in the personal present, can be equally vivid as an experience of past or future. What we do, in the doing, has an entirely different meaning than it does in the telling, then or, especially, later. As Hannah Arendt phrases it, "Action reveals itself fully only to the storyteller, that is, to the backward glance of the historian, who indeed always knows better what it was all about than the participants."[15] It is not that the historian (understood as the one who later contextualizes the story, not in a narrow professional sense) has deeper insights into the experience in itself than the person involved, but that only from outside can the place of the experience in even the involved individual's life begin to be ascertained. "What the storyteller narrates must necessarily be hidden from the actor himself, at least as long as he is in the act or caught in its consequences, because to him the meaningfulness of his act is not in the story that follows."[16] The storyteller and the actor may be the same person, but not at the same time; or, more precisely, the actor is the one who acts and as such is fixed within a specific set of circumstances (the immediate experience), whereas the storyteller continually recreates the meaning of the acts, and is constrained only by the bounds of coherence in regard to conjoined experiences. Hence the character of Wells's future histories, which attempt simultaneously to explain elements of the process of reconfiguring the meaning humanity gives collectively to its situation and to help initiate the process of that reconfiguration at the level of discrete individuals. Wells attempts to act and to contextualize the act within an imaginative portrayal of a future within which that act has acquired a particular meaning; as Arendt has noted, "Even though stories are the inevitable result of action, it is not the actor but the storyteller who perceives and "makes" the story."[17]

As Northrop Frye wrote, "The utopia is a *speculative* myth; it is designed to contain or provide a vision for one's social ideas, not to be a theory connecting social facts together."[18] Theories must account for the causal links between their facts; imaginative writing need merely allow the reader to *create* those links, to define the importance of those facts in a way independent of their place in any objective setting. Yet most people's imaginations have been shriveled and stunted by one means or another; therefore, in a world in which meaning must be created, there will need to be those whose task it is to suggest the fundamental social myths: the writers. In the absence of deity, writers must become like gods. As William H. Gass expressed it,

> Thus so many of the things which are false or foolish when taken to the world — in religion or philosophy — become the plainest statements of what's true when taken to fiction, for in its beginning *is* the word, and if the esthetic aim of any fiction is the creation of a world, then the writer is a creator — he is god — and the relation of the writer to his work represents in ideal form the relation of the fabled Creator to His creation.[19]

It is the writers (and, by extension, artists in general) who, in the beginning, create new worlds; here, "in the beginning was the word" is once again literally true, but without a metaphysical assumption underneath it.

This freedom is not absolute, at least for the artist working toward utopia; Wells expects creators to be aware of the ethical aspect of their work. This, too, is a constant theme within his work. In the little known 1894 story, "A Misunderstood Artist," for example, the title character is a cook, who engages in a dialogue with a poet. "A man sent to me only a week ago to ask what my sonnet 'The Scarlet Thread' *meant*?!" says the poet; "I gave him answer.... 'Twas a sonnet, not a symbol."

The cook empathizes. "They are always trying to pull me to earth," he complains.

> "Is it wholesome?" they say; "nutritious?" I say to them, "I do not know. I am an artist. I do not care. It is beautiful." ... "Cookery ... is an art." ... I tried — it was an altogether new development, I believe, in culinary art — the Bizarre. I made some curious arrangements in pork and strawberries, with a sauce containing beer. Then I produced some Nocturnes in imitation of Mr. Whistler, with mushrooms, truffles, grilled meat, pickled walnuts, black pudding, French plums, porter — a dinner in soft velvety black, eaten in a starlight of small scattered candles. That, too, led to a resignation: Art will ever demand its martyrs.[20]

The moral, though implicit, is clear: Art has consequences, and it behooves the artist to be aware of them. We laugh at the idea of poisonous food designed for a purely visual effect, yet ignore the moral, emotional, and intellectual consequences of bad art designed for a purely fiscal reward.

Wells regards it as the primary responsibility and task of authors (and, by extension, other artists) to expand the range of human sympathies and connections, but this is, as with much else in his project, a temporary situation. Later, as the utopian process expands and develops, this task will become the common property of all. It is this, if anything, which may be defined as the purpose of a Wellsian utopia: to allow each person, to the utmost degree possible, the freedom to create, shape, live, and tell their own story in their own manner. "World-pax, economic efficiency, universal education, all these things we find in the long run have but one objective, to make the world safe for artists," writes William Burroughs Steele, or, rather, for "'Art — the undying explorer.' And with that emendation," comments Wells, the purported editor of Steele's posthumous papers, "it seems to me most of the distinction between art and science disappears."[21] Science is largely an exploration of the material world in which we live and of which we are a part, but such explorations are important only within some sort of theoretical (narrative) structure. These structures, as it turns out, need not be scientific at all.

This does not by any means require that all people be writers, or that all writers produce science fiction, or even that all writers must have explicit utopian visions. For one thing, science fiction is not in itself utopian, nor are science fiction authors necessarily interested in themes of compassion or humanism; the free-market libertarianism of Robert Heinlein or Poul Anderson comes quickly to mind here, for example, as does the explicitly anti–Wellsian Christianity of C.S. Lewis's *That Hideous Strength*. Indeed most of the lesser sort of action-oriented science fiction, fun though it may be to read, is implicitly in favor of the economic and social status quo of the time during which it appeared. Poor writing of any sort makes utopianizing difficult in any case, as it reduces the depth of the possible connection between author, reader, and characters. Part of the utopianizing process is an increasing understanding of what it means to be human, which perforce includes being human under the present circumstances (whatever point and condition is taken as "present"). Such an understanding, which it might be said lies in the realm of sociology or anthropology to develop, is inextricably tied in with imagination; "economics and sociology can only be made *hard* sciences by eliminating much of their living content."[22] Indeed, "in the field of sociology it is impossible to disentangle social analysis from literature.... It may be doubted if constructive sociology and educational science can ever be freed from a certain literary, aesthetic and ethical flavouring."[23] To say that Wells believes in "the impossibility of justifying the imagination as more than a distraction from serious public concerns"[24] is therefore to miss its role in his utopian vision altogether. The imagination is what allows for prescription to begin with. Descriptive sociology, economics, and so on have their place and their value, yet it is only prescription which will move humanity away from the current, unsatisfactory, situation. As George Santayana remarked, "All observation is observation of brute fact, all discipline is mere repression, until these facts digested and this discipline embodied in humane impulses become the starting-point for a creative movement of the imagination, the firm basis for ideal constructions in society, religion, and art. Only as conditions of these human activities can the facts of nature and history become morally intelligible or practically important. In themselves they are trivial incidents, gossip of the Fates, cacklings of their inexhaustible garrulity."[25] All social prescription that is not purely prohibitive requires imagination; it cannot be rigidly scientific, because it cannot control for all the possible variables, and experiments on any but the smallest scale are impossible. This restriction does not apply to literature, to imaginative writing. Here the experiments can be done on the broadest of scales as well as the smallest, in such a manner to at once encompass the reader and to allow her or him to remain outside as a critical observer. Although these are thought experiments they remain experiments nonetheless, albeit in a different sense; what matters here is the internal coherence of the vision being offered, as well as its ability to convey a convincing or at least persuasive vision of possible futures. Hence the importance of a utopia's connection with what its readers know and, at least initially, believe; hence also, however, the importance of a utopia's acknowledgement, and encouragement, of other possibilities, other thought experiments to be performed by the reader him or her self. Wells takes this latter point quite seriously, and his utopias show the result. In addition to the multitude of dialogues between characters representing opposing, or at least differing, visions of the steps needed toward the utopian path, Wells's writings are filled with subtle undercuttings of his own prior positions, or even with similar undercuttings of the central narrative by Wells himself, or at least someone speaking in his name. An example of the latter can be found in *The Shape of Things to Come*, wherein Wells, the ostensible editor of a future history book transcribed from dreams by a friend of his, does not hesitate to criticize the (presumably fixed) course of the history yet to unfold. For an example of the former, see *Apropos of Dolores*, where the publisher Stephen Wilbeck comments on his previously Wellsian views as valuable, but "not steps toward the salvaging of civilization." This triggers a parenthetical note: "(I forget whose phrase that is; it sounds familiar; one of my various authors may be responsible, manifestly he meant well, but it is not the precise right phrase. It suggests a sort of rescue of old masters from a burning country house.)" The title to which he is referring is Wells's own, from the 1921 book I have already mentioned.[26] Such a distantiation is vital to the evolutionary utopian project, as it encourages, if it doesn't compel, the reader to read beyond the text at hand, to see beyond the vision offered. If I could have been wrong then, the author suggests thereby, I could be wrong now; but so could you, in your acceptance of what is, or of only one method for changing it, be wrong. As Wells insisted in a public lecture, "My reply to the superior critic has always been — forgive me — 'Damn you, *do it better*.'"[27] Again we see a contrast with critical philosophy, where the ideal is absolute clarity (one thinks here of Descartes's "natural light," for example, or of the intentions behind much of modern symbolic logic) and the intent is to demonstrate the validity, often with no interest in the truth, of the position taken. In evolutionary utopian thought, on the other hand, that about which the author is writing is always subject to change, not least in the case where the author's writings are themselves influential; the clearer the analysis, therefore, the less interesting the utopia as a vision, and evocation, of previously unimagined possibilities.

It is therefore here that the distinction between imaginative literature and critical literature becomes most significant. Wilbur Marshall Urban has acutely commented on the underlying distinction in character of our response to imaginative literature as opposed to scientific:

> Poetry [by which he means all imaginative writing, including the novel], then, whether as intuitive, metaphorical, or dramatic language, always says certain things explicitly about man and about human life. What it says explicitly is manifold and varied and often contradictory; but in so far as it is authentic, all explicit assertions have one common character — they are assertions about *persons*. This may seem to be the veriest platitude, but it is, properly understood, of the utmost significance. For science, rightly understood, never speaks of persons and has no interest in them as such. Indeed it has no interest in the individual as such, but only as an exemplification of a universal.[28]

Where philosophy is scientific, whether intentionally or accidentally, the same strictures of necessity apply. As modern philosophy is largely scientific in its outlook, it perforce must avoid what to its practitioners appears as too strong a focus on individuals (save as exceptions which disprove some general rule), and must operate at the level of the general. The novel, on the other hand, is concerned, whether written about a group or even humanity as a whole, with the nature and character of individuals, as persons and as independent moral agents. Hence, for Wells, all types of fiction, indeed all types of imaginative narrative, are at least potentially available as utopian materials, as each narrative offers the same resources for reshaping the individual's moral consciousness. He placed special stress upon the role of the novel and the novelist, though, because he saw the novel as allowing the broadest possible development of an imaginative vision; Tolstoy or Victor Hugo can take a thousand pages and more to develop their narratives as deeply and consecutively as necessary, a detail (and length) unavailable to other forms of narrative presentation.

Wells defines the novel quite broadly; it is, he said, "any sort of honest treatment of the realities of human behaviour in narrative form."[29] Wells wrote so many different narratives because he was challenging the hold of one particular classification on the means of exciting the human imagination. In this he was paralleling the contemporary avant-garde, yet for vastly different purposes; accordingly, he has rarely been considered as having mapped out significant new ground for the novel. Only later did views quite similar to his become more commonplace, so much so, perhaps, that his originality once more can be missed. Compare his views with the attitude of Jean-Paul Sartre toward his own study of Flaubert: "I would like my study to be read as a novel because it really is the story of an apprenticeship that led to the failure of an entire life. At the same time, I would like it to be read with the idea in mind that it is true, that it is a *true* novel."[30] There have been various arguments over whether or not Sartre's work is a biography or a novel or something else altogether; Wells would say, of course it's a novel — and all the other things besides; they're not mutually exclusive, whatever the classificatory pedants say. Impact, however achieved, rather than a strict adherence to formal canons, matters most for Wells. He saw the novel as "an important and necessary thing indeed in that complicated system of uneasy adjustments which is modern civilization,"[31] a thing with "inseparable moral consequences."[32] Georg Lukács said something similar not very much later, in *The Theory of the Novel*: Compared to other literary forms, "In the novel, on the other hand, ethic — the ethical intention — is visible in the creation of every detail and hence is, in its most concrete content, an effective structural element of the work itself."

Lukács further claims that "as form, the novel establishes a fluctuating yet firm balance between becoming and being; as the idea of becoming, it becomes a state."[33] Wells would never have written in this manner, but the content of the two discussions is here not very far apart at all. The impact of writing of any sort, he thought, was underrated; "The power of the book, the possible function of the book in the modern state is still but imperfectly understood."[34]

Wells noted the conflicts between various elements of human interests which had been gathering force for decades (and which remain of paramount importance). "And today," he said in a lecture in 1910, in words still, or perhaps even more, relevant a century later,

> while we live in a period of tightening and extending social organisation, we live also in a period of adventurous and insurgent thought, in an intellectual spring unprecedented in the world's history. There is an enormous criticism going on of the faiths upon which men's lives and associations are based, and of every standard and rule of conduct. And it is inevitable that the novel, just in the measure of its sincerity and ability, should reflect and co-operate in the atmosphere and uncertainties and changing variety of this seething and creative time.
>
> And I do not mean merely that the novel is unavoidably charged with the representation of this wide and wonderful conflict. It is a necessary part of the conflict.[35]

The conflict hinges upon the growing recognition by various human beings that the forces of individuation and collectivization are both growing in strength as a necessary consequence of the development of human society. The expansion of government and industry and the rationalization of matters military, technical, and distributive require large-scale organizations of a sort hitherto seldom, if ever, seen. Yet at the same time the spread of liberal democratic and democratic-socialist ideologies,[36] with their enormous stress on the goal of individual freedoms, has generated a great demand for recognition of each person as unique by the very organizations which have sprung up to serve the mass demands themselves connected to these growing individual freedoms. The conflict between the two forces is generating a wide range of destructive social and psychological problems.

Wells sees the novel as providing "the only medium through which we can discuss the great majority" of these problems; each among them "has at its core a psychological problem, and not merely a psychological problem, but one in which the idea of individuality is an essential factor."[37] Wells claims for the novel the role of mediator between an individual reader and a comprehensive and sympathetic understanding of the multitude of roles played by other individuals within the increasingly complex structure of modern society; "the complicated social organisation of to-day cannot get along without the amount of mutual understanding and mutual explanation such a range of characterisation in our novels implies." He goes on to make the claim even stronger:

> The success of civilisation amounts ultimately to a success of sympathy and understanding. If people cannot be brought to an interest in one another greater than they feel to-day, to curiosities and criticisms far keener, and co-operations far subtler, than we have now; if class cannot be brought to measure itself against, and interchange experience and sympathy with class, and temperament with temperament, then we shall never struggle very far beyond the confused discomforts and uneasiness of to-day, and the changes and complications of human life will remain as they are now, very like the crumplings and separations and complications of an immense avalanche that is sliding down a hill.[38]

Wells considers and rejects the abilities of other forms of literature, such as drama, poetry, and biography, to attain his goals. Biography, he says, is restricted first by consideration for the living, and then by ignorance of the inner forces which molded the life at hand. What is left is either rigorously true to fact, and thus as dead as its subject, or speculative regarding motives, and thus half-way to fiction. Autobiography, though potentially more effective as a study of human motivations (assuming the writer to be honest, whether by intention or otherwise), suffers from some of the same limitations, as well others of its own. As Wells notes, "The novel has neither the intense self-consciousness of autobiography nor the paralyzing responsibilities of the biographer. It is by comparison irresponsible and free. Because its characters are figments and phantoms, they can be made entirely transparent."[39]

The modern reader (that such a word—"modern"—might come to be used against Wells is an irony which he would have savored fully) might reject the importance of the novel. It will be said that serious literature is scarcely significant at a societal level any more, and that successful thriller writers such as Clive Cussler, who *are* significant (at least in terms of sales), will never so much as propose ways of making more profound connections between individuals, let alone envision better societies. Something more up-to-date is needed. One might suggest, as has been done for example by Alan Wykes, that "any One World State idea that had ever come to fruition would, one feels, have been ideally suited to the cinema,"[40] which can present images so much more vividly than ever the novel can. Indeed, Wells himself appears to have thought so at one point; commenting in 1929 on the general vapidity of the contemporary motion picture, he foresaw, in rather Wagnerian terms, "the possibility of a spectacle-music drama, greater, more beautiful and intellectually deeper and richer than any artistic form humanity has hitherto achieved."⁴¹ In the lack of visual limitation, the detachment of color from form, and the similar independence of sound from image Wells saw "intimations of a means of expression, exceeding in force, beauty and universality any that have hitherto been available for mankind."⁴² He leapt at the opportunities he detected for using films as an educational aid; "The possibilities of certain branches of teaching," he wrote in 1921, "have been altogether revolutionized by the cinematograph."⁴³ And in 1936 he wrote and was otherwise very largely responsible for the landmark science fiction film *Things to Come*, a vision of the future based largely on his own novel *The Shape of Things to Come* of three years earlier.

It was this last experience which may have tempered Wells's enthusiasm; certainly the film itself points up the problems with film as a medium of presenting a utopian vision. Wells himself recognized some of these:

> It was easy to write of a Dictator, splendidly clothed, seated at the head of his council, and then go on with the speeches. But when it came to the screen, you have to show him from top to toe. And how was he going to dress his hair? Would he be clean-shaven?... And what sort of clothes would he be wearing?... And was our Dictator going to sit down to a wooden table with a wooden chair?... We did our best, but in fact we could never get beyond contemporary modernism. [The film] began in the present time with an intense realism. At the end it culminated in scenes of the intensest detailed improbability.⁴⁴

Speculative film dates far more quickly than the novel, as the trappings of location, set design, and visual style are necessarily more specific than those left to the reader's imagination (science fiction films of any era but the most recent invariably seem more quaint, at least visually, than other films of their own era, save perhaps so-called horror films). The viewer is expected to conform to the vision, rather than the vision being shaped by the viewer. Think here, for example, of the attitude of certain fans of *Star Trek* and its many spin-offs. The original series and its immediate successor are clearly utopian in their aspirations (the later and lesser spin-offs, neither so popular nor so influential, are arguably less so). They dress as the characters, speak as the characters, get married as the characters, and in general live at times in accordance with rules laid down entirely by someone else. Instead of working toward the creation of such worlds (however improbable they may be), these individuals are working towards re-creating themselves in order to more closely experience the products of someone else's imagination. Without wanting to push the analogy too far, this approach is not so very different from the devotees of pornography who purchase ever more elaborate costumes and perform ever more complex scenarios in order to overcome their own certainty that such a reality does not exist. The result is a withdrawal from larger social concerns, to a greater or lesser degree. Ironically, the increased virtuosity of special effects artists militates against the usefulness of film to the utopian project; the better the production values, the more firmly film fixes a specific utopian vision (much more firmly than any novel possibly could), and thus is even falser to the idea of utopia as process. Even in regard to contemporary matters, images specific to the time and place of the reader, film is of necessity faithful to one imagination only, whereas the novel allows for as many experiences of its imaginative aspects as their readers. Finally, film production, at least as regards presentations of a utopian future, entails enormous expenses, and the resultant films are thus unlikely to offer serious critiques of the foundations of the culture in which they were produced, as opposed to specific details within it. A talented writer needs only a pen or pencil and some paper to begin a novel; the same is hardly true of an aspiring utopian director. And it must be admitted that utopian film all too often encourages, or perhaps even demands, passivity on the part of its viewers, whereas the novel, or at least the serious novel, requires an active participation. As it is this latter which is necessary if the reader is to be gotten to move mentally toward the utopian society, the art form most helpful will be one which requires already a sense of imaginative participation and thought.

The novel, then, is seen by Wells as offering the best possible opportunity to attain two goals simultaneously. First, the creation of serious novels will help provide the grounds for a growth in human sympathy, compassion, and understanding. Second, through the reading of novels (reading understood in an interactive and highly involved sense), the individual reader will at one and the same time be broadened and strengthened as a self-consciousness. The novel provides a means for focusing aspects of a particular social self-identity within the reader, creating a new and wider sort of self-identity through empathetic linkings with other human beings (who, because imaginary, are potentially more clearly demarcated as exemplars of specific sorts of relations and emotional/intellectual states), yet it does so through allowing the reader's consciousness to become, to a degree, something that it is not already. "The truth of art," as Marcuse recognized, "lies in its power to break the monopoly of established reality (i.e. of those who established it) to *define* what is *real*. In this rupture, which is the achievement of the aesthetic form, the fictitious world of art appears as true reality."[45] The utopian form, or set of forms, is already in itself a challenge to the present social and political structure. Similar claims occur elsewhere. Karl Mannheim, e.g., considered only visions which, "when they pass over into conduct, tend to shatter, either partially or wholly, the order of things prevailing at the time" to be genuine utopian orientations.[46]

The result is that the reader (and, by extension, the author who can engage the reader in a genuine experience of this sort) is led to a wider definition of what it is to be human, of what the possibilities are for others, and therefore for her or his own being. Again the apparent contradictions resolve, but at a higher (which is to say more fully developed and mutually interactive) level; "these considerations lead us toward mutual understanding," as Wells avers, to which he adds that "They clear up the deadlocks that come from hard and fast use of terms, they establish mutual charity as an intellectual necessity."[47]

The novel works because it mimics and intensifies the very process which we all must undergo as individuals forming a persona in the first place; "Conduct systems of reaction require a story or stories of what we are in order to hold our *selves* together and to put our *selves* over to other people."[48] Wells is by no means alone, or outdated, in holding this position. For a recent restatement of the idea, for example, see Mark Turner: "Narrative imagining, often thought of as literary and optional, appears instead to be inseparable from our evolutionary past and our necessary personal experience."[49] Storytelling helped make us who we are, but who we have become has allowed the extension of storytelling into new and extremely complex forms such as the novel. The narrative structure of the novel, itself analogous to the narrative structure of individual lives as lived, provides an experience which is at one and the same time sharable and unique; it provides a model for unifying the self-consciousness and a focal point for so doing. As Martha Nussbaum describes the process,

> Stories have shaped and continue to shape the readers' desires, giving them a preference for onward movement over stasis, for risk over self-sufficiency, for the human form of time over divine timelessness. They play upon and nourish the emotions — fear, anticipation, grief, hope — that presuppose the form of life of a being both needy and resourceful, both active and finite — and that seem to have their point and function only within the context of such a life.[50]

Stories — narratives of human endeavor — serve simultaneously to recreate and strengthen our self-conceptions; they give us ways through which to experience ourselves as sharing truths with others, truths about each, and all, of us. This is a major concern of Wells's. "Throughout my life," he admits, "a main strand of interest has been the endeavour to anchor *personas* to a common conception of reality."[51] Only through a shared narration can we truly share our separate realities, share the experiences and emotions by which the fragmentary facts of our existences are made coherent and meaningful. Nor is it an objection here to say that no life is lived exactly as the any novel unfolds; the point is that the experience of the novel maps onto the structure of relations within the reader's life and helps to reinforce, or to weaken, these ones or those. Any narrative structure which is vividly experienced can serve this purpose; therefore any novel, whatever technique of writing is used, is potentially available as a means of strengthening one side or another of a persona. It may be true that certain avant-garde styles communicate with only a small number of readers, but this is no *a priori* truth about all readers across time. So long as the text remains there remains a possibility of communication. As Robin Morgan movingly commented to her imagined reader, "We are as close, you and I, as one megaparsec — a mere 3.26 million light years — and as distant as the possibility of these words coming to rest photonically on your retina long after I have gone, electromagnetic dust, into the field of energy."[52] The message is eminently Wellsian; Wells's character Stephen Wilbeck, in *Apropos of Dolores*, expressed a similar point:

> And when I plan and publish books — or write this stuff I am writing now — I do that also for an unseen intimate. Someone whom I hope I shall never meet to quarrel with, or disappoint, or experience his or her everyday inadequacy, will read this. Maybe human intimacy is escaping from the prison of the present and the visible, the prison of our current life ... our invisible tentacles will stretch through time and space to an altogether deeper and different fellowship. A man who sits in a quiet room reading or writing, listening or thinking, may seem to be solitary and isolated. But in fact he is in contact with myriads of intimates. He has a thousand intimacies, each closer and a thousand times finer than those of a peasant with his wife or with his dearest boon companions....[53]

The shared narration *creates* the ground for mutual understanding in a way often not open to critical reason, which requires that the shared ground be already present. As Urban noted, the aesthetic symbol "evokes feeling for the reason that values cannot be appreciated except through feeling."[54] A utopia, the most overarching of symbols, evokes a feeling of wrongness about its contemporary setting and a feeling of rightness about some perceived goal toward which to change the contemporary social structure. This change will in turn give force and meaning to a variety of arguments previously ungrounded; it will also create new ways for other symbols to gain meaning. Any writing about a society, or even a person, which or who does not exist must of necessity partake of the symbolic (the same is probably in fact true of history, but to explore this point would take us too far afield here). Its aesthetic test is the degree to which it convinces the experiencer of its own inner truth; its moral test is the degree to which it provides a sense of projective universal necessity (that things *should* be this way, and *could* be this way for all). I will explore this point further below.

The novel, as Wells sees it, provides as well a moral and political challenge to the individual as constituted at any given moment. Again a parallel point is made by Marcuse: "Art cannot change the world, but it can contribute to changing the consciousness and drives of the men and women who could change the world."[55] To enter into the world of the novel is to become, for a time, unified in a way not possible in real life, and then to confront one's self with the self as recreated by the novel. "But life is always more complicated than any account or representation of it can be."[56] The dissatisfaction with what is portrayed compels the reader to supply what is missing, which in turn requires introspection and thought. In modifying the experience one is having, one is of necessity modifying oneself. The re-visioning of one's place in the world, and of one's self as being in a place, points the way toward a further re-visioning of one's attitudes toward one's fellow human beings. The novel confronts the reader with "Problems of association between men and women and an infinitude of opportunities for mutual charity."[57] The act of will necessary to enter into the world of the serious novel transfers itself, through the text of the novel in hand, to the act of will necessary to enter into the life of another person, and enlarges the number of our opportunities for developing and expanding our range and breadth of sympathies.

This concern for the expansion and development of human sympathies is what led Wells to make so many experiments with the form of the novel. Given the enormous range of human attitudes, interests, emotional states, and personal situations, it would be wrong to assume that any one form will be the key to expressing this or that state, to connecting with this or that person. In the famous controversy between Wells and James, Wells did not so much reject the Jamesian novel of formal perfection as insist that such an approach "no more exhausts the possibilities of the novel, than the art of Velasquez exhausts the possibilities of the painted picture."[58] The form must be shaped by the need to convey the utopian or quasi-utopian or proto-utopian message of mutual charity and cooperation to the widest range of people. The mechanisms will vary, but the project will remain the same; "The *apparatus of moral suggestion*, the people who write, preach, and teach that is, needs only too evidently the discipline of a common ideal."[59] Wells will say that the novel, in its many forms and with its many potential audiences, provides the best means to the common end. Intensely experienced, the novel expands the personality, and renders it thus more open to a wider and richer range of experiences contingent upon a refreshed ordinary life.

Thus far I have been writing of the effect of the novel, or of any work of art, as if all that a person has to do is sit back and enjoy the ride. This is misleading, and it is important to consider the obverse: the responsibility of the reader. This, it turns out, is not only considerable, it points the way into the responsibility of the utopian citizen as a citizen.

Although Wells was and is enormously popular as an author, he recognized and insisted upon a distinction among different types of writing, his own and that of others. "My scientific training," he declared, "disposes me to state and publish "the truth, the whole truth and nothing but the truth," but my unavoidable practical entanglement in the world crisis makes me acutely aware of the strategic and tactical disadvantages of that course."[60] As a utopian, Wells needs to be as detailed and thorough as possible; as an author, Wells wants to be read by more than a small coterie of admirers. His solution took form through the multitude of his writings, from brief newspaper articles to massive histories, from sparkling short stories and comedies to nightmarish fables and complex fictional epics. Even so, he insisted that his readers, at whatever level they were joining him, needed to provide a portion of the requisite work of understanding. In his essay on "The Contemporary Novel," he declared that a lazy reader, especially a male one (caricatured as "the Weary Giant"), would find little support among modern authors; "we are all out with one accord resolved to exercise his higher ganglia in every possible way." (Wells here deliberately distinguished men from women; "Women," he wrote, "are more serious, not only about life, but about books. No type or kind of woman is capable of that lounging, defensive stupidity which is the basis of the tired-giant attitude....")[61] "[R]ead it hard," he likewise demanded in the Preface to *'42 to '44*.[62] Wells wanted criticism, but he wanted it to be informed rather than merely a loud restatement of the reader's unexamined prejudices.

Wells's utopian commitments require this approach, for utopia, under this view, cannot be imposed but must be willed (a fact to which I shall recur several times as the discussion unfolds). The writer, and in particular the novelist, begins by enticing the reader to keep reading, but sooner or later the reader must actively participate in the process of reading if anything of lasting value is to ensue. This entails certain responsibilities, regardless of the reader's actual position regarding the vision presented.

A serious response to any work of art involves understanding and entering into the work's own presuppositions as much as possible and engaging with it on those terms. This by no means requires that one accept those presuppositions, or agree with such conclusions as may follow therefrom, but it does mean that one works as hard as possible to set aside one's own presuppositions in advance. This latter goal is impossible to achieve fully, for we can never be entirely aware of all the forces which have gone into shaping our composite consciousness, yet the mere fact of the effort allows us to expand our range of understandings and their concomitant responses. Nor is it any objection to argue that no work of art exists completely in isolation from social circumstances, and therefore no work of art deserves contemplation purely in itself. Quite the opposite; the more deeply grounded in its context a work is, the more effort is required to grasp its underlying intention and meaning from outside that context. We are probably better off confronting something not from our own traditions than something familiar, for it is in the former case rather than the latter that we are most likely to recognize the need to shift our perspectives in order to expand our understanding. But the process is the same in each case; we encounter the work and, to the degree that we open ourselves to it, we discover the new ways of feeling and thinking that it suggests. The greatest works are those which continue the longest to invite the widest and strongest range of possible responses. But, and this is vital here, the greatest experiencers are those who actively seek out the broadest aspects of themselves in responding to works of art. The best works of art, therefore, do not merely invite active commitment, they reward it repeatedly by never being the same, in part by insuring that those who engage with them are never quite the same afterwards.

It is no accident that one of Wells's favorite novels was Laurence Sterne's rambling comic masterpiece *Tristram Shandy*, and no surprise to find Sterne prefiguring Wells:

> Writing, when properly managed (as you may be sure I think mine is) is but a different name for conversation. As no one, who knows what he is about in good company, would venture to talk all;— so no author, who understands the just boundaries of decorum and good-breeding, would presume to think all; The truest respect which you can pay to the reader's understanding, is to halve this matter amicably, and leave him something to imagine, in his turn, as well as yourself.
>
> For my own part, I am eternally paying him compliments of this kind, and do all that lies in my power to keep his imagination as busy as my own.[63]

Wells's version of Sterne's approach, though often applied in a comic manner, reflects his allegiance to a foundational aspect of progressive utopianizing: that the worlds to come cannot be imposed, for to the degree that they are they are not utopian. This accounts for a typographical oddity that anyone who has read more than a small number of Wells's writings will have noticed: his frequent practice of ending a paragraph with a set of ellipses. Writing is different from conversation in one obvious and unavoidable manner, that there can be no direct dialogue between author and reader. Wells's solution is to write in pauses, places where he is explicitly using the manner of presentation to encourage the reader to go off on their own train of thought. It is up to the reader to take advantage of these opportunities (or any others which they insert for themselves). It is not agreement with his ideas which is primary for Wells, but engagement with the basic idea, that of creating a freer and more utopian society. To the degree that one genuinely argues with Wells or any other utopian author, as opposed to simply ignoring them, one is acting so as to further the process of utopia, for one must, in the process of the argument, deepen one's understanding both of the ideas one rejects and the ideas one espouses. One is enriching one's imagination, and therefore, in at least a small way, the world in which and with which it functions. The reader is perforce but by choice being taken out of her or his narrower sphere of being into a larger one, one in which considerations beyond the personal become ever more important. The engagement with literature, with art of any sort, takes on a dual quality, a sheen of universality which emphasizes, because it is inextricably grounded in, the personal response, It becomes a form of love, and in so doing takes on the mantle of religion: "Love is personal always; inalterably preferential; it is an intensification of personality in ourselves and in our Lovers. It is the qualification, the corrective, of religious universalism. By religion we become Man [sic], by love we remain individual, and as our religion rises and widens to the world community and the starry mind, so the subtlety of our appreciation of the individual difference in ourselves and others must intensify to keep pace with it."[64]

As the individual broadens their emotional and intellectual horizon, they discover new calls upon their mental energies, calls made not in the name of art, or other persons, or even of utopia, but in the name of their own self-conception. What we discover will echo the wisdom of George Santayana's comment introducing his discussion of philosophical poets:

> The sole advantage in possessing great works of literature lies in what they can help us to become. In themselves, as feats performed by their authors, they would have forfeited none of their truth or greatness. We can neither take away nor add to their past value or inherent dignity. It is only they, in so far as they are appropriate food and not poison for us, that can add to the present value and dignity of our minds.[65]

As we learn what we are capable of becoming, we realize that it is incumbent upon us to seek out ever richer and deeper experiences, aesthetically, emotionally, and intellectually, and to understand ourselves, with the aid of those experiences, in ever richer and deeper ways, to avoid what is poisonous to our greater being. It is not that we become incapable of taking pleasure from light entertainments, say, but that we come more and more fully to see them for what they are. Aspects of our personalities scarcely suspected will be freed to develop, but as these various aspects combine in ever more complex ways we will find ourselves less and less willing to accept mediocrity in the arts, in education, in political discourse and action, in our daily lives. Along with this with comes a growing compulsion, powerful because it is internally driven rather than externally imposed, to understand ever more of our interconnectedness with the world, and especially the individuals, around us. We will be experiencing in fact what Kant described in theory as Enlightenment: "man's emergence from his self-imposed immaturity." Wells's link with the Enlightenment is never clearer than here; Kant's description could easily be that of Wells. "Immaturity is the inability to use one's understanding without guidance from another. This immaturity is self-imposed when its cause lies not in lack of understanding, but in lack of resolve and courage to use it with guidance from another."[66] With growing understanding will come resolve and courage, and with resolve and courage will come an increasing unwillingness to be used for the ends of others, whether through systemic manipulation or outright force, through mindless trivia conceived and marketed solely for private gain or vacuous, perhaps even vicious, theories developed and applied without humane intent.

A number of points which have already appeared may now be seen in a new and more revealing light. Utopian thought deals primarily in political generalities, however much their import may be illustrated through the depiction of individual lives; a literary work dealing with the improvement of but one person's life, in the absence of encompassing political concerns, is not in itself utopian, however profound it may be in other ways. But the political choices which would lead to the establishment of a given utopia are made by individuals, and individuals must of necessity be operating within some pre-existing moral scheme of their own (that is to say, one which applies to them uniquely in their situatedness in the world, not one that they must necessarily have created themselves). The utopia and its components will be judged by reason according to prior moral commitments, rather than the other way around. The same is true of the political systems within which the utopia is created; as I have already noted, claims about the moral status of the reader's society presuppose a set of values, and no philosophical reason external to those values (or, if you will, that value system) can have moral weight.

Hence the overblown rhetoric often found in attacks upon utopian thought. Take the notorious assaults on *Republic* by Karl Popper and R.H.S. Crossman, for example, the latter of whom described Plato's philosophy as "the most savage and profound attack upon liberal ideas which history can show,"[67] or for that matter Friedrich Hayek, whose attacks on Wells we shall encounter later. It is not that these writers have misunderstood Plato; rather, they have understood, even if only unconsciously, the need to counter his tremendously evocative vision with strong words which may help to undermine the reader's emotional acceptance of it. Plato cannot *establish* his utopia on grounds of philosophical reason (though he can give reasons for desiring it if one's moral commitments point in something like his direction); therefore no attack on Plato's *foundations* (as opposed to particular factual claims or logical entailments) which is purely philosophical and critical can work either. As Dr. Johnson is somewhere reported to have said, you cannot reason a man out of a position into which he was never reasoned. Crossman and Popper, having a moral commitment to a system (or separate systems, for I suspect that they would disagree with each other's political views as well as with Plato's) other than Plato's, must find some way to threaten it at its base, at the point where Plato might evoke the moral sympathy he needs. Hence their rhetoric.[68]

The converse is also true. The creation of a utopia is not only a political act, but a moral act as well. Utopian schemes, indeed melioristic political schemes of any sort, require compassion: an emotional concern for, and involvement with, the needs, desires, and sufferings of others. No argument can create compassion where none exists; without compassion no proposed scheme of social change on a vast scale (which is one of the distinguishing marks of utopian thought) stands much chance at all of being desired, let alone implemented (one thinks here, for example, of the conservative attitude toward the rights, and specific needs, of women and minorities, an attitude which refuses even to see that there might be a problem worthy of being addressed). Such positive changes as have occurred have usually been driven initially by a small group of morally compassionate individuals, who used all the resources of rhetoric and emotional appeals (and sometimes of threats and violence) to shift the moral stance of those with the power to make the desired changes: the destruction of the slave trade is a case in point. Thus any utopian must strive to awaken compassion in her or his readers.

This recurs in turn to the reason why utopias must be fictional, or at least take on trappings other than those of critical philosophy. If an attempt is being made to convert the reader to a new moral position, or even one significantly different from her or his present position, then something other than factual and logical reasons must be used. The emotions must be awakened and steered in the desired direction, a direction which will lead to the perspective whence the proposed utopia looks better than the old system freshly viewed. As Hume famously said, "Reason is, and ought only to be the slave of the passions, and can never pretend to any other office than to serve and obey them."[69] The moral emotions (approval, disapproval, love, hatred, and so on) must be ignited before any set of factual propositions about the character of the world and the desirability of some major political and social change therein can have any weight at all.

Authors of dystopias know this well. This is why, for example, the tone of the presentation in, say, *Brave New World* is so important. The treatment of the citizenry therein is, as I have noted, at least arguably more humane than the treatment of vast numbers of people in our own society, yet Huxley manages, through careful writing (and through an equally careful playing upon the norms of his intended audience) to suggest that it is far worse. Exactly the same set of facts could be made considerably more palatable, even to the same audience, through a different literary approach.[70] The moral distinction comes through the difference in emphasis and description, not through any innate moral quality. Thus the author of a dystopia, for reasons of her or his own, chooses to work toward making the readers react one way, and the author of a utopia chooses to work toward making the readers react in another way. The former has an easier task, as most people are deeply suspicious at least of schemes labeled "utopian," if not of significant progressive change altogether. Thus only a few qualities need be seized upon and exaggerated in order to make the reader feel the desired revulsion, whereas in the creation of a successful positive utopia a vast number of small details need to be given at least some attention in order to create the sought after sense of approval and desire.

The foregoing, finally, explains also another aspect of the ultimately unsatisfactory nature of most, if not all, utopias. Any utopia is, to some degree at least, the creation of two minds: its author and its reader. All utopian writings are the product of a particular time and place, a time and place which begin to recede and grow vaguer as soon as the utopia is fixed in writing. No utopia can overlap completely with any reader's moral presuppositions. Although the author will do what she or he can to make the utopian vision attractive, invariably some elements will seem, or over time and among readers distant culturally from the author, alien or even repulsive. To that extent the reader will become detached from the vision offered in a way not possible where the 'real world' of daily life is involved. To that extent the same 'real world' will provide a drag upon the utopian urge. Since proportionally few persons ever encounter and engage with serious and detailed utopias in the first place, this factor of what I might call social drag will render even the strongest utopias all but impotent to cause the will to change among their readers.[71] It therefore then becomes the task of those readers to do what they can to awaken the desired moral attitudes in others. From the person to the society is a large step, and making it requires elements of individual transcendence traditionally considered to be in the realm of religion.

Imaginative literature has connections beyond the person as individual; nor does the writer operate in a vacuum. The novel, and the imaginative processes linked with both its creation and its reception, will find further echoes in revivified religious attitudes. These, though, have little to do with contemporary theistic beliefs and practices. Wells's religion is thoroughly atheistic. The only exception to this is Wells's brief and tendentious digression into theism, which began about 1916 (e.g., in *Mr. Britling Sees It Through*) and ended shortly after World War One, to the stresses attendant upon which it largely owed its origin. Wells himself regretted the phase; "What we have here," he wrote later, "is really a falling back of the mind towards immaturity under the stress of dismay and anxiety." He did point out, however, that his God was "a heartening God but not a palliating God. At his best my deity was far less like the Heavenly Father of a devout Catholic or a devout Moslem or Jew than he was like a personification of, let us say, the Five Year Plan." Shortly afterwards, "my phraseology went back unobtrusively to the sturdy atheism of my youthful days." He explicitly disavowed the divagation; "I wish, not so much for my own sake as for the sake of my more faithful readers, that I had never fallen into it; it confused and misled many of them and introduced a barren détour into my research for an effective direction for human affairs."[72]

Appropriately enough, Wells's religion finds its roots in the philosophy of another atheist, Arthur Schopenhauer, "surely at once the most acute and the most biassed [sic] of mortal men."[73] Wells inverts Schopenhauer's notorious pessimism, yet accepts his conclusions, seeing "our wills only as temporary manifestations of an ampler will, our lives as passing phases of a greater Life, and [arguing that humans should decide] to accept these facts even joyfully, to take our places in that larger scheme with a sense of relief and discovery...."[74]

Wells accepts one of the conventional claims about the importance of religion: "its presence seems to have been necessary for collective life. Without it morality was baseless and law unjustifiable."[75] This, however, is an empirical social claim, not a metaphysical one. Religion did not provide the basis for law and morality because of its truth, but because of its usefulness;

"the survival value of a religion to a community has lain always in the practical assistance it afforded in the subordination of self and the achievement of co-operative loyalties not otherwise attainable."[76] Those compelled by loyalty to a religious view, any religious view, surrender their individuality to its demands, and then begin to define that individuality along new lines, as shaped by the religion to which they have given allegiance. Religion seen thus includes three elements: "self-disregard, then service, and then this reconstructive creative urgency."[77]

The previous religious structures of the world have been grounded in, and oriented toward, the prejudices of various groups. Although the major religions claim hundreds of millions of adherents, each still defines itself as against the others, theologically even if not, as is so often the case, legally, politically, and even militarily. Most still cling to a view of a personalized deity, or world-force, into a relationship with which the individual enters by means of particularized beliefs and actions. Wells will have none of this; "The histories and symbols that served our fathers encumber and divide us. Sacraments and rituals harbour disputes and waste our scanty emotions."[78] Instead, some other source and inspiration for the urge to self-transcendence must be found. The authority which was once held by supernatural religions must be transcended and expanded.

The answer, as Wells sees it (and as we have seen already in another context), is the idea of humanity, and indeed of what humanity may become, as a whole.[79] Not, he is quick to assert, humanity as it exists now, or at any other temporal point, but as a process in itself. That most of his writings concentrate on the nearer future is to be expected; much of his intended audience could scarcely imagine the next year, let alone the next millennium. The contrast, however made, remains clear; Wells's focus is on the future, while most religions are grounded in events in the past (creation, the "Fall," and various other historical or quasi-historical or pseudo-historical events, etc.). Religion in its essence, providing "an escape from the distressful pettiness and morality of the individual life,"[80] must turn now toward the future. "There was no Creation in the past, we begin to realise, but eternally there is creation; there was no Fall to account for the conflict of good and evil, but a stormy ascent. Life as we know it is a mere beginning."[81]

There is an acknowledged connection with Comte here, but Wells goes far beyond Comte in his vision. Comte wrote without any apparent sense of evolutionary history; "if he was not totally ignorant of its existence, he was, and conscientiously remained ignorant of its relevancy [sic] to the history of humanity."[82] This led to a failure of imagination on Comte's part, a failure echoed by all subsequent positivists. "Since he could imagine nothing higher than man, he had to assert that humanity, and particularly the future of humanity, was the highest of all conceivable things."[83] Humanity needed only to pass one last barrier to arrive at a final happy and cultured state, one needing no further adjustments. This flies in the face of the understanding opened up by evolutionary science (given Comte's almost worshipful attitude toward science, there is an irony here which Wells does not develop); "our imaginations have been trained upon a past in which the past that Comte knew is scarcely more than the concluding moment.... And when, from that retrospect, we turn again toward the future, surely any thought of finality, any millennial settlement of cultured persons, has vanished from our minds."[84] (Wells admitted, "Probably I am unjust to Comte and grudge to acknowledge a sort of priority he had in sketching the modern outlook." This dislike he attributed to his response to Comte's glorification as a leader, which irked Wells no matter who was being so honored. Karl Marx fell afoul of Wells in the same fashion.[85] His main point, however, whatever its origins in his personal psychology, remains valid. Comte clearly neither knew nor guessed the implications of the new understandings of the age of the earth in his lifetime, let alone the possibility of biological evolution).

Religion, then, must survive in a manner stripped of excrescences of cult or sect or textual fundamentalism if it is to remain valid, yet its validity is itself a necessity. The utopian project therefore includes a cleansing and humanizing of religion. Religion becomes subordinate to, and part of, the educational structure of society — "Education is the preparation of the individual for the community, and his religious training is the core of that preparation."[86] — where it continues to serve its earlier function of grounding morality and law, only now without theistic illusions. Religion abandons its claims to factual matters, about which it can prove nothing and which provide only grounds for social fragmentation, and takes its place as a means of enhancing the humanistic outlook. This is, according to Wells, what religions already do anyway, save that their practitioners, and especially their promoters, don't always recognize the fact. As William Clissold saw, "Religion is only formally a thing of the intelligence; its substance is feeling and a way of life. Every religion pretends to rest upon facts and statements, but no religion really does so."[87] Once this is widely acknowledged, religion will at once contract and expand its importance to the human mind. It will contract, in that all the little distinctions in ritual and belief which now set humans against one another will vanish; it will expand, in that the greater sense of shared humanity will take on a larger part in shaping and creating the individual's emotions, attitudes, and actions. Religion is a means of social control toward a desired end; only when that end no longer entails conversion, but rather implies inclusion, will religion become the force for the overall human good that it has always had the potential to be. Religion, for Wells, is always a strong educative force; what he wants is to render it a means of educating all of humanity about their own commonalty. He even recruits Jesus Christ into his service; meeting him in a fictional dream, he discovered that "His scorn and contempt for Christianity go beyond my extremest vocabulary." Nor is God Himself exactly pleased with the human approach to religion:

> I *hate* pious people. I hate their abject prayers. Almost always they are mean demands for preferential miracles. Whenever I get a chance, I do them bad turns. I never, if I can help it, answer their prayers. Then they say I am *trying* them and they crawl more than ever. Where do they get these ideas about me? When have I countenanced any of these verminous saints?

God sails aboard a new Ark, but only as a passenger and harmonium player.[88] The humorous satirical point is, like most such, serious at heart; Wells is acknowledging, and building upon, the narrative core of virtually all religions. The difference is that he seeks cooperation rather than either divisiveness or coerced unity.

It is this attitude, incidentally, which explains Wells's testy attitude toward Judaism, an attitude occasionally mistaken for anti–Semitism. As with Wells's views on eugenics, a topic of minor significance within his writings has attracted undue attention as a result of later events, yet in this case Wells is more to blame than in the other. Certainly a writer expects, or ought to expect, that the most obvious meaning is the one which will be taken by the ordinary reader, and equally certainly a writer should expect that most readers will be of the ordinary sort. Thus it is no surprise that some of Wells's more vigorous strictures against Judaism should raise the hackles of some of his readers. "The whole question turns upon the Chosen people idea," Wells argues, "which this remnant cherishes and sustains, which it is the 'mission' of this remnant to cherish and sustain. It is difficult not to regard that idea as a conspiracy against the rest of the world. It is essentially a bad tradition, and the fact that the Jews on the whole have been very roughly treated by the rest of mankind does not make it any the less bad." Nor was Wells any less rough with the religious texts, as his description of the Book of Isaiah, complete with what now seems an appalling comparison, shows: "Much of it is ferocious; extraordinarily like the rantings of some Nazi propagandist." Worse still would appear to be his summation of the relations of Jews and gentiles: "I argue that the Jews make themselves and that Gentile intolerance is a response to the cult of the Chosen People." And just in case one might be tempted to defend him by arguing that he is referring to things drawn from ancient history, he addresses the refugee problem of the late 1930s in this manner: "Why should any country want these inassimilable aliens bent on preserving their distinctness?"[89] Wells must surely be blamed at the very least for almost offensive carelessness in producing such passages, especially at the historical moment when he did so.

There are actually two questions posed by Wells's statements. The first is simple: are Wells's writings such as to encourage or support anti–Semitism in the mind of a careful reader? The second is broader and more serious: is what Wells is saying on the whole true or on the whole false, however we might dislike his manner of saying it? After all, if I tell you your house is burning and it is, then even if I say "Your house is burning, you rotten bastard," the fact conveyed remains the same despite my choice of descriptive terms.

The first question is fairly easily answered. Although Wells is writing within a specifically English tradition of suspicion and misunderstanding about the Jewish religion, a tradition going back at least to Shakespeare (think of Shylock), and although he has not critically examined his own beliefs, it is clear that his statements amount to nothing more than common prejudices carelessly articulated rather than wholesale anti–Semitism. This is not to defend them, but merely to indicate that they fall into the same category as jokes about jolly fat people or limp-wristed homosexuals in our own society; such things stem from unexamined prejudices absorbed from social context, and can often be found in people who are otherwise free of hatreds. The charge, then, dissolves into the claim that Wells failed to avoid all of the social prejudices of his time. This is certainly unfortunate, but hardly reprehensible in any strong sense. They play no part in his larger agenda; remove every single testily phrased comment about Judaism from his work, and the utopian project will remain unchanged.

Once this is understood, the reason for that testiness becomes evident, and the context for the comments becomes clearer. Wells is trying to establish the grounds, and create the desire, for a world state. Any insular viewpoint stands in opposition to this, so if Wells is serious — and he most definitely is — he must find some way around or past the given insularity. Any group which, on metaphysical grounds, claims to be in some manner genuinely distinct from the rest of humanity is, for Wells, a force operating against the world commonwealth. Such groups regularly aroused his wrath, and he was often intemperate in expressing it; the comments on the Jews are scattered throughout his writings, and do not in fact add up to much, but the peak of his anti-religious invective is reached in *Crux Ansata*, a book-length blast against the Roman Catholic Church. Here his terminology is even less temperate: "To propitiate the Roman Catholic organisation with political office or power is like establishing friendly relations with the area sneak by handing him the family silver." He describes Pius XII as "an open ally of the Nazi-Fascist-Shinto axis," and describes the "Axis Pope" as "clamouring for a bitter conflict against something "Unchristian" called "Bolshevisation," which will destroy every decent thing in existence, superiors and inferiors, the family — the Catholics are always very great on the family — and dividends."[90] It is ferocious, but all to the same end: to help convince the reader of a claim which by now should be quite familiar: that "the Pope, any Pope, is necessarily an ill-educated and foolish obstacle, a nucleus of base resistance, heir to the tradition of Roman Catholicism in its last stage of poisonous decay, in the way to a better order in the world."[91]

The foregoing suggests that the main problem with Wells's comments regarding Judaism is the change in historical context; later readers known what happened in the Holocaust, whereas Wells knew only the bare beginnings of it. Since such an evil has been done to individuals within a particular group solely because of their membership therein, we tend to associate any attack on the general ideology of the group as an attack motivated by attitudes similar to those which underlay the Holocaust. Wells's comments on Catholicism would scarcely rile anyone today, because there is no emotional context which goes beyond the comments themselves, while quite the opposite is true of his scattered references to Judaism.

One need not defend these outbursts to understand the reasons behind them and the context within which they were voiced. Wells is trying to convey a sense of urgency in a limited space. He lays out his claims brusquely and avows doing so, because he's making factual claims and believes very strongly that "they are facts that have to be stated, even though matters are now coming to a complexion which gives a flavour of ruthlessness to their bare statement."[92] Wells is concerned with what appears to him to be impending disaster on a scale hitherto unseen, and he is not going to take the time over niceties of expression as regards any particular group. In fact, part of his project is to warn the Jews as well; "I have enlarged upon their case because it is not only conspicuously challenging at the present time but because it brings into the picture most of the elements of the present human situation, the general disposition of any established community to adhere to forms and traditions of living long after their survival value has disappeared, the normal blindness of human beings to the onset of novel and more exacting conditions until disaster actually supervenes, the swiftness with which social balance can now be overturned."[93] Ironically, it was Wells who failed to understand the swiftness of the approaching catastrophe, for he failed to understand the equally outdated, and much more vicious, views on which Nazi racial policy was based.

Wells's attitude toward religion as practiced historically stems from, and is required by, his overall commitment to humanity as a whole. Wells is largely right, in fact if not in approach; any religion, deistic or secular (e.g. Marxism, against which Wells railed on many an occasion as well) with a specific set of doctrines, which is truly convinced of its own truth must hold all others to be in error, at least doctrinally. When it comes to determining what should be taught, and even by whom it should be taught, the advocate of a given religion who holds that it does not matter is displaying a surprising disregard for the value of her or his purported truths, since an education which says that Y and Z are of equal weight implies that it doesn't much matter which is believed. This, then, either says that the "truth" doesn't matter, or that it isn't really *the* truth. Neither conclusion supports the claims of the particular believer, or of the religion. But it is precisely this at which Wells is driving. There may be a truth out there somewhere, but it is not something which we can know completely or with absolute certainty. We have to make moral commitments (even attempting not to make a commitment is already to do so), but there are no guarantees, and Wells thinks that therefore there can be no justification for allowing any group to maintain its particular set of dogmas otherwise unchallenged, especially if those dogmas help maintain the moral and social fragmentation of humanity. In other words, wherever Wells sees errors compounding the confusions militating against utopian possibilities for humanity he challenges those errors as forcefully as possible. To return to the burning house analogy, it is as if you had been warned not to use a space heater with a frayed electrical cord prior to the fire; now I am both calling your attention to a fact (the fire) and venting my frustration at the fact that the fire could have been prevented had you heeded the previous warning. The language may be intemperate, but the context reveals that it is not in fact personal.

It will probably be clear that Wells's ideas here are squarely in the tradition of classical liberalism, save that classical liberals, and especially their modern descendants, don't recognize, or at least prefer not to make much of, the fact that true liberalism requires denying the possibility of socially applicable fundamental knowledge to traditional supernatural religion as well as to anything political; universal claims ostensibly obtained through revelation have no place in deciding what should be policy in a pluralistic liberal society. In this sense modern conservatives are quite right to fear liberalism, for it poses an extremely difficult challenge to their fundamentalist metaphysics and the implicit theocracy it entails. It is, as we have seen, largely supernatural religion which buttresses our social morality; liberalism, if followed through consistently, entails a challenge to the presumed veracity of any so-called revealed religion, and thereby to the moral systems based upon those revelations. It is not that an individual cannot choose to hold particular beliefs under such an account, but rather that they have no grounds for imposing regulations based solely upon those beliefs on others. Pluralism and revelation are in irreconcilable conflict. Revelation, taken seriously, excludes pluralism altogether; if there is a God, and if that God does speak to certain individuals in order to lay down a variety of moral laws, then there is no arguing with those individuals. The idea of truth or falsity, right or wrong, simply doesn't exist here, as there is no possible ground for questioning the rightness of an infinite and omnipotent being. Those speaking for that being are backed by infinite power; whatever they say goes, and damn the rest of us, quite literally.

Conversely, pluralism excludes revelation as a basis for political or moral claims beyond the ambit of the individual, because pluralism requires the possibility of dialogue and criticism. In revelation there is no ground for examining the truth claim of the presumed revelation. If someone tells me that god has commanded them to burn Wells's books, I have no factual grounds whatsoever for affirming or denying their statement. Likewise, if I assert the opposite — that god told me to preach Wells's ideas from the rooftops — the skeptical opponent can only say something like "I doubt it." Neither situation is resolvable; neither is useful. While this might not matter much at the personal level, when taken to the level of public policy it creates, as history all too clearly shows, the conditions for the worst sorts of theocratic or fascistic tyranny. This problem is basic to teleological utopias, and is usually swept under the rug by their authors. Plato, for example, uses myths to convince the craftspeople that they ought to trust the philosophers, but they — the craftspeople — do so only because of their upbringing. They cannot in fact tell the difference between a true philosophical claims and a false one, so they tend to laugh at them all, as Socrates says. What is needed is a clean slate mentally and a very effective program of education. But since the bulk of the citizenry is excluded from an understanding of the reasons underlying the structure and operations of the state, their connection thereto is only as strong as the propaganda mechanisms of the philosophers, and the weapons of the Guardians, can make it. Even Plato admits not only that his ideal society will decay, but that it will eventually, and necessarily, turn into a tyranny. In ancient times amidst a horde of city-states with much comparatively empty space between each of them, this might have been more or less acceptable, but modern technology has made the cost of tyrannies in human suffering too high to be borne in good faith.

Wells's putative anti–Semitism can now be understood clearly. Whatever most deeply divides us, he insists, is to be condemned most deeply. Religion, which Wells sees as primarily a matter of emotion rather than intellect, divides humanity very deeply indeed, and it does so not at the level of discourse but at the level of feeling; to challenge its power, to overcome the divisive attitudes derived from it, will require an equally powerful emotional counterweight. Part of this is creative — the utopias, and various satirical passages on religion in the conventional novels — but part of it is rhetorical. Wells is trying, in the space of one lifetime of writing, to help create the will, on the part of diverse individuals of differing backgrounds, to think of humanity as a whole rather than as a collection of necessarily conflicting subgroups, tribes, nations, religions. To do this he resorts to strong language, language often derived from the very groups he is attacking. Consider his strictures against Isaiah; Wells, himself something of a prophet, is indulging in the good old-fashioned prophetic habit of abuse, very much in the language, suitably modernized, of his target. As Isaiah insists of the days to come, "Through the wrath of the Lord of hosts is the land darkened, and the people shall be as the fuel of the fire: no man shall spare his brother. And he shall snatch on the right hand, and be hungry; and he shall eat on the left hand, and they shall not be satisfied: they shall eat every man the flesh of his own arm...." Similarly he warns of the fate of Babylon: "Every one that is found shall be thrust through; and every one that is joined unto them shall fall by the sword. Their children also shall be dashed to pieces before their eyes; their houses shall be spoiled, and their wives ravished.... Their bows also shall dash the young men to pieces; and they shall have no pity on the fruit of the womb; their eye shall not spare children."[94] Had Wells used these words instead of his own, a reader unfamiliar with Isaiah might have been yet more offended, but this is indeed the language of fundamentalism. On the other hand, had Wells referred to "the rantings of some Hyde Park lunatic" rather than a Nazi, probably no one would even have noticed. His choice of comparisons seems odious only in hindsight; when he made his comment the Nazis were widely, though quite wrongly, seen as a set of thugs who had somehow gotten their hands on the levers of power but who posed little real danger. Only later did the extent of their atrocities become known.

The context changes the impact of the words, but the message, stripped of irrelevancies, remains worth consideration. Wells knew of historical anti–Semitism and its consequences, but, as he wrote,

> All the countervailing evil in the world cannot make a bad tradition a good one. Killing or ill-treating a man does not put him in the wrong, but also, we have to remember, and that is not so easy for the liberal-

minded, it does not put him in the right. The idea of the solidarity of the Chosen People, evade it or not, remains the fundamental Jewish idea, and this fundamental Jewish idea, like any other nationalism, is an offence against the unity of mankind.⁹⁵

That is to say that any group which sets itself apart from the rest of the human commonwealth, no matter what the reason, is acting against the best interests not only of humanity as a whole, but even against the interests of each individual within the group, since, no matter what each person believes, that person is a human being above all else. Both persecutors and persecuted tend to forget this fact. Thus Wells's comment about refugees was not a demand that Jews be rejected; in fact, the statement merely remarks on the likelihood of their being rejected rather than recommending such a rejection. Rather, he was pointing out that any person who begins their life in a new country by setting themselves apart from those already there is not offering a great incentive to those prior inhabitants to welcome them. He is explicitly writing against a small group of die-hard conservatives, and using his warnings to them as yet another in his educative campaign to awaken a sense of humanity in the rest of us.

Education, for Wells, is the inheritor of the religious and political motivations behind the creation of states and communities; its aim, for utopian purposes, must be to transcend them. "The community of will is limited in size by the limitations set upon the possibilities of a community of knowledge."⁹⁶ As the community of knowledge in utopia will necessarily be all of humanity (a point already suggested, and to be developed at greater length in the following chapter), the foundations of educational theory and practice must themselves be as unrestricted by traditional national or cultural attitudes and practices as possible. Accordingly, Wells distinguishes "four chief factors" in education:

> *One*, the training of all the individual faculties to as high a level as possible, speech, drawing, the full use of hands and body generally.; *two*, the development of a persona and of the self-knowledge and the practical psychological commonsense necessary for happy personal conduct and the filling of a distinctive role in life; *three*, the establishment of a picture of the universe in accordance with reality, the realization of the great adventure of humanity and of a personal role in that drama; and *four*, the special technical training and experience needed for the due enactment of the individual role.⁹⁷

Of these four factors, only the third is primarily a function of ordinary schooling. The first begins in infancy; the second, though examined briefly here, will be examined in greater detail later; and the fourth requires both specialized schooling and individual initiative.

The foundation of education is social and moral in nature. Two thousand years from now Sarnac, in describing his dream, or really nightmare, of having lived in our century, mentions one of the signal differences between his world and ours. "We are trained from earliest childhood in the world," he comments, "to be tolerant and understanding of others and to be wary and disciplined with our own wayward impulses, we are given from the first a clear knowledge of our entangled nature." As he later adds, "In this world we breathe mercy with our first fluttering gasp. In this world we are so taught and trained to think of others that their pain is ours."[98] The recognition of the multifarious character of the human personality forms the basis both for training which works to focus that personality more clearly in a cooperative direction and for an education which allows the creative aspects of that personality to develop themselves most acutely. Knowledge of self and of others go hand in hand, in order to develop a sympathetic understanding of our relations, both with others and with our own shifting personae. "An extraordinary amount of unhappiness has been and still is caused in the world by the failure to recognize the fluctuating quality of personality,"[99] Wells comments; one of the first functions of education is to ameliorate this potential unhappiness. Unhappy people are not good subjects for later and further education, which they will be likely to resist.

Along with a sense of social connectedness comes a welter of information. Wells has provided a detailed blueprint of the scope and structure of the informational side of his educational system, at least as it approximates to conditions now and in the realistically foreseeable future; his system includes a wide range of scientific, as well as historical, material. Unlike those of most prior utopian writers, who at least assumed, and often specifically insisted upon, a rigid hierarchy of educational levels, Wells's system is aimed at every possible citizen; "What," he asks, "is the irreducible minimum of knowledge for a responsible human being today?"[100] Finally, and this is surely among the most important distinctions between Wells's educational proposals and those of the majority of his predecessors, Wells's are designed to be inserted into an extant educational system, presuming only that it is minimally coherent and functional in itself. Wells expected close and critical scrutiny of his proposals, and acted accordingly; again and again we see Wells doing his best to render his proposals not only plausible but practical.[101] Here he is not utopian in the futuristic sense, but rather contemporary; his suggestions are, at least initially, designed to strengthen and expand the character, and focus the personality, of citizens within the present state, in such a way as to prepare for that state's peaceful obsolescence and subsumption into the world state. Compassion, in its fullest sense, requires humanism; humanism requires an understanding of the forces which shape us as human beings. Understanding requires education.

Wells begins by making an interesting assumption: that "whatever we propose as this irreducible minimum of knowledge must be imparted between infancy and — at most, the fifteenth or sixteenth year." In this he remained consistent; regarding the education of the citizenry in *A Modern Utopia* the narrator's host said "our schooling period ends now about fourteen ... the rest go on to college or upper school," out of which they pass at eighteen. Only the leaders, the samurai, are actually required to attend upper school, and to pass the final examination, the nature of which is unspecified.[102] These age limits are in part based on practical concerns, but in the main they mark a recognition that the education in the early years is more likely to have a lasting effect than that in the later years. Freedom afterwards is worth the price of a solid, though flexible, regimen beforehand. Pursuant to this assumption, Wells restricts himself to a small portion of ten years worth of schooling, 2400 hours in total. Into this he inserts what he considers the requisite informative content.

The process is divided into a base, three levels of primary study, two levels of secondary study, and the level of "new knowledge and thought."[103] The base is the child's natural curiosity, which leads easily to simple lessons in natural science and history; significantly, the formal aspect of education begins with "true stories of the past and other lands. We open out the child's mind to a realization that the sort of life it is living is not the only life that has been lived and that human life in the past has been different from what it is today and on the whole that it has been progressive."[104] The latter claim may be disputed, but Wells is not insisting on some law of historical development, so his position is not so easy to attack as a more historicist one. The burden of proof would seem to be on the person who claims that humanity was better off, *on the whole*, at any given period prior to our own. Wells includes the darker elements of history, but still as narratives rather than collections of dates and names. Our education in history is, in a sense, an education in the means of developing our own story more fully by grounding it in the broader story of human development.

The same sort of approach applies to the sciences; those which can most easily connect with the expanding external world of the youngster come first, and are taught in ways intended to make the pupil feel at home in the natural world. "I think we might easily turn the bear, the wolf, the tiger and the ape from holy terrors and nightmare material into sympathetic creatures, if we brought some realization of how these creatures live, what their real excitements are, how they are sometimes timid, into the teaching."[105] Here Wells is seeking to more fully ground the person in the physical world, to make the person realize their own links with that world, rather than to deny its value altogether.

Alongside these early stages (about 400 hours of education), Wells includes the child's own reading and play, which develop the imagination. In support of this, Wells therefore excludes much "of what has hitherto figured as *history*. I do not see," he declared,

> either the charm or the educational benefit of making an important subject of and throwing a sort of halo of prestige and glory about the criminal history of royalty, the murder of the Princes in the Tower, the wives of Henry VIII, the families of Edward I and James I, the mistresses of Charles II, Sweet Nell of Old Drury, and all the rest of it. I suggest that the sooner we get all that unpleasant stuff out of schools, and the sooner we forget the border bickerings of England, France, Scotland, Ireland and Wales, Bannockburn, Flodden, Crécy and Agincourt, the nearer our world will be to a sane outlook on life.[106]

These things, Wells says, have no importance in themselves for the proper shaping of intelligent and thoughtful human beings. Wells wants education to be ultimately subversive of tradition and stability (again a point of contrast between his views and those of most other utopians). "The Old Education," according to the future history textbook in *The Shape of Things to Come*, "existed to preserve traditions and institutions.... But the New Education, based on a swiftly expanding science of relationship, was no longer the preservation of tradition, but instead the explanation of a creative effort in the light of a constantly most penetrating criticism of contemporary things."[107] Education, then, should set its face toward the improvement of human conditions, not merely a raking over of long dead disputes, conspirators, and cabals.

Wells is not by any means rejecting the teaching of history altogether. Wells simply wants history to be proactive, not reactive. "I put it to you," he says,

> that if we want the world to become a consistent whole, we must think of it as a whole. We must not deal with states, nations and empires as primary things which have to be reconciled and welded together, if we want world peace, we must deal with these divisions as secondary things which have appeared and disappeared almost incidentally in the course of a larger and longer biological adventure. Education can wipe them out completely.[108]

What he wants in place of trivia about royalty and border disputes is an examination of the large scale forces and movements which have shaped human societies and attitudes. The subject of history, properly designed and taught, will serve as a corrective to that "crazy combative patriotism that plainly threatens to destroy civilization today,"[109] a patriotism which draws a large measure of its sustenance from the way history is presently taught. As Wells says,

> Our schools take the growing mind at a naturally barbaric phase and they inflame and fix its barbarism. I think we underrate the formative effect of this perpetual reiteration of how *we* won, how *our* empire grew and how relatively splendid *we* have been in every department of life. We are blinded by habit and custom to the way it infects these growing minds with the chronic and nearly incurable disease of national egotism.[110]

There is an ironic contrast with Plato, whose restrictions on the poets (that is, the imaginative writers) are such an important aspect of his ideal state, here; where Plato will have myths and stories glorifying the foundation and stability of his society,[111] Wells celebrates change. He wants the true story of the long struggle for what little humanity has attained, and as close and hard a look as possible at the forces which have made that struggle much harder than it need have been, and which continue to do so. But it is, he recognizes, a *story*. History is a narrative in the way no other discipline can be, and thus understood offers tremendous possibilities to writer and teacher. "History explains the community to the individual, and when the community of interests and vital interaction has expanded to planetary dimensions, then nothing less than a clear and simplified world history is required as the framework of social ideas."[112] History reveals the inconsistencies within human character and development; history helps explain actions otherwise incoherent or ridiculous; history allows the individual to understand not only the imperfections in the social and political structure, but the reasons for them, and from this understanding can suggest ways to address those problems peacefully and constructively. Wells's challenge to Plato (and any other authoritarian utopianism) is this: even assuming that your poets can be coerced into repeating these pleasant stories and embellishing them with all their skill into things of power and beauty, how will you keep the citizens from seeing that they are false? The first argument which ends in fisticuffs will carry more conviction than a dozen fairy tales; the first disgruntled guardian reject will reveal the weaknesses and falsehoods upon which the society rests. Only if criticism is an innate part of the educational and political structure will you avoid the harsher criticism, the criticism which is merely rejection, that follows hard on the heels of broken faith. There is no zealot like the new zealot, and those who turn against your state will do so with the firm conviction that it is *they*, and not the philosophers, who have seen the truth. Even if they might be wrong, as Plato is sure to insist that they are, the problem is that their actions will undercut the purpose of the just society: the overall happiness of its citizens. Plato might respond that the training of his citizens will be such as to, in fact, prevent arguments from degenerating into fisticuffs[113] and that the other guardians will use whatever means necessary to make sure their sullen former companion does not cause unrest. Apart from the questionable nature of such assertions in themselves, they require an implausible degree of watchfulness on the part of at least the guardians; sooner or later some flaw is likely to appear which cannot be contained, and the city will begin its inevitable decay.[114] This decay stems from the static and reactive nature of the city's political structure; since perfection has been attained, there can perforce be no improvements, and all that anyone can do is either contemplate the good, or watch out for the bad.

Wells's theory of education, on the other hand, is that education is itself an ever-changing process keyed to an ever-changing understanding of the natural and social worlds, an understanding which it helps, and should help, to implement and modify on a continuing basis. Here we see again the influence of evolution; in a world which is everlasting but stable, or in a world created but a few thousand years ago, it makes some sense to speak of permanent institutions and practices. As members of a species we know to have existed for hundreds of thousands of years in a world which we know to be billions of years old, and yet whose entire recorded history spans less than 10,000 years, what sense does it make for us to speak of permanence? What sense, then, does it make for history teachers to parrot lessons learned in decades past without examining the content of those lessons to see if it still holds value under present conditions? In a later portion of the utopian process, the answer at which these questions aim has become common property: "Nowadays every schoolboy knows that the essential and permanent conflict in life is a conflict between the past and the future, between the accomplished past and the forward effort."[115] Conservatives are correct in their suspicion, best demonstrated in repeated attempts to ban or dilute the teaching of evolution in science classes, of education (what Wells remarked satirically regarding English traditionalists, "English people have an instinctive perception of the corrosive effect of knowledge and intelligence upon sound dogma." applies well beyond the bounds of England).[116] Even a mediocre education can raise many more questions than it can answer, and a good one is inherently an invitation to the learner to challenge the status quo, to reach beyond the boundaries of their teacher's knowledge and opinions. The best teachers know and encourage this.

Education is far more than what takes place in a schoolroom. Wells warns against identifying the process with one of its manifestations. "People are too apt to identify schools and education," writes William Clissold. "Never was there a more mischievous error. Schools may merely fix and intensify those adolescent qualities it is the business of education to correct." Clissold goes on to criticize his "distant cousin Wells," who has written much on the topic of education. He agrees with his cousin, but doubts "if he has sufficiently separated the idea of education from the idea of schoolmastering. He was, I believe, for some years at an impressionable age, a schoolmaster, and he has shown a pathetic disposition throughout a large part of his life to follow schoolmasters about and ask them to be more so, but different." (Again we see Wells doing his best to create a sense of uncertainty and openness about his proposals and exactly who we are to take as having found the proper ones).[117] Education requires mechanisms through which the social elements connect with the intellectual, through which thought connects with feeling, ways in which the personal develops into, and connects with, the public. "Order, discipline, health, are nothing except to make the world safe for the aesthetic life."[118] Education requires something beyond facts, something which gives those facts an emotional resonance which makes them of concern to all. Facts require a setting which transcends their facticity, a setting which can be only that of the imagination; as Oswald Sydenham asks schoolmaster after schoolmaster, "Don't you *know* that education is building up an imagination?"[119] Education, to fulfill its highest potential, requires the support of imaginative literature.

Even to raise such questions regarding the nature of education points to another necessity: that present conditions be understood as thoroughly as possible by those who teach within and about them. Wells begins here to press contemporary education toward utopian, rather than quotidian, considerations, and in the process to expand its boundaries. The formal education of children, which is what we have thus far been considering, does not take place in a vacuum; "We are parting from the old delusion that learning is a mere phase in life."[120] Even as the teachers are teaching, they are learning; Wells made a special point of demanding "those reconditioning courses that *must* somehow be made a normal part in the lives of working professional."[121] To become a teacher is to become something like one of the fictional samurai in *A Modern Utopia*, of whom we shall hear much more presently; one is, or ought to be, a member of a class with both remarkable privileges (surely an apt description of the position of influence on the minds of the young in which many teachers find themselves) and stringent responsibilities, one of which is to be kept up to date, along the same broad lines as all the other teachers of the same subject, with recent developments or discoveries which effect one's subject area, whether directly or indirectly.

History passes over into anthropology on one side, into geography on another, and into evolutionary studies on a third. Each of these is important for situating the student in time and place. Each shades off into other disciplines, which the student who shows an aptitude in a particular direction may choose to explore as they progress to the advanced educational levels, where individual initiative plays a much greater role. At this point, the formal structure shifts from something mandatory to something voluntary; "Individuality is becoming conscious of itself and specialization is beginning."[122] Wells says remarkably little about this component of education, which comprises what we think of as the university years. Although Wells himself set great store by getting his doctorate from the University of London in his later years, he seems not to have thought highly of universities as sources of support for utopian thought. He regarded the narrowness encouraged by academic politics as fertile ground for opposition to larger visions, as an extended description of the typical academic personality in *The World of William Clissold* shows:

> Perhaps there is something innate that in the first place disposes a man to become a University teacher or specialist. He is, I suspect, more often than not by nature and instinctively afraid of the insecure uproar of things. Visit him in college and you will see that he does not so much live here as lurk. He must find infinite assurance, infinite compensation for the threatening indignities of life, in the development of his lucid counter-world, so much simpler, so much clearer, so entirely logical. Once he has secured his cell he encounters little opposition; he may bid good-bye to his worst timidities, and set to work secreting his soul's protection. To deny a fact in that withdrawn and protected atmosphere becomes more and more like defeating it, and to impose a system on the confusion almost as good as conquering it. In his classrooms, his lectures, his written controversies, the theorising recluse can soon grow fierce and contemptuous enough; he can at last down and out with his facts that are so intractable in practice, to his own complete satisfaction.

The point is not merely satirical; there is some truth here, especially as regards the tendency of academics to elevate theory over practice. Wells saw the danger clearly; "to live in agreement with a theory for any length of time is like what the Americans call a common-law marriage; you and it are wedded by habit and repute. A man wedded to a system is less and less able to apprehend contradictory realities. He becomes like the dogs and pigs people here in the South of France specialise to hunt truffles; he can at last discover his system at the merest hint of evidence, and all that does not countenance it ceases to interest him, ceases to exist for him; he thrusts past it heedlessly, scornfully."[123] Wells did not foresee the increasing involvement of the modern university with large scale scientific and technological projects, whether funded by industry or government. Given the corruption of scientific honesty so often associated with the former, and the all-too-frequent attempts by the latter to dictate the definition of scientific method, it may well be wondered whether Wells would find reason to change his position significantly. In any case, he left such matters mostly to one side, preferring to concentrate on creating a solid foundation, which he presumed would at least partially ameliorate traditional academic tendencies.

One common misapprehension regarding Wells is that he expected everyone to calmly wait for the state to put them in their place. The preceding description of what happens after the required formal educational process should help refute such beliefs. This, though, only begins the conversation; various other objections to Wells's approach have been raised, and these, too, must be considered. They fall, broadly speaking, into two categories: those who think Wells is too naive in his assessment of the possibilities, as opposed to the realities, of the practical aspects of designing educational systems, as well as in his expectations regarding the effects of education upon the educated[124]; and those who find the Wellsian educational vision totalitarian in nature, a prelude to fascistic brainwashing or its equivalent. An obvious line of attack in the first category is that raised, for example, by H.L. Mencken; "popular education, no matter what efforts are made to improve it, must inevitably remain but little more than a device for perpetuating the ideas that happen to be official — in other words, the nonsense regarded as revelation by the powers currently in control of the state."[125] That this is a danger with any state-supervised educational system must be admitted, but the charge seems both a bit needlessly cynical and considerably unfair to Wells. No educational system is free of the dangers of ossified authority — of the "it's true because I said so" approach. But Wells has made serious attempts to address this concern: first, by emphasizing, within the educational process itself, the provisional nature of the knowledge being presented; second, by requiring the regular retraining of teachers, which will in itself indicate to the students both that knowledge is not something one acquires during an unpleasant but limited portion of one's early life and that everything which the teacher declares to be a matter of fact may be subject to revision or even overthrow; and third, by connecting education to the idea of utopia — that is, to a social system which is itself seen and known to be a process, subject like all processes to change, renewal, and revision. Plato's system contains no mechanism for correction should things begin to disintegrate at the top of the hierarchy; Wells's system contains a number of self-correcting elements, not the least of which being its self-professed imperfection (or else why the need for the process at all?).

A second objection, one which is both stronger and, if true, quite damaging, regards an aspect of the Wellsian educational philosophy which I have deliberately withheld thus far: the role of science. As W. Warren Wagar, himself a committed Wellsian, puts it, "The problem makes its presence felt in almost everything he wrote.... Wells let himself be drawn into a messianic scientism that short-circuited democracy, menaced civil liberty, and guaranteed that in a Wellsian world order supreme power would be wielded by technocrats."[126] Wells, misled by the promise of clarity held out by science, rested his entire utopian system thereon, and in so doing allowed a vicious chimera to dominate an otherwise humane system. Wagar extends the problem by identifying Wells's supposed scientism with his educational process in itself; "it may be argued that the principal flaw in Wells's prophetic vision was his philosophy of education."[127] The indictment concludes on a strong note:

> Wells was dangerously wrong. The sciences, as they flourished in his years in South Kensington, or as they flourish today, give us no wisdom, no justice, no grace. Nor do the experts schooled in their conflicting mysteries. The dream of an automatic utopia that any fool with a modicum of proper training can plainly see and build is nothing but a foolish dream. The sooner we wake from it and get on with the serious business of world democracy, the better.[128]

A similar critique of Wells, though developed at greater length and in more detail, is offered by Leon Stover. Indeed, Stover's book *The Prophetic Soul*[129] is almost certainly the harshest intellectually respectable judgment of Wells written since his death; although it takes the form of a commentary on Wells's film *Things to Come*, a large number of Wellsian texts are summoned before the court in order to provide evidence that, as Stover asseverates, "Scientism is in fact the very essence of Wellsism."[130] It is even worse than this; "The Communist Revision of H.G. Wells, then, is no more than Leninism with Marxism subtracted from the Communist Party's official propaganda."[131] This entails chicanery on Wells's part, in that he must disguise the naked power politics of his characters, the more vicious and powerful of whom may be taken as standing in for his own views. "Thus in the rhetoric of Wellsian socialism, the collective mind and will of "Man" stands for the power of Direction over Labor, and Direction (or the World Council) stands for its number one party member, its king bee and dictator of a one person state."[132] Stover gives the example of John Cabal in the film; "With saintly mendacity, Cabal denies that he is his party's individual leader. "No more bosses." He rather asks that Gordon [another character] give himself to the collective cause of human civilization and world unity. In this he mystifies the personal power of his Air Dictatorship by displacing it onto society at large, the familiar rhetorical trick of all totalitarian creeds."¹³³ The result can be only catastrophic for the interests of human beings:

> The technocratic state-monster dreamed of by the saint–Simonians and celebrated in Wellsism is a Frankenstein's monster. To design a society and model it by command is first to demodel the existing order. It is like tearing a living body to bits in order to build a new one out of the dead parts. To make Collectivism a fact one must first kill off all forms of independent group life standing between the individual and the state. The condition for mobilizing all citizens for direct public service is the death of civil society. A forced social division of labor replaces the spontaneous division of labor rooted in voluntary social ties, and the total state is built on the ruined soil of that uprooting. The result is totalitarian poverty.¹³⁴

Any sort of planning for the future of humanity, as opposed to individual plans made for purely personal purposes, will invariably lead to the destruction of the very thing which is purported to justify the collective planning in the first place: the betterment of individual lives.¹³⁵

If Wagar and Stover are right, it is difficult to see that anything of value remains in Wells's system, so closely tied together are its elements. Pleasant visions of utopian life turn out to be dangerous poisoned traps for the unwary reader, and the synthetic approach turns out to be the construction and sealing of a prison from inside. "It is thus significant that in nearly all his plans for a utopia," notes Roslynn Haynes, "[Wells] depends for leadership chiefly on the scientists of the society."¹³⁶

The charges Wagar and Stover lay may be summed up as, first, that Wells identified clear thought, and therefore the purpose of education, with science; second, that Wells places too much power in the hands of scientists ("technocrats"); third, that Wells identifies human beings as merely another objective fact within science, and thus devalues individuality altogether, undercutting in the process the whole purpose of his own utopian thought¹³⁷; and, fourth, that Wells is advocating a mechanistic view of human beings which will lead to horrendous consequences involving mass murder on a tremendous scale. "In its [the Wellsian state's] conquest of society, the preferred method is colossal homicide on an industrial scale."¹³⁸

Certainly, on the surface, there are grounds for supposing Wagar and Stover to be right. Their charges regarding the disjunction between science and morality are quite true (a point I have already touched upon more than once, and will touch on again). There can be no doubt that Wells respected science greatly, and thought that education would be all the more valuable for including a large component of scientific training. Indeed, at times he writes as if that is all that is needed:

> The scientific vision of life in the universe and no other has to be his vision of the universe. Any other leads ultimately to disaster. And since the existing organization of the world does not provide anything like that vision nor establish the necessary conceptions of right conduct that arise out of it, it needs to be recast quite as much and even more than the political framework needs to be recast.[139]

"Science," cries the king in *The World Set Free*, "is the new king of the world."[140] Proper education, says Mr. Preeder, a minor employee of the Camford University Press, will always lead to the appropriate results. Egotism struggles, "but sound thinking and sufficient knowledge can dominate feeling. Most of this stuff about incurable differences of opinion is nonsense, brains are as alike as eggs. You can beat them or boil them hard or scramble them or poach them or let them go rotten. But cook them the same way and they will come out very much alike."[141]

Wagar and Stover, and those who share their views, have missed, or perhaps elided, an important distinction, however — although to be sure Wells does not always write as clearly as he should on this point. Such criticisms make a mistake very close to that of which they accuse Wells: they equate the problems stemming from the *products* of science, primarily including technological achievements, with the underlying *method* of science. Yet it is the latter to which Wells is appealing as a support for (but not the purpose underlying) the utopian process, not to the former. Mere facts are not what interest Wells; to be significant, they must be situated within a context of humanistic social concerns. Science, for Wells, is in fact the opposite of a hard core of fully ascertained facts; as he puts it, in rather quaint language,

> Science never professes to present more than a working diagram of fact. She does not explain, she states the relations and associations of facts as simply as possible.... She has always been true, and continually becomes truer. But she never expects to reach Ultimate Truth. At their truest her theories are not, and never pretend to be, more than diagrams to fit, not even all possible facts, but simply the known facts.[142]

So Wells was writing in the 1930s, but the position was not one to which he had recently come. Consider one of Wells's most famous statements on science, dating from 1891:

> Science is a match that man has just got alight. He thought he was in a room — in moments of devotion, a temple — and that his light would be reflected from and display walls inscribed with wonderful secrets and pillars carved with philosophical systems wrought into harmony. It is a curious sensation, now that the preliminary splutter is over and the flame burns up clear, to see his hands lit and just a glimpse of himself and the patch he stands on visible, and around him, in place of all that human comfort and beauty he anticipated — darkness still.[143]

The point many people miss is that for Wells, science will *always* be in this relation to the whole of human reality; science, by its nature, is always more interested in what it does not know than what it does, however important the latter is in understanding the former. As Wells described it somewhat less colorfully during the First World War, "Science is very largely analysis aimed at forecasting. The test of any scientific law is our verification of its anticipations."[144] Forecasting involves error, for it is about that which has not yet happened, and detecting error is vital to improving anything, whether it be self or society, for it is only through errors that we correct ourselves and avoid repeating them in the future. Wells welcomed the better products of science, it is true, but recognized, often in advance, the dangers of technological innovation unguided by clear thought coupled with humane social purposes. Wells knew fully the human propensity to use science and technology as a means to violent ends. He wrote of gas war in 1898, of air war in 1899 and 1908, of tanks in 1903, and of atomic war in 1914, among other misuses of technology for destructive purposes. Science, for Wells, means the scientific method, not its specific, and especially technological, results.

Similarly, Wells was usually careful to distinguish thought and its thinkers. "It is *science* and not *men of science* that we want to enlighten and animate our politics and rule the world."[145] That is to say, utopia must be guided by the principle that every experiment in living, every attempt at a broader, fairer, more humane approach to the problems of humanity, is to be regarded as provisional. The purpose of education, beyond its practical and informative content, is to inculcate this approach, this application of the scientific method to matters both personal and political. It is not to turn us into scientific workers in the narrow white lab-coated sense (while there are no doubt those who equate science with this image, Wells was not among them, although biology is the science most influential on his own thought and imagery).[146] While it is undeniably true that Wells, the human being who had escaped the rigors of the lower middle class, shows a fascination with technological devices, this fascination operates at the personal level, not at the level of society; he no more expects salvation from the products of technology than he does from the workers who build them.

The related charge concerning the putative Wellsian dictatorial technocracy requires a slightly different approach to refute. Part of Wells's answer has already been given above; Wells has no interest in assigning the rule of society to a body of scientists, or any other intellectual elites; he quite specifically states that "men of science, artists, philosophers, specialized intelligences of any sort, do not constitute an *élite* that can be mobilized for collective action." As he comments, "A professor-ridden world might prove as unsatisfactory under the stress of modern life and fluctuating conditions as a theologian-ridden world."[147] While it is true that many of his utopian novels depict just this sort of elite taking, or even seizing, the reins of power, this is in part an artifact of the literary structure and intent of his novels (and even more of the necessarily compressed expression of ideas found in the film *Things to Come*). He is writing of societies intended to be seen as in some fashion connected with ours over time and history; in order to suggest the need for thoughtful and experimental education and governance he must, if the plot is to have even a semblance of plausibility, situate its origins in the groups most likely to provide it. Indeed, much the same can be said of his non-fiction speculations to the same effect: if they are to suggest what is likely to happen, or to stimulate action by those concerned that it not happen that way, they need to be grounded in some sort of believable representation of at least some of the possibilities out of which the actions will come.

Even so, and this is a point overlooked by Wagar and Stover, he is always careful to show the true scientists (that is, those who follow scientific method) as eventually abdicating the power which they recognize as no longer necessary. While this may be idealistic, and even perhaps a little naive, it is a far cry from advocating rule by a technocratic elite. "Thus Wells's utopias," concludes Roslynn Haynes in completing her consideration of the political role of scientists therein, "unlike almost all that have followed them, pursue the actual policies of scientific method, not some authoritarian travesty of these, stressing the equal responsibility of all citizens, and working towards the elimination of any separate governing class."[148] Wagar and Stover have, albeit no doubt unwittingly, provided such a travesty.

It should also be noted that many of those who criticize Wells for his anti-democratic proclivities presume the agreement of the reader to the proposition that the idea of an imposed minority rule is inherently unacceptable. This is in itself a questionable assumption, both on the grounds of history and political theory. All external rules are imposed, by definition; historically, there has never been a time when such external rules have not been in place, and there has likewise never been a time when the rules have not been devised, established, and enforced by a minority or their representatives, however selected. One may object altogether to the idea of an "elite" body of individuals running the world, but objection to an idea is not disproof of its necessity or even probability. Wells might respond by indicating that such a situation exists presently anyway, except that the supposed elite is based on power and wealth, not knowledge, service, and integrity; nor is entrance to the ruling elite available, on grounds clearly and universally understood, to all who wish to join, regardless of their social, economic, or other class. The process has already begun, scarcely noticed by the bulk of humanity. The choice posed by Wells, and unacknowledged by Wagar or Stover, is stark; "between socialization by compulsion or socialization by enlightened consent."[149] A self-defined and virtually unregulated elite now has their hands on the levers of power. It remains to be seen whether the entrepreneurs and corporate executives who now control so much of the world will apply scientific method, and whether they will vanish when their task, none too clearly defined in the first place, is done. That this is probable may, one suspects, be doubted. Wells is by no means the only thinker in the liberal humanitarian tradition to consider the possibility that a limited period of rule by a strict minority may be necessary (not merely probable) if humanity is to survive the destructive trends of the present. Robert L. Heilbroner, for example, offers the disturbing suggestion "that the passage through the gantlet ahead may be possible only under governments capable of rallying obedience far more effectively than would be possible in a democratic setting. If the issue for mankind is survival, such governments may be unavoidable, even necessary." His conclusion is that "the revitalization of the polis is hardly likely to take place during a period in which an orderly response to social and physical challenges will require an increase of centralized power and the encouragement of national rather than communal attitudes."[150] Heilbroner fails to recognize the part that nationalism has played and will continue to play in generating the problems to which he refers, and thus weakens his overall argument in some ways, yet it is clear that, from a position clearly opposed to such a government, his argument, together with the empirical data behind it, leads to the end Wagar and Stover seem to assume may be dismissed without qualm. The query Wells would pose to all three authors is whether, should such a process be either necessary or inevitable, we are to *allow* the process to happen on terms dictated by a small group of oligarchs, or *arrange* for it to happen on terms congenial to the higher human aspirations.

The charge that Wells objectifies human beings within a scientistic technocratic world-view has probably by now been sufficiently refuted. Nonetheless, a further point may be made here. Consider the quote about brains being like eggs. Wells is clearly right; on the whole, people brought up under similar circumstances, even within the loose and chaotic social systems which have henceforth existed, systems defined as much by what they are opposed to as by what, if anything, they are intended to achieve, do think alike; the majority of North Americans are Christian in their general outlook, while the majority of Iranians are Muslim in theirs, for example. Indeed, the whole premise of shared education of any sort is that pupils treated in a similar manner will react similarly. Where this premise fails in not in the educations received *per se*, but in the fact that much of what is propounded in school is contradicted elsewhere. Science classes are countered by newspaper horoscopes and "factual" accounts of ESP, UFOs, angelic visitations, and other paranormal rubbish. History classes are countered by bigotry at home and jingoism in the press. Literature classes are countered by the easy availability of trivial bestsellers and by aesthetic relativism in academia. And so on. Both Wells and Plato would agree on this point: that education, to succeed, must be something behind which the society as a whole consistently and forcefully rallies. Until then, its achievements will be mere shadows of its possibilities.

But education is far more than what takes place in a schoolroom; it requires mechanisms through which the social elements connect with the intellectual, ways in which the personal develops into, and connects with, the public. Education requires either the support of imaginative literature, or its suppression. This does not occur in a political vacuum; much will rest on how the state within which the education takes place functions.

3

The State

Once an understanding of the individual utopian citizen has begun to evolve, the political structure(s) under which, or within which, that individual will live, evolve, and develop must be taken into account. There is no one structure or even type of structure of human relations which must be envisioned and presented in order to count as utopian; only the results are of importance here. Nonetheless, there is no way of escaping the presentation itself; it is inherent in any utopian scheme. People must interact, and some means of overcoming or making use of conflicts, or of rendering conflict obsolete, must exist. To describe a society, for instance, in which private property no longer exists is already to presuppose a kind of political structure: one in which certain mechanisms of acquisition and retention of material goods no longer function, or have been superseded. Again, the political structure envisioned may be sketched only or drawn in detail, but its existence, at least initially, is unavoidable, since (for one obvious reason) it is implicit in the sorts of human relations depicted. The structure envisioned, then, will be influenced by the conditions under which the envisioning occurs; certain modes of presentation, and certain ideas concerning social possibilities, will be seen as less attractive, or even as less plausible, at one time than at another. Some ideas may always remain merely fantastic, and retain a charm for readers quite unconnected with their former utopian value, while other ideas will come to be seen, perhaps even by their originator, as not only improbable of execution but as actually regrettable or repugnant.

The structure of society has many components. Not all of them need be thought out in detail for a utopia to hold together, but clearly the more that are, and the more large questions that are answered, the more solid the utopia will come to feel to the reader, and the more likely it will be to influence her or his own thoughts and actions. In this chapter I will provide an examination of some of these components. I will begin with an examination of the structures of the state(s) under review. Following that, I will take up some particular aspects of those state(s); a state structure, indeed any social structure, even the most static, can be examined in itself for only so long before questions arise about its interactions with the citizens which comprise, or which live under, its operations. It must be understood, however, that such a discussion is itself already false to life as lived, since the political and social structures under which an individual lives are not genuinely distinct from that individual's character, and it is from the interplay of individual characters taken as a whole that the society derives its structures. Much which is found here, therefore, must be understood as part of a whole, a whole which involves both what has been discussed already and what has yet to be discussed.

One vital aspect of utopian imagining which cannot be avoided is some conception of the character of authority in the society envisioned. This is fundamental; without some reason(s) for the citizenry to act one way rather than another, and further to act in consort where necessary for the attainment of goals beyond the scope of the individual's powers, the society cannot function at all, whatever the value of the impulses behind its creation. Further, the character of the authority conceived will itself dictate, or at the very least strongly suggest, the character of the society to be attained. Where the nature of authority in the given utopia is not at least implicitly developed, it is difficult to comprehend what it is that is seen as holding the society together at all, beyond the author's imagination. In that case, anyone who finds the author's vision attractive enough to advocate practical moves in that direction will themselves have to develop a conception of the necessary authority; in any case, for a utopia to have relevance to social policy and individual action it will need to include justification for its own authority.

Hannah Arendt has argued that authority, as traditionally understood, occupies a specific ground of its own, one all too often mistaken for something else. Authority requires that those subject to it obey, yet it does not, and cannot, rest on either violence or persuasion. As Arendt says,

> authority precludes the use of external means of coercion; where force is used, authority itself has failed. Authority, on the other hand, is incompatible with persuasion, which presupposes equality and works through a process of argumentation Where arguments are used, authority is left in abeyance. Against the egalitarian order of persuasion stands the authoritarian order, which is always hierarchical. If authority is to be defined at all, then, it must be in contradistinction to both coercion by force and persuasion through arguments.[1]

As seen by Arendt, authority must rest on something internal to the relation between the authoritarian figure or political structure and the person or person obedient thereto. It is this which causes trouble for Plato; he wishes to ground the political authority of the philosopher-kings upon their superior reason and knowledge, yet he must admit that the majority of the ordinary citizens will not be capable of distinguishing between a true philosopher and a false one.[2] "The trouble with coercion through reason," as Arendt indicates and as Plato well knew, "is that only the few are subject to it, so that the problem arises of how to assure that the many, the people who in their very multitude compose the body politic, can be submitted to the same truth."[3] Violence is not, at least within the bounds of Plato's political theory (and Greek domestic political practice in general), an acceptable alternative, and persuasion is unlikely to work. Plato wished to avoid the sorts of disasters he would encounter with the tyrant Dionysius II, yet he could not trust the decisions of the philosophically incapable. He needed to find a means of establishing authority, of coercing the citizenry, without appearing to do so.

Plato turned therefore to myths. These manage to suggest that a superior force guarantees the weight of the authority while allowing the authority itself to escape from the need to use either violence or persuasion. They operate on a number of levels; the Myth of the Metals serves to legitimate the political hierarchy itself, for example, and the Myth of Er ("a myth which Plato himself obviously neither believed nor wanted the philosophers to believe," according to Arendt)[4] serves to inculcate the expectation of an afterlife of rewards and punishments. The myths serve as the practical equivalent, for the ordinary person, of the formal realm for the philosopher. They ground authority in something seen as external to both the rulers and the ruled.

Two objections here are clear. The first is that the myths themselves are merely a sublimated form of violence, not different in character (albeit vastly more complex in description) from a bank robber using an outstretched finger in a jacket pocket as a simulacrum of a revolver to obtain obedience from an otherwise healthy, husky, and strong teller. The second objection, which stems from the response to the first (that no violence is in fact possible, since these are just bluffs), is that when these myths are recognized for what they are (falsehoods) the authority riding on them is irrevocably diminished. Once doubt regarding the truth of the myths arises, the same doubt will quickly corrode the political structures dependent thereon. Since Plato expects that his rulers will know that the myths are myths, and since Plato indicates that a constant watch needs to be kept out for potential rulers who are in fact, clever but for one reason or another innately unworthy of ruling, the possibility exists always that some disgruntled former candidate for the guardians or even the philosophers will blow the gaff, so to speak. What the outcome of this would be is hard to say, but it is at least possible that the result would be unrest among the citizenry; if one thing is revealed to be a lie, why not others? What would exist would be, as Lyndon Johnson knew the term, a credibility gap.

Wells clearly recognizes this fact, which provides something of a problem; he needs to find a way toward a particular political condition without using means which undercut the purpose of that condition altogether. Wells's goal, then, is straightforward: to provide a means of persuasion which does not topple over into tyranny or a totalitarian dictatorship. It must be admitted that his solution, at least as regards the transitional phases between the present and a considerably more enlightened future, is not entirely more successful than Plato's. Nonetheless, Wells has at least helped indicate the sort of path a thoroughly humanistic mythology will need to follow; by getting rid of the strong teleological base required by Plato, he has subverted at least some of the dangers which arise when one recognizes that any foundation for a state or society must always rest on something fundamentally beyond the purview of critical analysis; a strictly critical approach to utopia needs always to be supplemented by an imaginative one.

Wells rejects "this irrational idea that there can be some single person, a wonder leader, a divine inspired individual who will know what everything is all about and will gather up all our poor wits into his stupendous noddle, to which everything can then be referred."[5] Even if there could somehow be such a person in terms of mental capacity, the resistances of ordinary persons would eventually weaken and destroy such authority as the leader might enjoy, or the imbalance between the leader's responsibilities (which would require an ever-changing set of responses to the ever-changing human situation) and the leader's personal weaknesses (which everyone has to some degree, regardless of their other abilities) would make it impossible for him (or her, but Wells never depicted a woman in a genuine dictatorial capacity) to function.[6] In any case, the authority of even the most successful dictator will not outlast that dictator's life, and thus will not provide a useful basis for social or political authority. Even the apparent exceptions to this (e.g. the embalmed icon Lenin) rest on an equivocation between the dictator as symbol and the dictator's actual positions as authoritative. Stalin appealed to Lenin's presumed wishes whenever convenient, but only as a cover for carrying out his own will. The actual aims of Lenin were quickly forgotten, except where they happened to coincide with those of later Soviet leaders. Similar processes occur even in republics, as the intense but rarely helpful arguments about the "original intent" of the authors of the Constitution of the United States demonstrate.

To help obviate the problem of authority, Wells turns from individuals to humanity as a whole. Time and again he makes such assertions as, "The modern tendency has been and is all in the direction of minimising what one might call self-centred devotion and self-subjugation, and of expanding and developing external service."[7] The focus of the individual becomes less personal, so to speak, and more human; the social comes to commingle with the individual in motivation and self-definition, such that the individual is less driven by purely atomistic needs and desires and begins instead to think of her or himself as primarily a part of the greater entity that is humanity. As we have already seen, the underlying attitude, apart from its lack of a theistic backdrop, shares much with that commonly considered religious. William Clissold's lover asks him why he values this World Republic he will never see; his response indicates the ground on which Wells is seeking to establish authority: The answer, he says, "is that I have grown up."

> I have become fully adult in a world in which as yet most human beings do not press on to a complete realisation of their adult possibilities.... I have grown at last altogether out of regarding myself as the prime concern of my life. I am no longer vitally impassioned by my own success or failure. I have done with my personal career as my chief occupation.... William Clissold dwindles to relative unimportance in my mind and Man arises and increases. And though William Clissold, my narrow self, will surely die before any great portion of this present revolution [he means the move toward the world state, the first step into the utopian process] can be achieved, yet just as surely will man, that greater self in which my narrow self is no more than a thought and a phase, survive.[8]

There is considerably more of this, expanding powerfully on the mindset under review; I have presented enough, I hope, to give the flavor of it. What Wells is trying to do here is to equate the motivations for personal action and the motivations for public action, to meld the private sphere with the political. The authority against which a person will measure their actions becomes the whole of human good yet to come. One extends oneself to the fullest because in that way one is contributing to the atmosphere in which humanity will develop, even if one is not contributing directly to the process oneself. As William Clissold puts it, "The attainment of the World Republic and the attainment of the fully adult life are the general and the particular aspects of one and the same reality. Each conditions the other." He expands the point: "In the service and salvation of the species lies the salvation of the individual."[9] We act for the best for ourselves, but that best is defined through a socialization of ourselves such that our action is also such as to benefit, in whatever small way, the whole of humanity after us.

Wells recognizes the pull of egoism, and knows that without some internalized force acting against individual egoisms the hope of a progressive world society is a slim one. "If we are to have any Utopia at all," he writes,

> we must have a clear common purpose, and a great and steadfast movement of will to override all these incurably egotistical dissentients. Something is needed wide and deep enough to float the worst of the egotisms away. The world is not to be made right by acclamation and in a day, and then for ever more trusted to run alone.[10]

The utopian process must be one which includes as many people as possible, and the number eventually needs to be a vast majority, lest accumulated resistances drag the whole of society down. Indeed, the number may have to encompass all of humanity. As Sartre commented on the need for both eradicating material scarcity and establishing genuine emotional and intellectual openness among human beings, "Such a society, of course, would have to be worldwide, for if there remained inequalities and privileges anywhere in the world, the resulting conflicts would little by little take over the whole social body."[11] The person, therefore, needs to be encouraged (but not coerced, which would defeat the purpose) into taking a broader view of their self, a view which includes the interests of humanity as their own.

All of this, it will be objected, sounds rather vague. It does, and it is. Among other things, it points to perhaps the central problem for any utopian ideal: the nature of the transition period. In order for the utopian process to reach beyond a few lonely avatars crying out in the political wilderness it needs to reach and energize a large number of people; yet the people must, in order to be reached, already be open to one of the central tenets of the utopian ideology: the idea of subordination of the self (selves) to the utopian ideal(s). Utopian thought is, of necessity, thought which deals in political generalities, however important the individuals as individuals may be seen as being within the final structure. Again we see, as Plato saw but preferred not to emphasize, and as Wells insists, the need for foundational mythologies, for reconfigurings of the moral bases whence stem the decisions of the readers. Such things are, if not uncoercive, at least not coercive in any but the most peaceful sense; the reader has chosen to enter into the given utopian/literary world and been transformed thereby, even if unexpectedly. Wells's process is therefore not merely a challenge to traditional teleological approaches, it turns out to challenge also traditional concepts of authority such as that espoused by Arendt. Arendt's views, and the many like them, presume the continued existence of some external force compelling obedience, however gently or smoothly integrated into the political lives of persons that force may be. Wells accepts this as one stage in the process, and seeks to ensure that it be as uncoercive as possible, yet he wishes to go much further, to a political structure in which authority is entirely universal and entirely shared. Here he has clearly modeled his approach on the impact of art, which is both completely authoritative (the work itself provides the only true basis for its own interpretation) and open-ended (the greater the work of art the more interpretations it can sustain). The transformative power of the novel stems from its ability to take readers from widely differing backgrounds and channel them toward a shared set of emotional responses to non-existent situations. As I have already noted, the choice to read is free, but the transformation which can follow is no longer entirely in our control nor completely predictable in its nature, even by the author.

Whether such transformations will be enough is a matter for debate. The transformative power of a great novel or other work of art is indisputable, but for its transformation to have a practical impact on society as a whole requires additional power, this time political. This raises still further, and equally important, concerns.

Closely linked with the idea of authority is the question of power, a question which recurs time and again in any discussion of utopian development. Where decisions affecting society have to be made, someone must make them. The grounds for determining the ruling class are a fundamental aspect of the overall character of the utopian society envisaged. It is that class which sets the agenda to which the others must respond, or it is the proposed absence of that class which allows for a full egalitarianism, should such be desired. To put the point more strongly, egalitarianism *necessarily* follows from the genuine absence of a ruling or guiding class because otherwise what is proposed amounts only to an anarchistic interregnum, during which elements among various other classes dispute for control. If no class or its representatives can attain power, then egalitarianism is a fact of political life, even if it is an egalitarianism of pure chaos, a Hobbesian state of nature. If a single tyrant achieves complete power, then again egalitarianism is the rule, as all are equally powerless. If a class does achieve hegemony, then it becomes the new ruling class, whatever its propagandists may say to the contrary.

Plato's division of power is well known:

> The society we have described [i.e., the whole of the *Republic*] can never grow into a reality or see the light of day, and there will be no end to the troubles of states, or indeed, my dear Glaucon, of humanity itself, till philosophers become kings in this world, or till those we now call kings

> and rulers really and truly become philosophers, and political power and philosophy thus come into the same hands, while the many natures now content to follow either to the exclusion of the other are forcibly debarred from doing so.[12]

The philosophers must rule because true philosophers, as a condition of being true philosophers, have a number of magnanimous and incorruptible qualities which equip them best to descry and deal with the needs of the state. Having a "love of any branch of learning that reveals eternal reality, the realm unaffected by the vicissitudes of change and decay,"[13] and thereby being best "able to guard the laws and customs of society,"[14] the philosophers will naturally see and hold the best interests of the society as their goal as rulers. Leadership, in the political sense, requires "good memory, readiness to learn, breadth of vision and grace, and [that the person] be a friend of truth, justice, courage, and self-control."[15] These qualities the philosophers have in abundance, and thus they naturally should form the ruling class.

The logic of Plato's position leads him inexorably to the idea of a distinct ruling class with virtually unlimited powers over the others in the state. This raises a number of problems; the only one which need be mentioned in this context is the idea of succession. Plato must assume that a regular supply of persons innately gifted for philosophical thought will be forthcoming, either through natural means or eugenic engineering; without this supply, his state will have nowhere to turn for its leaders, and without the leaders the state will be unable to survive, as it is they who guide and keep it from harm, and only they who can do so. This assumption seems unwarranted, as even Plato appears to recognize. He is insistent that philosophers will be rare in any case, and ends by invoking divine aid:

> To produce a different type of character, educated for excellence on standards different from those held by public opinion, is not, never has been, and never will be possible — in terms, that is, of human possibility, and short of a miracle as they say. For, make no mistake, to escape harm and grow up on the right lines in our present society is something that can fairly be attributed to divine providence.[16]

Later, in discussing the process by which this miracle might be achieved short of divine intervention, he assumes that power is held by "one or more true philosophers,"[17] who would begin the process of establishing the ideal state "by sending away into the country all citizens over the age of ten,"[18] and educating the children along rigidly controlled lines. Socrates thinks that "This is the best and quickest way to establish our society and constitution, and for it to prosper and bring its benefits to any people among which it is established."[19]

His interlocutor Glaucon agreed; others may be more skeptical. The problem of how the philosophers are to convince the citizenry to decamp without their children, for example, is not addressed. But then, as Socrates himself has said, "Does practice ever square with theory? Is it not in the nature of things that, whatever people think, practice should come less close to truth than theory?"[20]

Throughout his utopias and sociological writings Wells grappled with the problem of political leadership. His concern was similar to Plato's, but without the metaphysical base to fall back on: how are the majority of human beings as they are now composed to be gotten to accept whatever leadership is necessary to properly begin the utopian process? His answers, although considerably influenced by those of Plato (at least as he understood Plato), show distinct differences as well.

"Leaders I feel," wrote Wells, should guide as far as they can — and then vanish. Their ashes should not choke they fire they have lit."[21] Thinking it probable that some sort of minority would have to point the way into the utopian process, Wells nonetheless looked for ways to restrict the powers of that minority, and to ensure that they represented as much as possible the interests of humanity, rather than their own. At the same time, Wells remained suspicious of electoral democracy, which he distinguished from democracy proper. "Modern Democracy," he said in a lecture at the Sorbonne in 1927, "is not a permanent form of political and social life, but a phase of immense dissolution."[22] Democracy is the product of the loosening of social controls rather than its avatar; as a result, it in fact leads to self-contradictions. The modern multinational corporation is clearly a product of "the lack of control and restriction the ascent of Democracy has involved." Yet the hegemonic natures of these very corporations "run counter to the more intimate feeling of Democracy that every man is as good as every man, that every man should be his own master and live his life in his own fashion after his own heart."[23] Wells took the period of Democratic expansion to be winding down; the releases from various codes of behavior and various types of social restrictions need now to give way to a broader, more comprehensive reorganization. Democracy as presently constituted, he thought, had no effective response to the three interrelated problems of war, monetary instability, and the growing economic unification of the world. These problems are of such a nature as to alienate the interest of the ordinary voter, who votes reactively, not creatively; "The vote is an instrument of defence, and not a constructive tool."[24] If these problems are not to overwhelm the world, or lead to an ever more powerful plutocracy of international business leaders concerned only with profits, some further constructive force will have to arise and be used in response to them. Wells points to the rise of the fascists in Italy and the communists in Russia as vastly flawed symptoms of the sort of movement he sees as one possible answer to the problem (it is necessary to remember Wells's corollary to this claim: "I am anti–Communist and anti–Fascist. But what I am discussing now is not the mental content of these two movements, but their quality and spirit as organizations."). He well understood the mental state which gave rise to these approaches; "The pain of aimlessness and ineffectiveness can be aroused at any age with the realization of insecurity," he notes. "The search for a consuming objective ends only with life."[25] What is needed, then, is some way to channel these energies into a constructive movement, one grounded neither in resentment, as with the communists, nor a lust for power over the weak, as with the fascists, for the freeing and development of human abilities and interests.

One of his answers (long before the fascists or communists had made much of an appearance as more or less disciplined political movements with some power, it might be noted) took the form of the samurai, the "voluntary nobility" in *A Modern Utopia*, a leadership class as fully worked out as Plato's. The samurai arose, it is suggested, because "the large intricacy of Utopian organisation demands more powerful and efficient method [sic] of control than electoral methods can give."[26] Their creation was intentional, the result of "a clash of social forces and political systems" much like those of present-day Earth.[27] Those who established the samurai were confronted with "the problem of combining progress with political stability;"[28] their response was to maximize personal freedom for everyone *but* the ruling class, and to make that class open to as many people as possible without sacrificing its particular qualities. The result is at once to provide a source of social guidance, to make it possible for as many able people as possible to participate in that guidance in a thoughtful manner, and to weaken the structure of the ruling class as a class, thus helping mitigate the risk of an oligarchy arising. The emphasis is thrown on the possibilities of the individual citizen, rather than on any person by virtue of their membership in a given class. Wells insists that any such movement may be judged by this component; the truly progressive ones will "find the ultimate significance in life in individuality, novelty and the undefined"[29] and structure their plans for society accordingly. What is important here, though, is the character of the ruling, or guiding, class.

The samurai class is voluntary, not hereditary (or based on specific inherent qualities). It is open to anyone over the age of twenty-five for men and twenty-one for women, provided that they follow the "Rule." There is an echo of the age restrictions for mating placed on Plato's guardians here, although, as the samurai describing the regulations says, "Now there is a feeling that it ought to be raised."[30] As always, Wells tries very hard in his writing to give the feeling of something incomplete, something evolving, here, so as to counter any charges that this is a fixed Rule and ruling class. The "Rule" itself is a complex and always evolving catalogue of restrictions and requirements, not all of which need be examined here; it "aims to exclude the dull and base altogether, to discipline the impulses and emotions, to develop a moral habit and sustain a man in periods of stress, fatigue, and temptation, to produce the maximum co-operation of all men of good intent, and, in fact, to keep all the *samurai* in a state of moral and bodily health and efficiency."[31] What is interesting is that the restrictions on the samurai, together with the fact that any violation of the rule entails permanent expulsion from the samurai, are all intended to make membership something really rather unappealing. The samurai, and no one else, are forbidden a variety of foods, all tobaccos and alcohol, "Acting, singing, or reciting, ... though they may lecture authoritatively or debate,"[32] gambling, participating in or watching public sporting events, and a variety of other pleasures, mostly small. "We think that a constant resistance to little seductions is good for a man's quality."[33] There are positive requirements as well, among them the intriguing order that "Every month they must buy and read faithfully through at least one book that has been published during the last five years."[34] The purpose of this is obvious; a monthly reading of recent literature or science or historical reinterpretation would at the very least serve to keep one's mind up to date, and probably serve as well to suggest the impermanence of a great many ideas inculcated in childhood. It would also decrease the likelihood of decisions being taken in utter ignorance of current conditions of daily life and the types of knowledge which effect it. Finally, in yet another attempt to emphasize the importance of the inner life of the individual, "the most striking of all the rules of the *samurai*"[35] requires that "For seven consecutive days in the year, at least, each man or woman under the Rule must go right out of all the life of man into some wild and solitary place, must speak to no man or woman, and have no sort of intercourse with mankind."[36] Without books, weaponless, bearing no maps or fire-making tools, each samurai, carrying only enough provisions for the week, must "draw their minds for a space from the insistent details of life, from the intricate arguments and the fretting effort to work, from personal quarrels and personal affections, and the things of the heated room."[37]

Such, in brief, is Wells's detailed attempt to suggest a transitional ruling class, one devoted to its own supersession. The samurai are the organizers of the world state, but they have remarkably little personal power or specific power over others as individuals. Their responsibilities are in the nature of broad social policy planning. One must presume that the temptations to corruption found in any governing group are present here as well, but Wells has provided a number of plausible devices to at least mitigate the problem. The samurai are responsible only for general social restrictions. They are constantly on trial, so to speak, so as to ensure their self-control and lack of self-indulgence; conversely, there is no one way into the class (save adherence to the Rule, which is voluntary). There is little to be gained by being a member, and much to be lost, except by those whose desires are already inclined toward subordination of the self.

Wells's critics have made much polemical hay from the presumably violent nature of the creation of the Samurai, as well as the anti-democratic implications thereof. I have already attempted to show reasons why their views misrepresent Wells's intentions; another such reason is grounded in the once famous Wellsian conception of the Open Conspiracy. Wells knew the danger of corruption inherent in seeking and maintaining power, however benevolent the motivations, as a number of his novels show. He recognized, though, that some sort of power would have to be consciously applied to the social mechanism in order to turn it to utopian purposes; the march of history would not invariably supply the needed events. "The accident of a great opportunity," he held, "has happened to our kind. It is opportunity and not destiny we face."[38] Accordingly, he looked for ways to spread the progressive use of power as widely as possible while at the same time minimizing the temptations to misuse that power. One of his answers took the form of an appeal to those who thought, at least generally, along similar lines to operate openly and, if need be, defiantly in the interests of the world state. By remaining in the open, these actors, and their actions, can at one and the same time be checked for anti-utopian tendencies and serve as examples, or provide exhortations, inviting others, more timid, to join the process. But that the actions must never be hidden is a central tenet of the Wellsian approach; "a movement to realise the conceivable better state of the world, must deny itself the advantages of secret methods or tactical insincerities. It must leave that to its adversaries. We must declare our end plainly from the outset and risk no misunderstandings of our procedure."[39] Indeed, secrecy is not just wrong; it is fundamentally inimical to the utopian ideal or anything like its realization. Utopianism requires candor; "It is lost if it goes underground. Every step to world unity must be taken in the daylight, or the sort of unity that will be won will be found to be scarcely worth the winning."[40] Nor, contrary to the claims of Wells's libertarian critics, is anything like a unity under dictatorship either necessary or acceptable:

> A world Cæsar is hardly better from the progressive viewpoint than world chaos; the unity we seek must mean the liberation of human thought,

experiment, and creative effort. A successful conspiracy merely to seize governments and wield and retain world power would be at best only the empty frame of success, it might be the exact reverse of success. Release from the threat of war and the waste of international economic conflicts is a poor release if it demands as its price the loss of all other liberties.[41]

The Wellsian utopia, it bears repeating, may come about in part through the work of a small elite, but it cannot remain in their hands without dissolving into something not at all utopian. A test of their commitment to utopia, then, is found in the willingness of its avatars to invite others into the chambers of power promptly, wholeheartedly, and on a basis of complete equality. Hence the eventual creation of the voluntary ruling class, the Samurai.

Nor is the Open Conspiracy to be a rigid body, open only to those who surrender themselves utterly to its hegemony. Although Wells does see self-subordination as the essence of all religion, he recognizes that few human beings, especially under present conditions, can even aspire to, let alone attain, such purity of will. Isolated commitments are seldom productive; too often they are instead destructive, of individual sanity if not of other things. Community reinforces meaning; a single system of beliefs held alone, however strong, will eventually be crushed or imprisoned or defined as crazy or eccentric and forgotten by the society in which it occurs. Held in tandem with another person, the system grows stronger; as the network of connections expands, the system becomes progressively less liable to being dismissed or destroyed by external systems of belief. Enough such systems in cooperation can remain secure against all but the strongest social counterforce; each person is supported by the presence of the others. This is all well known as a matter of contemporary human psychology; Wells adds to the idea of such a system the purpose of permanent self-change (rather than mere maintenance around a permanent ground of presumed facts). The Open Conspiracy is an attempt to create an open-ended support system for the view that a global humanistic approach is necessary for all, even those who are not avowed members of the system. Wells excludes "thugs and burglars" and "race-course bookmakers," the latter of whom "provide the minimum of distraction and entertainment with as maximum of mischief," from membership in the Open Conspiracy,[42] but his criteria are otherwise quite generous (one may perhaps quarrel with the latter group's exclusion, but surely not the former. On a large scale, only the fascists based much of their political power on the recruitment of thugs). Anyone committed to expanding freedom for all, and to openly striving for the attainment of the world state, is welcome. Wells's assessment of his potential collaborators follows his assessment of the human personality; "In nearly every individual instance we should find a mixed composition, a human being of fluctuating moods and confused purposes, sometimes base, sometimes drifting with the tide and sometimes alert and intellectually and morally quickened. The Open Conspiracy must be content to take a fraction of a man, as it appeals to fractions of many classes, if it cannot get him altogether."[43]

Nor does Wells see this as anything but a stage in the enlargement and freeing of human society; I have examined the idea in such detail because, for one, it connects well with the concepts behind Plato's guardians (to the idea of which Wells avowed his indebtedness),[44] and for another it is, being very close to the first step on the infinite utopian road, of perhaps more pressing interest than some of the later formulations, which are more purely imaginative, however evocative they may be.

Two obvious concerns may be raised here, from opposing viewpoints: first, that Wellsian freedom, since it is apparently meant to be illimitable, is in fact meaningless, and, second, that what Wells is seeking is in fact merely a form of brainwashing.

The first concern is the more easily addressed, in part because it rests on a misconception. Wells is advocating an endless expansion of human freedom over time, not the idea that any given individual at a particular point in the ongoing evolution of humanity will be totally free of all constraints. Were he to advocate this, he would indeed be falling into the position which the Marxists in particular accuse him of adopting: that human beings are not, at least in large measure, products of their social and economic setting. As we have already seen, Wells holds the contrary position (it is this, in fact, which will lead to the problems behind the second objection).

But the emphasis on freedom may still seem disturbing. Where all is permitted, even if only in potential, does not everything lose its value? Aren't freedoms freedoms precisely by virtue of being contrasted with restraints? I shall examine the theoretical components of these questions later, but for now I want to discuss freedom in the specifically political and organizational sense — that is, the sense in which it connects most closely with the role of the state.

The political challenges to Wells rest on an elision of the distinction between freedom from restraints and freedom to act autonomously. As Erich Fromm has described the distinction, "Freedom does not mean freedom *from* all guiding principles. It means the freedom *to grow* according to the laws of the structure of human existence (autonomous restrictions). It means obedience to the laws that govern optimal human development."[45] Wells would place less emphasis on the law-like character of the relations to which Fromm refers, but otherwise the intentions of the two authors are similar. Any given person will, at any given time, be in a position to extend and develop his or her intellectual, emotional, and physical being in a creative manner in particular directions, and will have the innate urge to do so. This, for both authors, is a societal fact grounded on a biological reality; human beings, like all other living beings, seek to expand the boundaries of their existence as best they can. Even a person living under appalling conditions of scarcity or oppression will still strive to reach beyond what they have been forced to become, just as a seed which falls into a crack in the sidewalk will struggle to become a viable plant. What is lacking in the atomistic individual qua individual is a reason to pursue any particular goal in preference to any other. Only in the presence of society, that is to say of a network of secure interpersonal relations, can goals beyond the merely atomistic be formulated. Only in the absence of scarcity and the violence attendant thereon can individuals begin to formulate and act upon goals not defined by external necessity (external necessity including such exigencies as the need to eat, to find shelter, to 'get a good job,' etc.). In a Wellsian society the restrictions are restrictions upon the forces, internal and external, which would tend to atomize society through conflict (hence, for example, the restrictions on private property, restrictions which Plato and More upheld for much the same reasons, which I will discuss below). Once these social constraints are in place, then individuals will be free to develop and expand desires scarcely imaginable now (because they will be desires and projects free of any necessity but the internal). Some hint of this can be found in the products of the artists and writers who have existed thus far; Wells sees in these, and in the many attempts, too often pathetic and laughable by the highest of aesthetic standards but completely sincere nonetheless, of ordinary persons to brighten the atmosphere of their drab poverty-stricken homes. He calls the reader's attention to "a row of yards behind a row of mean houses in the same great city."

> Scarcely one of these yards is neglected or purely utilitarian. In more than half of them are evidences of effort to make some sort of garden or arbour or such-like pleasant and orderly arrangement. You rarely see people playing in these yards or resting in them; they are overlooked by a railway and very noisy. But nevertheless there you have the plainest evidence of an impulse to order and make, the rudiment of the house-building, garden-making impulse. In most of these yards it has been an unprofitable, useless, and perhaps disappointing effort, but it has been at work there. In nearly every man and woman there is something of this same garden-making, arbour-building impulse.[46]

It is these impulses which a Wellsian society seeks to set free, while restraining those impulses which lead to the vandalism and destruction of even such efforts as already exist.

Wells is not naive in this matter, though; he sees clearly the countervailing tendencies to which a competitive society gives birth. The Open Conspiracy requires, at the least, that one strive always to increase one's self-awareness, that one watch for anti-human thoughts and activities within oneself. "The Open Conspiracy will be no more free from rivalries, heartburnings, distrust, touchy suspicions, mutual interference and disingenuous negligences, that any other great human co-operation," Wells acknowledges. "The disciplines, the trainings and methods of organisation that must be evolved as the movement grows may be effective in restricting the mischief of such humanities; they will certainly not suppress them altogether."[47] But the warning already suggests the answer, partial though it must necessarily be: a self-consciously evolutionary system is, to the extent of that self-consciousness, less likely to assume, or to allow its members to assume, any position of certainty or infallibility regarding itself, its members, or the world they seek to change. To the degree that the Open Conspiracy is truly open, it allows room for ongoing intellectual, emotional, and personal expansion; "the Open Conspiracy will grow as science grows, greater at last than all its outer antagonisms, than ancient tradition or instinctive resistance, greater than the conscious or unconscious loyalties of its adherents, greater than all the present vices of mankind."[48]

The second concern is a darker one, especially given the history of our century. Freedom will vanish in a Wellsian state (which will in fact be a state, whatever he calls it), it says, because the vast majority of people will be merely mechanical drones carrying out some purpose developed by the ruling class which they do not understand, yet which they obey mindlessly, being unable to do otherwise. It is something of this sort of concern, no doubt, which underlay Aldous Huxley's *Brave New World*, clearly an attack on a version of Wellsian thought.

The attack has the strength of vagueness. Precisely what *human* freedoms, as opposed to individual privileges, are being lost is seldom specified. Why killing is better than exile is never explained. The assumption is made that the treatment of the ordinary citizens in *Brave New World* is so obviously heinous that no further argument is necessary. But in fact the moral distinction is in the presentation, not in the actions themselves (why this is so will become clearer as the discussion develops). Nor is it difficult to see the justice behind the claim that even such a treatment as Huxley describes is vastly preferable to the treatment of the underclass populations in our society, whose members starve, or are slaughtered, by the hundreds of thousands across the globe. Critics of a presumably worse alternative to present reality should make certain that the alternative is indeed worse before taking the assent of their readers for granted. As Theodor Adorno remarked, "It is idle to bemoan what will become of men when hunger and distress have disappeared from the world."[49]

But these matters are comparatively minor; the main charge, that the Wellsian vision strips humanity of freedom altogether, is far more serious. After all, if, as I have been claiming all along, morality requires freedom, then a society in which freedom has ceased cannot be a moral society, and thus cannot be said to be better than some other society, any more than one star undergoing trillions of natural changes over millennia can be said to be better than another. (I leave aside here the peculiar, though not perhaps entirely implausible, idea that the goal of morality is in fact the cessation of free action; while exploring this might be interesting, it is too far from the argument here, too broad a topic, and, even if successfully defended, too easy an escape).

Arguments about the role of freedom in any given utopian, or even political, vision are easy but often unilluminating; the putative attitude of the author may reveal what he or she *thinks* would be the case under their regimen, but an examination of probable specific results may reveal an entirely different consequence. With this in mind, I shall discuss at some length a major theme in utopian thought: restrictions on private property. Private property, as we shall see, is often taken as the *sine qua non* of freedom; where there are stringent restrictions thereon (or even, for libertarians like Robert Nozick, virtually any restrictions at all), this is taken as *a priori* evidence that freedom is minimal. By contrast, many, indeed nearly all, major utopias take some form of communism or socialism as both necessary and desirable. In More's *Utopia*, for example, "everything is divided equally among the entire population."[50] The *City of the Sun*, although strictly hierarchical, nonetheless is far less concerned with rank based on possessions than either Campanella's own time or ours; "since the services and the trades and all kinds of tasks are distributed among all, each one has to work barely four hours a day ... communal life makes all at the same time rich and poor; rich since they have everything, poor since they own nothing. At the same time they are not slaves to things; rather, things serve them."[51] In Jack Vance's *Big Planet*, the travelers encounter Kirstendale, a community in which each member exists partly as a grandee, partly as a servant, taking up the roles in rotation; "Every hour of swanking around as an aristocrat they put in two working — in the shops, the factories, in the homes. Usually all three. Instead of living one life, they live two or three. They love it, thrive on it."[52] Examples could be multiplied considerably.

Plato, who thought the matter through in far greater depth than most of his successors, likewise seeks to avoid civil strife by divorcing wealth from power. The ordinary citizens, who have no political power, may make money and own property, but not the guardians. Plato applies this rule stringently:

> First, they shall have no private property beyond the barest essentials. Second, none of them shall possess a dwellinghouse or storehouse to which all have not the right of entry. Next, their food shall be provided by the other citizens as an agreed wage for the duties they perform as guardians.... They must be told that they have no need of mortal and material gold and silver, because they have in their hearts the heavenly gold and silver.... They alone, therefore, of all the citizens are forbidden to touch or handle silver or gold; they must not come under the same roof as them, nor wear them as ornaments, nor drink from vessels made from them.[53]

Possessions divide; by preventing the guardians from owning anything, Plato hoped to create a balance between them and the classes who could. Eventually, though, Plato decided that even this did not go far enough in the right direction; in the *Laws*, he asseverated that a society could only be the very best "if all means have been taken to eliminate everything we mean by the word *ownership* from life; if all possible means have been taken to make even what nature has made our *own* in some sense common property, I mean, if our eyes, ears, and hands seem to see, hear, act, in the common service."[54] This idea connects with the social role of religion, which we have already discussed, although in Plato it is taken further than in most other utopian writers.

Wells placed similar, though less harsh, restrictions on the ruling class in the earlier stages of his utopian process. For the general public his restrictions were by some measures stronger than Plato's in *Republic*, though by all measures less strong than Plato's in the *Laws*. Wells begins typically, calling attention to an ambiguity overlooked by most writers, whatever their political agenda, on property. "The word "property," one must remember, is a slightly evasive word." As he points out, absolute property rights do not exist anywhere under any circumstances; "The extremest private property is limited to a certain sanity and humanity in its use."[55] Wells saw no need to expropriate the whole of what is owned; rather, he sought "the abolition of private property in anything but what a man has earned or made."[56] This is not so dramatic as at first appears; an individual's money will remain largely untouched, and Wellsian socialism "will equally sustain property in books and objects of aesthetic satisfaction, in furnishing, in the apartments or dwellinghouse a man or woman occupies and in their household implements."[57]

> Inheritances will remain untouched, so long as they remain in the possession of descendants of the original owner; There is a strong natural sentiment in favour of the institution of heirlooms, for example; one feels

a son might well own — though he should certainly not sell — the intimate things his father desires to leave him. The pride of descent is an honorable one, the love for one's blood, and I hope that a thousand years from now some descendant will still treasure an obsolete weapon here, a picture there, or a piece of faint and faded needlework, from our days and the days before our own. One may hate inherited privileges and still respect a family tree.[58]

The moral and economic balance is clear; there is no reason to limit the retention of things of personal value, for these are matters of individual concern. What matters is restricting the concentrations of wealth which allow one individual to control the life of another. "All that property which is an enlargement of personality, the modern Socialist seeks to preserve," Wells insisted; "it is the exaggerated property that gives power over the food and needs of one's fellow-creatures, property and inheritance in land, in industrial machinery, in the homes of others, that he seeks to destroy."[59] This attitude, too, is part of the utopian process, and both sides of it will change as society changes. Wells suggests that the fetishization of wealth stemmed from fear of loss; "the less there was in the past the more you had to have and hold.... You got with difficulty, and what you got you kept."[60] As abundance becomes the rule rather than the exception, the desire for possession fades. Not only does home ownership, for one example, become transient, houses do as well; people will come to think of them as temporary structures (which may last for only a few months, or for the duration of their lives). "We no longer think it meet to wear another man's abandoned house than we think it proper to wear the clothes of the dead," remarks one of Wells's future historians, adding that "it is only in the past century that man has learnt the real lesson of plenty, that far more important than getting things is getting rid of things. We are rich universally because we are no longer rich personally."[61] Wells rejects the idea that the desire for property is innate; he holds that as our social structures change their present emphasis on ownership as a measure of self-worth our putative need for possessions will fade.

An interesting corollary to Wells's approach to restricting private property is that he sees a corresponding need to ensure that some 'property' (by which he means large tracts of land) be altogether free of even human occupancy. Even where the control of such ostensible property is vested in society as a whole, it will be necessary that aspects of it be free of any but the most minimal social use. The process by which this develops covers several distinct steps. The first is quite contemporary; Wells saw a need for a growing ecological consciousness on the part of the citizenry. "The devastation of the world's forests," he wrote, "the replacement of pasture by sand deserts through haphazard cultivation, the waste and exhaustion of natural resources, coal, petrol, water, that is now going on, the massacre of important animals, whales, penguins, seals, food fish, should be matters of universal knowledge and concern."[62] Not only for practical reasons, but for aesthetic and moral ones as well, should these human depredations on the natural world be taken as serious and deserving of social attention, control, and, at the least, inhibition.

As the conditions become more utopian, "men will turn again with renewed interest to the animal world." The random extermination of species now underway would stop; "one of the first fruits of an effective world state would be the better protection of what are now wild beasts." The primitive instincts that find surcease in the mindless killing known as sport would be channeled into altogether more productive activities. A new interest in the animals themselves for themselves would arise, "leading to fresh and perhaps very strange and beautiful attempts to befriend these pathetic, kindred lower creatures we no longer fear as enemies, hate as rivals, or need as slaves." Recall that the inhabitants of *A Modern Utopia* are all but vegetarians (they still eat fish).[63]

In the final stage envisioned by Wells (which is not, it may be necessary to remind the reader, to say the final stage in a teleological sense), the animals are left altogether alone in special secluded parks. As one of his future historians notes of the world of 2106, "There are fifteen Major Parks of over five hundred square miles in which various specifically interesting faunas and floras flourish without human interference, except for the occasional passage of some qualified observer on foot or the transit of a specially licensed aeroplane overhead. Adventurous holiday-makers are excluded. The creatures in these areas are less affected by man than were their predecessors."[64] The vision which has been developing here reaches a logical climax, one generally alien to, and indeed unlikely of realization in, most prior utopian states (save possibly some pastoral utopias, though these seldom suggest any means, apart from the collapse of civilization, for reaching this stage). Wells, once more showing, and repaying, his debt to an evolutionary understanding of Earth's history, has hinted at a qualifiedly holistic view of the human relation to the earth and its other inhabitants. Wells foresaw the possibility of genetic engineering to produce new species, whether for aesthetic or agricultural purposes; he recognized, however, the necessity that such engineering be done not for private profit but with the welfare of humanity in mind, and that it therefore be subject to stringent regulations by the world community.

In any case, the need for restrictions on private property has a justification beyond the natural world; the pursuit and possession of things militates against wisdom, whatever that wisdom is taken to be. This is true for many utopians. More inveighs against the worship of gold, which leads to the sad result "that a man with about as much mental agility as a lump of lead or a block of wood, a man whose utter stupidity is paralleled only by his immorality, can have lots of good, intelligent people at his beck and call, just because he happens to possess a large pile of gold coins."[65] In Plato's case, a concern with particular things distract the mind from contemplating the eternal realms; the time spent in planning the actions necessary to acquire material goods is time wasted, for it produces neither true happiness nor true knowledge. In Wells's case, things anchor us too firmly in the system which produced both the things and our desire for them, which system is itself then taken as embodying, somehow, eternal principles. There are no successful avowedly capitalist utopias;[66] capitalism, which rests on the illusion of inclusivity and the fact of exclusivity, is not conducive to being utopian. Any utopia, if it is to appeal to more than a narrow range of readers, must at least appear to be more inclusive than the society in which it is produced, and to which it is in part a reaction. Since utopias are, by their very nature as imaginative productions, bound to take an external view of the society under examination, they will of necessity reveal the exclusions within the imagined society more clearly than might be seen by members of that society should it somehow become realized. The readers of an unrealized utopia will measure their own position against that proffered; if they find imagining themselves as part of it either unnecessary or unpleasant (if they already live under the circumstance imagined or if they see those circumstances as a worsening of their relative position), they will reject the vision presented. Utopias are, for the most part, a product of capitalist or proto-capitalist societies, the flaws of which the readers already can see all too clearly; a celebration and extension of those flaws is unlikely to appeal to a wide audience. Plato, writing long before capitalism, already knew this (hence his strictures on democracy, which in his version emerges looking very much like free market capitalism); Wells, writing from deep within the inequities of Victorian and Edwardian England, knew it as well.

But this attitude toward private property is also one which has been challenged almost from the beginning. Aristotle, for example, called Plato's strictures into question for several reasons. He doubts the truth of Plato's fundamental claim; indeed, he inverts it. Rather than private property dividing people, Aristotle says, it actually makes for greater public peace; "when everyone has a distinct interest, men will no complain of one another, and they will make more progress, because everyone will be attending to his own business."[67] Worse, the absence of private property will weaken the possibilities of good interpersonal relations; "No one, when men have all things in common, will any longer set an example of liberality or do any liberal action; for liberality consists in the use which is made of property."[68]

Similar attacks are lodged directly against Wells, as for example by F.A. Hayek. Private property supports freedom, he claims; "the system of private property is the most important guaranty [sic] of freedom, not only for those who own property, but scarcely less for those who do not. It is only because the control of the means of production is divided among many people acting independently that nobody has complete power over us, that we as individuals can decide what to do with ourselves."[69] Private property ensures that the state does not have total control over the direction the individual's life will take, since the competitive society based on private property is all that has given us any grounds for moral understanding in the first place; "What standards we have are derived from the competitive regime we have known and would necessarily disappear soon after the disappearance of competition."[70] Failing to recognize this fact has led to confusion and self-contradiction on the part of utopian writers; "The individual rights which Mr. Wells hopes to preserve would inevitably obstruct the planning which he desires."[71]

Aristotle's first claim is not so strongly expressed as might first appear; he himself modifies it by admitting that friends, and sometimes even fellow citizens, treat many supposedly private things as being in common. "Even now there are traces of such a principle, showing that it is not impracticable, but, in well-ordered states, exists already to a certain extent and may be carried further."[72] In fact, Aristotle is resting his argument here on an assumption of moderation on the part of the property owner. This assumption is an empirical claim which experience suggests is at least questionable; while many property owners do not attempt to acquire ever more property, many do, and it is those owners who create the class tensions with which Plato is concerned. The business of these people becomes domination of others in one form or another (as landlords, employers, slave owners, etc.), and thus tending to their own business implicitly entails attending to, and controlling, the business (and even lives) of others.

The second charge, regarding the absence of liberality, rests on a circular equivocation. To say that "liberality consists in the use which is made of property" is already, by an act of definition, to answer the question prior to raising it. But surely Aristotle is simply wrong here. One can be liberal with many other things than property: emotional support, one's time, one's skills, and so on. There is no reason whatsoever that even the total disappearance of private property would necessarily lead to the disappearance of such liberalities. Further, even on Aristotle's account, the presence of private property by no means guarantees liberality; he would need to show that the loss was not only real but significant.[73]

Hayek's defense of private property, which may be taken as an attack on the position of all thinkers, such as Plato and Wells, who doubt either its necessity or its justifiability, is a fairly conventional version of the standard inegalitarian view, and is subject to a variety of responses. I shall examine only what I take to be the two principal ones here: first, that Hayek's view, like many similar ones, rests on a set of assumptions and hidden connections which undercut its force considerably,[74] and second, that Hayek has reified a particular concept (private property) illegitimately.

In his argument, Hayek appeals to the Rule of Law, which he describes simply as meaning "that government in all its actions is bound by rules fixed and announced beforehand — rules which make it possible to foresee with fair certainty how the authority will use its coercive powers in given circumstances and to plan one's individual affairs on the basis of this knowledge."[75] He seeks the creation of permanent laws which are designed with no particular person or group of persons in mind; "they are, or ought to be, intended for such long periods that it is impossible to know whether they will assist particular people more than others."[76] Collectivist economic planning makes this impossible; the state will have to make *ad hoc* decisions involving particular people, and therefore involving judging between the claims and needs of individuals or groups. This in turn entails the impossibility of any given person being able to plan for the future, as they will be unable to predict what the government might choose to do at any point therein. Since only the individual can know what is best for her or himself in any given situation, it follows that, if the goal of a state is the best for its citizens (and few states admit otherwise), "the state should confine itself to establishing rules applying to general types of situations and should allow the individuals freedom in everything which depends on the circumstances of time and place, because only the individuals concerned in each instance can fully know these circumstances and adapt their actions to them."[77] This leads to Hayek's strongest point: that "if the state is precisely to foresee the incidence of its actions, it means that it can leave those affected no choice."[78] General laws address no specific circumstance, and therefore leave freedom, if not untouched, at least minimally affected; state planning, conversely, makes individual freedom impossible, as the state cannot plan if the choices of its citizens cannot be known in advance. Utopia, then, can exist only if its citizens are not free at all, and the restrictions on private property are but the most concrete example of this.

Hayek's argument here provides something of a caricature of the goal and nature of social planning, at least as conceived by most socialists and/or utopian writers. Certainly there is nothing in either Wells or More, Bacon or Plato, which is opposed to the Rule of Law, even as described by Hayek. The crux of the question, then, is this: is private property a necessary concomitant of individual freedom, as Hayek (and virtually all modern conservative socio-economic theorists after him)[79] will claim? The answer, even on Hayek's terms, appears to be no.

The whole point of the Rule of Law is to maintain the freedom of the individual to decide what to do with her or his life with a minimum of external interference. Hayek restricts his discussion to governmental interference (apart from occasional passing digs at unions), but gives no reason why his strictures do not, and should not, apply to *anyone* who holds coercive power over another putatively independent individual.[80] That is to say, if the question is one of enhancing individual freedoms by removing arbitrary external constraints, then there is no ground on which to build a case against any universally applicable constraint intended to maximize these freedoms (i.e., to prevent a potential arbitrary action on the part of someone which would make my planning for the future more difficult). But all such constraints are against someone (or else they are meaningless). All such constraints will prevent someone, at some time, from making gains at the expense of another's ability to plan effectively. This is to say that the maximization of individual freedoms requires a maximization of constraints. This is absurd, so Hayek must mean something else.

He does, but his answer here is not in fact any better; he admits the necessity of inequality. "It cannot be denied that the Rule of Law produces economic inequality," he writes, adding that "all that can be claimed for it is that this inequality is not designed to affect particular people in a particular way."[81] What happens to any given person is unimportant, so long as the Rule of Law is consistently maintained; "The important thing is that the rule enables us to predict other people's behavior correctly, and this requires that it should apply to all cases — even if in a particular instance we feel it to be unjust."[82] This, then, is the core of the defense of private property; Hayek means here private property under the Rule of Law, "private property as such, which all can acquire under the same rules."[83] Since it is private property which gives people the base from which to exercise their freedom, private property must be protected in order to most fully protect freedom.

Hayek has still failed to answer the central question: on what grounds are constraints against individual freedoms themselves legitimately the subject of government (public) interest and action? Indeed, he muddies the waters further by arguing that his own principles do not require government inaction.

> The state controlling weights and measures (or preventing fraud and deception *in any other way*) is certainly acting, while the state permitting the use of violence, for example, by strike pickets, is inactive. Yet it is in the first case that the state observes liberal principles and in the second that it does not. Similarly with respect to most of the general and permanent rules which the state may establish with regard to production, such as building regulations or factory laws: these may be wise or unwise in the particular instance, but they do not conflict with liberal principles so long as they are intended to be permanent and are not used to favor or harm particular people.[84]

In fact, Hayek accepts still further restrictions on the freedoms of individuals; such restrictions are "inevitable in wartime, when, of course, even free and open criticism is necessarily restricted."[85]

Where, then, is the force of his criticism? If the state acts so as to prevent arbitrary increases of rent, for example, is it acting liberally or illiberally? Certainly private property rights are being infringed, perhaps quite forcefully, yet unknown and unspecified persons unable to pay the increased rent are being protected (one can imagine a law which states that rents shall not exceed N amount, where N is an amount not yet being charged by anyone, and therefore effecting as yet no specific tenant, which is intended to provide a ceiling for the future). If the restrictions on freedom of speech and criticism are permissible in wartime, there is no clear reason why they should not be permissible under at least some other circumstances in peacetime (say, under conditions of civil disorder or major natural catastrophes). Indeed, it is hard to see to what Hayek is appealing in allowing for these restrictions; no state ever fell through internal criticism alone, and if the appeal is to the security of the soldiers in the field then it contradicts Hayek's own principles, considering as it does the needs of a particular group under particular circumstances. The argument may quite rightly be raised that, as private property leads to inequality (admitted by Hayek), and as inequality leads to resentment and social unrest (held by Plato and Wells, among many others, and not refuted by Hayek), and as social unrest leads to difficulty in predicting the outcomes of one's personal choices, then the state is acting in the interests of freedom by restricting the ownership of private property. If what is desired is rendering the individual free to make personal choices unfettered by external constraints, then allowing the massive imbalances of power which private property has historically entailed would be every bit as erroneous as granting the government plenary powers over all economic decisions.[86]

Hayek has imported another error into his discussion as well. In addition to assuming that it is only government action which can render individual choice difficult or nugatory, he has abstracted the concept of private property from the setting in which it has any genuine meaning at all. Indeed, here too he ends in self-contradiction. Having dedicated much energy to providing arguments intended to demonstrate the need for preserving individual freedoms through restrictions on arbitrary actions by external powers (explicitly governmental but implicitly others as well), Hayek then turns around and avows that true freedom requires a large measure of submission to forces beyond our comprehension. "A complex civilization like ours is necessarily based on the individual's adjusting himself to changes whose cause and nature he cannot understand,"[87] writes Hayek, in terms with which Plato would be quite at home. "The crucial point," he adds,

> is that it is infinitely more difficult rationally to comprehend the necessity of submitting to forces whose operation we cannot follow in detail than to do so out of the humble awe which religion, or even the respect for the doctrines of economics, did inspire. It may, indeed, be the case that infinitely more intelligence on the part of everybody would be needed than anybody now possesses, if we are even merely to maintain our present complex civilization without anyone's having to do things of which he does not comprehend the necessity. The refusal to yield to forces which we neither understand nor can recognize as the conscious decisions of an intelligent being is the product of an incomplete and therefore erroneous rationalism.[88]

Hayek's equation between religion and "the doctrines of economics" is not a joke, nor is he alone in making it. Frank Knight, another major free-market ideologue, actually claimed that economists should be taught that each aspect of free market economic theory was "a sacred feature of the system," and as such not to be debated.[89] It may be argued that such doctrines do indeed partake more of mystical than rational thought, but this is probably not the sense in which Hayek and Knight are writing. The point upon which Hayek is insisting, though, is factual rather than religious in nature, despite his language: "It was men's submission to the impersonal forces of the market that in the past has made possible the growth of a civilization which without this could not have developed; it is by thus submitting that we are every day helping to build something that is greater than any one of us can fully comprehend."[90] In other words, since civilization as we know it has arrived largely through the uncontrolled and unconscious operations of a free marketplace centered around individualistic action based on private property, we can only maintain it if, despite the apparent evidence to the contrary,[91] we accept the necessity of those operations and do not attempt to control them ourselves.

The argument fails; the operations and achievements of the marketplace simply do not exist in the kind of moral, political, and social vacuum that Hayek supposes. Since Hayek has failed to demonstrate the necessity of those forces for the civilization he is describing (or, for that matter, that that civilization ought to survive if the means are as he describes), his paean to those forces lacks the strength it needs. Indeed, if submission to forces we do not understand is a necessary criterion for progress, there is no significant difference between Hayek and any tin-pot demagogue with a Five-Year-Plan; Hayek cannot appeal both to our understanding of what is truly necessary and our ignorance of the same; if we can judge the dictator a hindrance to human progress without fully comprehending the proffered plan, it is at least possible that the same should be true of private property and the marketplace.

Nor does Hayek take account of the social setting in which the actions of the individual unfold. Hayekian individuals appear to make decisions based solely upon personal understandings of the economic forces around them (apart from illegitimate interventions by government and unions), decisions which are presumed to somehow always be rational and for the best. This is absurd; rational decisions in such matters require much more information than most individuals either have or can obtain. Defending against the charge that in a socialist world state the "Virtuous Small Man" would see his savings disappear, Wells addressed this sort of challenge directly, in terms still all too relevant. The present system, he argues, "does not guarantee to the small investor any security for his little hoard at all. He comes into the world of investment ill-informed, credulous, or only unintelligently suspicious — and he is, as a class, continually and systematically deprived of his little accumulations. One great financial operation after another in the modern world, as any well-informed person can witness, eats up the small investor."[92] Wells's examples, drawn from contemporary events, are now known only to historians of the Edwardian era, yet similar ones can be found throughout the intervening decades, especially during the great investment bubble and inevitable crash in the early 2000s, one which saw millions of people lose their jobs, savings, pensions, and homes to forces over which they had little understanding and less control.

Having depicted the actual situation of the small investor in a largely unregulated market, Wells preemptively strikes down another common solution still broached by economists of a certain bent, again in language all too contemporary in tone. "It is possible to argue that the small man ought to take more pains about his investments; but, as a matter of fact, investing money securely and profitably is a special occupation of extraordinary complexity, and the common man with a few hundred pounds has no more chance in that market than he would have under water in Sydney Harbour amidst a shoal of sharks."[93] The problem is simple: in a market regulated largely in the interests of the industry at hand the ordinary citizen is at a distinct disadvantage because the regulations themselves are designed to keep him or her from having the kind of control which would allow thoughtful participation, even assuming due diligence on the part of the regulators and honesty on the part of those ostensibly being regulated. The function of the taxpayer dwindles to little more than being a source of income for those cleaning up the mess left behind when the speculations collapse, or to providing the money for new, publicly funded but quickly privatized, investments. As Wells sardonically noted, "It is scarcely too much to say that a very large proportion of our modern great properties, tramway systems, railways, gasworks, bread companies, have been created for their present owners,— the debenture-holders and mortgagors, the great capitalists,— by the unintentional altruism of that voluntary martyr, the Saving Small Man."[94]

Hayek in fact does admit that individual economic decisions require an organized social network in order either to have purpose or to be judged successful or otherwise. But that network is not, and cannot be, purely impersonal; it requires and rests upon a further network of positive social structures and practices, all of them created by particular people to further particular ends. As James Bonar had already commented, long before Hayek wrote, in a book with which Wells may have been familiar,

> The labour in a civilized state can only go on when the right of property in tools or the *use* of them has been first conceded; and apart from that concession, the labour, when it does go on, owes its efficiency to the social surroundings of the workman, and to the division of labour and inventions, without which he as an individual would realize a very inferior product indeed. What he produces therefore is what society has helped him to produce; and in apportionment of property according to labour, even if the latter could be taken as the only standard of desert, the society would have a claim as well as the individual.[95]

The same holds true for all individual activities; their achievement and value holds true only within a pre-existing social structure. No individual, therefore, has any claim to be above the society within which she or he lives and creates. This does not mean, in any way, that they cannot criticize their society, but only that that criticism too must be understood within a particular context, as drawing its force from a conscious effort to control and reshape the forces or social structures criticized, and therefore of importance only in relation to those structures and their envisioned replacements.[96] Criticism, no matter how harsh, is in fact evidence of the belief that the society or aspect thereof under question is subject both to rational understanding and rational change. Similarly, it has long been observed that satire is at its best where the satirist both hates the target and loves what the target could be.

The point which follows is this: that private property holds meaning as a social fact only within a particular type of setting. In order for private property to be understood as being of positive fundamental importance to a particular type of society, the setting within which it has meaning and the forces operant within that setting must themselves be understood. Hayek has provided no means to attaining the latter understanding; indeed, he has denied that such an understanding can be reached. On his grounds, this makes sense; once the forces operant in a society have been understood the first step to controlling them has been taken, and it is this control against which he has ranged himself. But here a further contradiction appears: if it is the arbitrary action of external forces which prevent freedom from flourishing, and if it is the proper function of the Rule of Law and the governmental (or societal) mechanisms necessary to maintain that rule to remove or weaken those forces, then the Rule of Law must be turned against all such forces, including those which result from the operations of the marketplace. But to do this requires as much understanding as possible; one cannot control, save by accident, that which one does nor understand. Thus the Rule of Law demands as much understanding of social mechanisms as possible, and as much application of those understandings as necessary. Understanding is possible only in the presence of regularity; social understanding therefore requires as regular a social mechanism as possible. Such a mechanism requires in turn some touchstone whence to draw its purpose. It is this which utopian writers have attempted to provide.

In keeping with his gradualism, though, Wells is not proposing any sort of instantaneous or revolutionary expropriation of everything anybody owns. The process will operate mostly at the individual level; people will come to realize that most of that to which they now cling, or which they struggle to obtain, most desperately, is not necessary for them to live rich and fulfilling lives. Much of the social control will in fact apply to large scale enterprises rather than personal property. Some of Wells's comments here have a distinctly contemporary ring, especially in light of the market-driven boom and crash that threw the first decade of the twenty-first century into such economic chaos. "Is it not plain," he asked,

> that there is something profoundly wrong about the organization of money? Its business is to set things working. Combined with private property it should be the basic mechanism of the contemporary human community. There is no reason why human society should protect anyone with possessions, unless there is a corresponding social benefit. And since money is a mechanism to serve the human community, and not the human community to serve money, it is plain that if it works so as to stall the economic life it has hitherto sustained, if it is not forthcoming where property has to be liquidated in order that idle hands may work, something has to be done about it. It has to be altered.[97]

So doing will require significant structural changes, as the institutions controlled by a few give way to institutions controlled by, and serving, the whole of society. "A time may come, when profit-seeking banking will not be tolerated and all banking operations will be recognized as vital public services. That does not mean that banks will be 'nationalized.' They tend through the natural development of financial affairs to become quasi-public organizations side-by-side with the politician's governments."[98] Wells would have been disappointed, though unsurprised, by the length of the process, but he would recognize and welcome the recent trend toward public control of financial institutions, asking only that it be hastened and extended. He recognized that the more power held by the people as a whole the more likely an accelerating movement toward utopia would be.

Power exists only in relation to purpose, whether as potential or actual. Any political organization has at its core some sort of purpose, though it may be difficult for a given person to explain it; even if the purpose is only the maintenance of order and the avoidance of a presumed or real Hobbesian state of nature, the organization has come into being to serve the needs of at least some of its inhabitants, past or present. The largest organization possible under present circumstances is a nation-state, although the possibility that the state could encompass the world cannot be immediately discounted. Any imaginary state, standing as it does in a contrary relation to that (or those) already extant, will likewise have a purpose, which, in contrast to that of an actual state (which purpose may well have become obscure to the majority of its citizenry), will usually be one which can be summed up fairly easily.

For utopians prior to Wells, the state is coextensive with a nation, or even, as in Plato, a city. Exactly how big a city is not made clear by Plato; it ought to be allowed to grow, Socrates says, "so long as growth is compatible with unity, but no further." He adds that its constructors "are to avoid at all costs either making the state too small or relying on apparent size, but keep it adequate in scale and unity."[99] What this entails in numbers is never given (apart from the passing suggestion "that the minimum state would consist of four or five men,"[100] a number soon abandoned as a result of other considerations), but Plato's pupil Aristotle suggests that "you cannot make a city of ten men, and if there are a hundred thousand it is a city no longer. But the proper number is presumably not a single number, but anything that falls between certain fixed points."[101] There seems no good reason not to take this as Plato's view as well. The Platonic state, then, is about the population of a small modern city.[102] More's Utopia is geographically larger — about 200 miles wide — but is divided into fifty-four "splendid big towns" separated by a minimum distance of twenty-four miles.[103] The towns themselves have a maximum population of approximately 100,000 and a minimum of 60,000,[104] which is to say that they are each comparable in size to Aristotle's city, while the utopian nation as a whole has a population of about five million, or not much more than a middle-sized metropolitan region. In each case, the assumption is that the state, whatever its size, will be one among many, and thus subject to external conflicts, up to and including war.[105]

War, for Wells, is one of the fundamental forces mitigating against human well-being; where there are individual nation-states, there will be war. But on his account the utopian process, as we have seen, requires that individuals think of themselves first and foremost as human, rather than as members of this or that group or tribe or nation. The state, therefore, if it is to be utopian in purpose (that is, if it is to act as the engine behind the initial creation and maintenance of the utopian process), must be such as to preclude war and encourage humanism.[106] The Wellsian utopian state, by contrast with Plato, begins therefore by encompassing the world; "No less than a planet will serve the purpose of a modern Utopia."[107] Wells is profoundly concerned with eradicating altogether the conditions which give rise to wars. "A permanent world peace implies a profound revolution in the nature of every existing government upon earth, and in the fundamental ideas upon which that government is based," he wrote.

> Something very fundamental, something very difficult, important and formidable, is being shirked and evaded in all this peace discussion and all these contemporary peace proposals. This difficulty is the *sovereign independence of states*. That is the cardinal difficulty before us, and until we tackle it instead of walking round it and round it, we shall not make much further progress towards the organised peace of the world.[108]

Although quite colossal wars may be a part of the process by which utopia comes to be, they are neither necessary nor desirable, and one of the criteria for the existence of utopia at all is that wars shall have ceased.[109] Since "a state powerful enough to keep isolated under modern conditions would be powerful enough to rule the world," and would end up as the arbiter in all major political functions, passively by acquiescence if not actively by threats or force, "world-state, therefore, it must be."[110] This, therefore, allows for one of the few definite boundaries to be drawn around the Wellsian idea of utopia; whatever it is, it requires a global base. Everything beforehand is preparation, and everyone doing so, although they may have a utopian attitude, cannot be said in any way to live under genuine utopian conditions. This is to say that although the utopian process may not have a discernible end, it does have a more or less clear beginning. I say "more or less clear" because the exact point at which a genuinely functional world state in the utopian sense has been reached is bound to be a matter of some dispute. It should also be noted that the mere existence of a world state is by no means a guarantee of utopia; the world state is necessary for the beginning of the utopian process, but hardly sufficient. For an illustration of this see, e.g., *When the Sleeper Wakes*; the world state therein is clearly dystopian.

Two fundamental objections arise immediately here, one from the party of war and the other from the party of peace. I shall begin by examining the objection to the eradication of war.

War, the argument runs, is a necessity for a proper and fully human existence. Without war, any society is bound to stagnate; a stagnant society is a decaying society, which is to say that it is a society becoming worse, and thus, socially, the exact opposite of utopia. As the German philosopher G.W.F. Hegel has said, "War is not to be regarded as an absolute evil and as a purely external accident, which itself therefore has some accidental cause, be it injustices, the passions of nations or the holders of power, &c., or in short, something or other which ought not to be."[111] War is a necessary part of human existence, because war serves to keep human beings in touch with the necessary operations of universal laws of individual relations. In commenting on his own assertions here, Hegel expands the point further:

> In peace civil life continually expands; all its departments wall themselves in, and in the long run men stagnate. Their idiosyncrasies become continually more fixed and ossified. But for health the unity of the body is required, and if its parts harden themselves into exclusiveness, that is death. Perpetual peace is often advocated as an ideal towards which humanity should strive.... As a result of war, nations are strengthened, but peoples involved in civil strife also acquire peace at home through making wars abroad ... the fact remains that wars occur when the necessity of the case requires. The seeds burgeon once more, and harangues are silenced by the solemn cycles of history.[112]

One need not assume the truth of, or even understand, Hegel's metaphysics to see the force of such a claim. Plenty of other writers have reached similar conclusions, in language varying according to their predispositions; a similar one, for example, is found in William James, who was assuredly no follower of Hegel, though attached to a contrary position, as we shall see.

One answer, the weakest philosophically but of great relevance to many people anyway, is to say that stagnation is preferable to the sorts of things which wars, especially modern wars, entail. One wonders what seeds would burgeon after an all-out nuclear war, for instance, and whether even Hegel would approve of them. Based on compassionate emotions rather than any sort of argumentation, the position rests largely on an indication of the massive amount of human suffering in, say, the last century, and the assertion that only a demonstration that stagnation would result in greater suffering would overcome the fact of that suffering. This objection carries greater weight than at first appears, but presumes that the listener holds a world-view in which compassion is a dominant emotion (hence its lack of philosophical weight; compassion must be for individual suffering, and philosophy, at least of the "scientific" sort, is resolutely uninterested in individuals).[113] The claim regarding the value of war becomes, then, a matter of historical empiricism of the thorniest type.[114] It also remains difficult to prove. Unless one imports a necessitarian or deterministic metaphysical ground for war in any possible human society, the already questionable claim remains an inductive one based on empirical data, data regarding situations which are themselves only inductively related to the future. Such an argument will not automatically sustain any presumption in favor of war, as it verges on the circular: war is necessary because all human progress has been accompanied by war; therefore all human progress requires war. The contrary position is, if not clearer, certainly no less clear; since the facts are not enough to determine the situation, the opposing argument runs, it is better to act on the presumption that peace without stagnation is both desirable and obtainable. Further, no argument based on the previous conditions of humanity is in itself enough to demonstrate the future conditions of humanity, as the understandings of those conditions will themselves be changed by the character of the arguments applied to them, and thus what counts as an understanding now (and is therefore a basis for claims about the future) may change beyond all recognition later. Finally, there is at least some evidence that ever larger groups of human beings are living in social arrangements not requiring war or even a significant threat of external violence (unless one counts even trade wars as violent in this sense); this last point, while inconclusive, is at least suggestive.

A second response relates to this, though it is somewhat stronger. This is to attack the problem of war along the lines proposed by William James by finding substitutes. James recognized the powerful emotional and social impact of war upon individuals within society, and to some extent even agreed with the conventional view; "Militarism is the great preserver of our ideals of hardihood, and human life with no use for hardihood would be contemptible. Without risks or prizes for the darer, history would be insipid indeed; and there is a type of military character which every one feels that the race should never cease to breed, for every one is sensitive to its superiority."[115] He also recognizes the countervailing fact of the destructiveness of modern war; "And when whole nations are the armies, and the science of destruction vies in intellectual refinement with the sciences of production, I see that war becomes absurd and impossible from its own monstrosity."[116] James, who avowedly supported Wells's views, argued that what was needed was a "substitute for war's disciplinary function," or what he famously called a "*moral equivalent* of war."[117] The challenge to the advocate of the necessity of war as a stimulant to human existence and/or progress is, as James and Wells recognized, to justify their insistence upon war in itself, as opposed to some other highly challenging and even dangerous activity. One such activity, for example, is space exploration; Wells ended the film *Things to Come* with a moon shot, after which a central character gestures at the stars and offers the choice, "all the universe — or nothingness." I will not here take a stand on this particular choice, save only to mention that, taken seriously as an option for humanity, it would entail an effort more colossal than any hitherto undertaken for even the greatest of wars. If stagnation is the risk should war be superseded, then some consideration should be given to the nature of what it is that is thought of as superseding war; until this question has been thoroughly explored, the necessity of war remains at most a tendentious assertion.

There is another consideration regarding war, one rooted less in a view of the greater good of humanity than an acknowledgement of practical political realities which must also be taken into account. War, or warlike conditions, can be very useful for reinforcing or strengthening the position of the powerful, who often provoke, but rarely fight, military conflicts. The problem can be recognized from many perspectives. George Orwell drew out its consequences in *1984*, with its depiction of the eternal state of war which justified enormous state controls. Dwight Eisenhower saw it when he warned against the "military-industrial complex," although he failed to recognize the ironic fact that his support for covert operations against democratically elected governments which were not following the free market party line aided its growth immensely. The best recent examination of the problem is found in Naomi Klein's *The Shock Doctrine: The Rise of Disaster Capitalism*, in which she massively documents decades of use of disasters, natural or created, and terrorism, overt or half-concealed, by various governments in thrall to an outdated economic theory, to impose the consequences of that theory upon the citizens living under those governments. As she says, "Some of the most infamous human rights violations of this era [the last four decades], which have tended to be viewed as sadistic acts carried out by antidemocratic regimes, were in fact either committed with the deliberate intent of terrorizing the public or actively harnessed to prepare the ground for the introduction of radical free-market 'reforms.'"[118]

Such a situation creates a serious problem for utopian hopes; it seems to present not an arguable intellectual challenge but an insuperable factual one, summed up in a grim syllogism: the realization of utopia depends on freedom for all; freedom for all requires the elimination of the current structure of power relations; elimination of the current structure of power relations would undercut the wealth and power of those currently in control; people never voluntarily surrender power; therefore the powerful will never allow utopia to develop. Laid out so baldly, though, the situation looks rather less hopeless than logic might suggest. It is a matter of historical fact that all rigid power structures have limits, if only because of limited resources for application to an unlimited need for control; there comes a time when those structures can no longer be supported even with best efforts of those who benefit from them. They collapse, either on their own or with assistance from outside the structure (revolution, not necessarily violent, being a common factor; war another). Given this fact, and the concomitant fear that the collapse may, and probably will, be worse for the former rulers than a peaceful transition, there are always advocates within the system for gradual transformation of the system. They may not win over the leaders immediately (and collapses of various sorts occur with monotonous regularity due to the intransigence of various leaders), but their voices, along with the often barely audible voices of the majority of the citizenry, remain to be heard. This creates a powerful pressure for even the most rigid system to change in at least a marginally progressive manner, especially as new technologies make access to comparisons between one political system and others more difficult to conceal. The very violence with which potentially utopian ideas are repressed is an indication of their power; as Klein notes, "It is precisely because the dream of economic equality is so popular, and so difficult to defeat in a fair fight, that the shock doctrine was embraced in the first place."[119] Wells never says that the creation of utopia is going to be easy, but it is more difficult to suppress the utopian spirit for long than dictators and their pet economists imagine. Again, we see an advantage of the evolutionary approach to utopia; because it is a process rather than something fixed, it allows small advances to build up over long periods rather than requiring sudden massive change. The point is implicit in much of the discussion so far, and shall return in other forms as we proceed.

The second challenge is similar to that from the point of view of those defending the necessity of war, but without the catastrophic accouterments. Simply put, the claim is that national competitiveness is necessary to stimulate the best in artistic and intellectual endeavors. The situation is, or should be, as the great Russian composer Anton Rubinstein, free of overt political intentions, described mid-nineteenth century Germany as being:

> ... a kind of Eldorado for the arts and sciences.... Each court vied with the other in protecting science and the fine arts.... Each university strove to attract to itself the shining lights of science. The universal standard of intelligence and intellectual development in general was carried to a much higher pitch in divided Germany than in these later times, now that it is compressed as by an iron ring into a single great kingdom.... Howsoever absurd may have been the political aspirations of divided Germany, in the domain of intellectual development she knew no superior. Petty sovereignties as a rule progress more rapidly than those of greater extent. What was Italy before her unification, and what is she now?[120]

Again, the force of these charges is strong, and in this case they are apparently amply supported by historical examples. If the price of a world state is, say, the Americanization of world culture, surely this is a significant argument against desiring a world state.

The first response is a counterpart to that regarding war: if the cessation of the mass slaughters endemic to the last century requires the loss of a certain degree of "culture," then so be it. Without human beings around to enjoy them, all the efforts of creative intellects will amount to nought. One is reminded of Bertrand Russell's response when asked which of his works he considered most important. "If nuclear war is prevented," he wrote, "I should consider my opposition to it my most important work. If not, *Principia Mathematica* will not be able to enlighten anyone."[121]

On the other hand, if there is no necessary connection between the world state and cultural stagnation, then some further response is required. This second response takes the form of a challenge to the assumptions built into the account given of human creativity. What, we might ask, is at the root of that creativity? Surely it is the support given to the artists and scientists by individual states, support which allowed them a degree of freedom from sordid fiscal concerns and the attendant drag on mental liveliness. Why, then, must we assume that in a state where *all* are free of those concerns, and where ample opportunities exist for the exercise of creativity, that there will not be at least an equal amount proportionally, and thus a greater amount absolutely, of creative thought and effort? It is at least arguably true that in large nations such as presently exist there is limited freedom from fiscal constraints, and that many who would have been likely to find at least a margin of support from some patron or another a century ago are unlikely to do so today. But this merely points to a flaw in the system as presently constituted, not to a problem shown to be inherent in the world state itself. The problem with the present political situation is precisely that too much money and too many resources are wasted on military and patriotic purposes; where the need for such waste has vanished, and where the fear of destitution has likewise vanished, then an upsurge of creativity (even without the presence of an educational system dedicated to fostering such creativity) would appear a more likely event than the opposite.

The character of this world state will undergo a variety of metamorphoses over time, as the conditions under which human relations and attitudes unfold change. Wells was quick to realize the impact of modern technologies of communication; "the right size of an administrative area is determined by the operative means of communication and must vary as those means vary,"[122] he wrote, with the clear understanding that very soon all parts of the world will be within instantaneous communicative reach of all others. This in turn removes the need for an omnipresent central authority; the members of any ruling or guiding body as may be necessary may be anywhere at any time. This in turn mitigates the concentration of hangers-on found always near the seats of government, and lessens the appearance of concentrated power so useful for dictatorships and the like. More and more people can become involved in the process, as they need not travel to make a presentation or petition for justice.[123] Government dissolves as a presence, even as its presence within the social structure grows broader. Resistance to this sort of claim, and the process it represents, rests on an assumption that "government" is some sort of structure of rules and regulations imposed upon, and largely alien to, the individual. What Wells is postulating here is a social structure in which the more intensely focused individual consciousness has internalized the social needs (mostly involving a diminution of ego and an expansion of community-centered attitudes) and therefore needs a minimum of externally imposed behavioral controls.

The specific forms the world state will take are not entirely predictable, especially in the long run. Some form is necessary, at least initially, but part of the process is the discovery of what degree of organization is most effective. "You see all organisation, with its implication of finality, is death," says Mr. Britling.

> What you organise you kill. Organised morals or organised religion or organised thought are dead morals and dead religion and dead thought. Yet some organisation you must have. Organisation is like killing cattle. If you do not kill some the herd is just waste. But you mustn't kill all or you kill the herd. The unkilled cattle are the herd, the continuation; the unorganised side of life is the real life. The reality of life is adventure, not performance. What isn't adventure isn't life. What can be ruled about can be machined.[124]

If the problem of political stagnation is to be avoided, some sort of extensive leeway for individual freedom within the social order must be found. This freedom cannot be imposed, so its character, which will have to be a matter of individual choice under the circumstances of the utopia, can only be hinted at. Plato (and indeed any teleological utopian) can present one vision on the assumption that the vision is either right or wrong. Wells (and any evolutionary utopian) must offer a range of visions, so as not to appear to be granting finality to any among them. Thus, for example, in *A Modern Utopia* he presents a bureaucratic state much like the contemporary welfare state in many respects; in *The Shape of Things to Come*, among other works, he describes a series of states leading toward the most utopian thus far[125]; in *Men Like Gods*, he describes a society in which there is no discernible state at all, at least in the organized political sense as understood today. Each of these states offers some flaw, or set of flaws, which undercuts it, which makes it non-utopian for its inhabitants (by virtue of failing to allow them scope for the fullest development of their individual potentialities, potentialities which are different than could be imagined at some previous stage in the development of human society and being), and which requires therefore the rise of new utopian theorists to propel human society toward another stage.

The world state formed a vital component of Wells's utopianism, yet it was never meant to be an end in itself. For Wells the state is but a mechanism for achieving political goals which require more than individuals or small groups can achieve on their own. The political goal of utopia is the infinite expansion of human freedom and creativity. Any mechanism which interferes with this cannot be utopian. This, then, is the test for political proposals purporting to move toward utopia: do they serve to maximize freedom for all? Can this maximization be demonstrated? If the answer to either question is no, the proposal is likely not utopian. Errors will no doubt be made in judging this, but it is, at the least, the beginning of a beginning. The rest requires imagination, compassion, and love. Imagination, in order to see beyond what is given to us by our surroundings; compassion, in order to comprehend the straitjackets, moral, emotional, and economic, in which all of us live and will continue to live our lives, unless we care enough to act against those restraints; love, in order to transcend the self toward others, that we may desire their freedom as well as our own, and in so desiring strive toward both.

Despite the foregoing, it must be admitted that the Wellsian utopia is, in fact, aimed in part at a kind of stability. The forward motion of society should be infinite, but in any case there should be no regression. There is an amusing irony here: Wells and Hayek are in fact seeking the same goal, albeit one which Hayek's method and political stance cannot support. What both authors desire is to provide individuals a secure position from which they can make plans for the future. This base is in part financial, and the desired security can be obtained only when the external economic forces which now to a great degree control individual lives have themselves been tamed and regularized, a fact which Hayek's prior commitments cannot allow him to see; his support is thrown instead to the very structures and relations which most undercut genuine personal economic stability (planning at the personal level is difficult indeed if one cannot count on a specific job, or at least a specific wage, from day to day, let alone longer periods). Thus the stability for which he argues is illusory, while that projected by Wells is structured so as to change with the needs of humanity. For Wells what is sought is a stability provided by a base which rises continually to reflect and preserve new attainments, yet which can also allow for their abandonment when necessitated by changed circumstances or still further ones. Such a stability requires a certain degree of regulation, coordination, and uniformity of particular activities. This is not, Wells, insists, the same as removing all the variety in life:

> it really does not enhance the natural variety and beauty of life to have all the clocks in a town keeping individual times of their own, no charts of the sea, no timetables, but trains starting secretly to unspecified destinations, infectious diseases without notification and postmen calling occasionally when they can get by the picturesque footpads at the corner.[126]

Regularity ensures security; security allows freedom. Freedom is one of the key purposes of the Wellsian state, including eventually freedom from the Wellsian state.[127] Freedom turns out not only to be a goal but a foundation as well. Political freedom is meaningful only in relation to individual freedom, which in turn requires political freedom. I have discussed the specific application of restraints in order to create greater freedom above, but in so doing have deferred a discussion of precisely what it is that those restraints are supposed to require and guarantee. It is therefore to an examination of the nature and consequences of individual freedom that I shall now turn.

4

Freedom and Social Patterns

The specific applications of the rhetoric of freedom vary from utopian author to utopian author, but they tend toward a similar point, wherein freedom is seen as implying some sort of subordination of the majority to a (presumably wiser) ruling class. Wells inverts this traditional utopian approach; "To the classical Utopists freedom was relatively trivial," Wells claims.

> Clearly they considered virtue and happiness as entirely separable from liberty, and as being altogether more important things. But the modern view, with its deepening insistence upon individuality and upon the significance of its uniqueness, steadily intensifies the value of freedom, until at last we begin to see liberty as the very substance of life, that indeed it is life, and that only the dead things, the choiceless things, live in absolute obedience to law.[1]

Political action, for Wells, is inescapably tinged with moral qualities, and these can be subject to no universal deterministic law without becoming thereby devoid of the very morality under consideration. Political morality, like all forms of morality, requires freedom. Without the availability of choices with significantly different consequences, and without the awareness of those options and their probable consequences, what remains is mere purposeless action with no more moral content than has a volcano erupting and spraying burning lava at random over the landscape.

Given his emphasis on the importance of choice, it is to be expected that Wells applies the term freedom broadly. "Freedom," one of his fictional avatars asserts, "is the primary desire of living things." It, or its absence, motivates virtually every other desire or attempted action.

> Almost all that they desire either individually or in common, can be expressed as a freedom, as an escape from a limitation. When they want Peace it is really an escape from the intense preoccupation and danger of war. When they want plenty it is freedom from the irksomeness of want and toil. When they obey it is to relieve themselves of the immediate

penalties of compulsion. When they dance or drill or sing or shout in unison it is to free themselves from the lonely conspicuousness of initiative, the essential agoraphobia. "Men only willingly place themselves under the discipline of organized effort in order to remain, in some nearer and more essential respect, free."[2]

Freedom is both a goal and a premise, with each aspect demanding ever more complex support from the other.

Wells does not elaborate a full scale theory undergirding the role of freedom in his utopian structures, yet the outlines of such a theory are implicit in the way he uses freedom as both a means and an end. For purposes of clarity, though, it may be helpful to explore, in advance of discussing those uses of freedom in themselves, the sort of view Wells presumably (and, I would argue, given the nature of his project, necessarily) holds. Wells's philosophical approach regarding freedom, although never explicated in detail, shares numerous characteristics with that of the writers and thinkers loosely subsumed under the rubric "existentialist," particularly Jean-Paul Sartre. In what follows, therefore, I shall where necessary recruit Sartre (and Simone de Beauvoir, who at times makes Sartre's points for him in a considerably clearer manner than he does himself) as an aid to making concrete what is philosophically undeveloped in Wells. I shall not attempt to present the whole of a theory of freedom, which task is beyond my purposes and which accomplishment is beyond my ability, but I shall indicate the primary elements such a theory must have in order to accommodate an evolutionary utopian outlook.

Freedom is the foundation of morality because morality entails choice, and choice cannot exist without freedom. As de Beauvoir remarked, "Freedom is the source from which all significations and all values spring. It is the original condition of all justification of existence."[3] That is, in order to justify any action one takes, to assert of it any moral predicate at all, one must be able to appeal to one's freedom to have acted otherwise. A volcanic eruption neither justifies itself nor is justified; it simply *is*. "To will oneself moral and to will oneself free are one and the same decision."[4] Acts are either predicated upon the idea that they are the best action conceivable at the moment (the reasons for so judging are not yet relevant here), or they are random, or they are purely deterministic. The deterministic can have no moral weight, because it could not be otherwise; it is neither good nor bad. The random must either be the result of some freely chosen determining action (flipping a coin, say) or be itself deterministic in an unknown way. The latter is necessarily true because no action can be without a cause; therefore a random action must result either from a known cause or an unknown one. If the cause is known, then it must have been chosen or it must be determined and unavoidable. If the latter, morality again vanishes. If the former, then the choice to submit the determination of one's action to random forces is itself contingent, and becomes the bearer of moral weight; one can always retract one's commitment to accepting the indicative result of the random force chosen. One chooses the path one will take even in the act of abdicating one's responsibility.

Freedom is always relative to a state of being. Freedom requires both knowledge and opportunity; left alone in a room with a piano, someone who knows not how to play the instrument is not free to create music. Conversely, the finest pianist in the world can do nothing without the presence of a keyboard. These criteria are indefinitely expandable; the non-player can learn to play, and the pianist can learn another score, or learn to play the oboe as well. One must know not only that one has options in an abstract sense, but what those options might be; they are, naturally, options only if one has the knowledge necessary to render them genuine in the first place. Similarly, opportunity must be more than abstract as well; the non-player must have regular access to a piano, and the pianist must have the time to practice two instruments rather than one. Both, of course, must have enough to eat.

The first condition of freedom, then, is freedom from material scarcity. As Brecht wrote, "Erst kommt das Fressen, dann kommt die Moral."[5] Where a person is worrying about whether or not they will have enough to eat, or will be able to find shelter on a cold night, they cannot be said in a meaningful political sense to be free; if the conditions of deprivation are severe enough, they can be described as free even in a moral sense only at the level of philosophical discourse, since the conditions under which they exist are such as to vitiate the awareness necessary for genuine choice in the first place. It is this fact which allows courts and juries to recognize "mitigating circumstances" when passing judgment on certain persons who are charged with having committed a crime. It is in this sense that material scarcity motivates actions experienced as free but in fact largely determined. Individuals make choices toward attaining or retaining what are accepted as the conditions, personal and social, for the avoidance of material scarcity and the satisfaction of private needs. That these conditions, and indeed the needs as well, are very often historically contingent is a fact overlooked in the choices themselves, which are seen as extending beyond their immediate relations toward the personal and social stability deemed necessary for choice in itself. The degree and character of the scarcity involved in determining the choice at hand is unacknowledged, or seen as irrelevant; the individual experiences his or her self as acting independently of others whose existence is likewise responding to, and reinforcing, the scarcity, whether real or merely perceived.[6] Yet the actions prompted by the scarcity could not exist in the same way in the absence of other human beings likewise desiring an end to scarcity. As Sartre has demonstrated, each person in social relations so determined, "will see everyone in terms of the object of consumption or the manufactured product, and, on this basic level, he will recognise them as the mere possibility of the consumption of something he himself needs. In short, he will find each of them to be the material possibility of his being annihilated through the material annihilation of an object of primary necessity."[7] Who I am is in part determined, whether I will it or not, by what I have, and this in part is determined by what others want, and how much freedom each of us has to obtain what we seek. Scarcity creates conflict. No matter what one is in the process of becoming, one encounters on all sides limitations unchosen by oneself; one encounters the designs, intentions, actions, and needs of others as potentially deleterious, by virtue of their perceived demands on the available resources.

Material scarcity is foundational, but it is not the only scarcity which restricts freedom. The concept of scarcity expands, on the one hand, to include psychological needs and, on the other hand, to include that which is needed to allow the individual to express her or his experienced self to the fullest degree. As external possibilities multiply, individuals respond, or at least can respond, by expanding their range of behaviors and practices. Homophonic melodic music, for example, can be made by any individual alone, but even the simplest harmony requires an instrument, or two voices working together within the prior bounds of a musical structure. Complex harmonic or timbral structures present fresh needs, expanding at once the expressive potential and its underlying requirements, whether of performative skill or in the technique of instrument manufacture. As in music, so in all areas of human endeavor; these expansions demand a concomitant expansion of the availability of resources through which the practices, and the personas linked thereto, can be sustained. New resources are always limited in some fashion, whether by location or by difficulties in production or through the complexity of the skills necessary to control them.

Self-justification stems from subjective self-creation; self-creation, as an open-ended set of possibilities, requires freedom. A self which is entirely externally caused is no subject at all, as it merely exists without the possibility of being other than what it is; it is, so to speak, the object of its causations. It is merely a thing. Yet the boundaries of the self are, as has already been shown (and will, in the last chapter, be shown further), vague and flexible. They are also, in large part, the result of social structures and the congeries of contingent intersubjective relations experienced by the self at hand. Scarcity, then, except in its foundational aspects, is, like freedom, always relative to a given state of society. Utopia is the progressive eradication of scarcity. This goal is achieved first by changing the material conditions of human existence, and second by changing the conditions of intersubjective relations within human existence. The two changes are linked; the conditions for each require the presence of the other.

Regarding the former I shall say little more here than I have already said. The provision for all of ample nutritious food, of adequate shelter, and of similar necessities, is included in the conditions for beginning the utopian process at any other than the purely personal level. Similarly, the tensions entailed by being dependent upon another for the means to these ends (that is, the subordination of the employee to the employer) must be at eliminated. These goals, though, and others like them, in themselves change only the surface of human relations and individual being. True freedom requires changing the inner character of those relations. It requires the recognition of the other as one whose freedom is entailed by mine, and mine by theirs. In a sense, Wells's entire project stems from this consideration; his moral sympathies are most engaged by those least able to act upon their own desires for freedom. Thus, for example, he will take the side of the tenant over the landlord, for many must live as tenants while no one has ever been forced to become, or remain, a landlord.

If freedom is relative to an individual's situation, and if the situation of an individual is at least in part relative to the state of social relations between that individual and others, then freedom can be understood fully only through an understanding of the situations of others. Choice is moral only to the degree that it is free. To desire morality, to will self-justification in one's acts, is to desire to be free. But freedom requires knowledge; to desire to act in a truly moral fashion, therefore, requires desiring to know the conditions of one's choice, and this requires knowing the intersubjective relations within which one's choice(s) are made. This is to say that while an action taken in complete ignorance may be received as having moral significance by those external to the actor, it cannot have true moral significance for the actor themself, as it cannot be justified by appeal to alternate possibilities. As the degree of ignorance lessens, the possibility of moral choice widens; the process of lessening such ignorance includes the progressive expansion of one's understanding of the consequences of one's actions for oneself and others. To assert of an action that it is morally the best possible, then, is to assert that, in light of its consequences fully considered, no other action would have better results, and that the action itself is maximally free (since it is only the free elements of the action which are morally relevant).[8]

It is this which lies behind Sartre's claim that, in "willing freedom, we discover that it depends entirely upon the freedom of others and that the freedom of others depends on our own."[9] Where our actions are taken in light of others seen as opponents, either directly or indirectly, those actions are already constrained, and thus less than maximally free, *even where we think to have chosen the others as opponents*. This is clearly the case in games or sporting events, although there the opponents presumably have mutually chosen the competition and each other, and thus their participation in the event is itself contingent and grounded in freedom. It is no less true, though not always so clear, in actions taken in other spheres of human interaction, where one person may well be altogether unaware that they are, in the eyes of another, an opponent. Wotan and Alberich, in Wagner's *Der Ring des Nibelungen*, are knowing opponents, for example, each in some measure constrained by the actions of the other (Alberich lost the Ring to Wotan; Alberich's curse drives Wotan to commit actions he would not otherwise have chosen, etc.); Siegfried, Wotan's grandson, is unaware of his competition with Hagen, Alberich's son. And so on. Such competitions restrict freedom because they constrain the individual, even where the individual is aware of the competition, to act in ways defined by the other. Since all individuals in the present state of human society are to some degree affected by a multitude of these competitive relations, no individual is completely free. This does not, however, mean that freedom does not exist, nor that one can abdicate from one's responsibility for at least one's attitude toward one's relations with others. Indeed, it is from within such attitudes that the evolution of utopia will, or will not, begin. The first step, as always, remains with the individual. It is the task of the utopian author to encourage an appropriate one.

Wells holds that the utopia attitude is both possible and desirable. Freedom, therefore, is an existential given for Wells:

> For all practical ends your liberty and your sense of your personal responsibility for what you do is ineradicable. Even if you fling yourself down and say, "I am the toy of destiny; I can do nothing that I am not compelled to do," you know all the time that you will be doing and saying this of your own free will. So soon as you have said it, you can say: "That was silly of me. I did not mean to say that."[10]

This is a central tenet of Wells's thought, and it takes many forms. Perhaps the clearest and most dramatic formulation is found in his 1910 novel *The History of Mr. Polly*, which might be described as a bucolic idyll. Referring to "the paper walls of everyday circumstance" through which it is possible to break, Wells emphasizes the free relation of the individual to their attitude toward the world, and the possibility of actions based thereon.

> If the world does not please you *you can change it*. Determine to alter it at any price, and you can change it altogether. You may change it to something sinister and angry, to something appalling, but it may be you will change it to something brighter, something more agreeable, and at the worst something much more interesting.... There are no circumstances in the world that determined action cannot alter, unless perhaps they are the walls of a prison cell, and even those will dissolve and change, I am told, into the infirmary compartment at any rate, for the man who can fast with resolution.[11]

True at the individual level primarily as a potentiality, as a project, this ability to alter reality becomes more powerful as humans begin to act collectively. Knowledge of this, in turn, impels individuals to join with others in order to increase their own freedom. "A man," says Dr. Martineau in *The Secret Places of the Heart*, "isn't a creature in vacuo. He's a surface of contact, a system of adaptions, between his essential self and his surroundings."[12] Despite the use of the word "essential," it is clear that what is meant is that the essence of the person being discussed (in this case, the central character, Sir Richmond Hardy, but by implication the reader as well) is what he has chosen to strive toward: the development of his projectedness toward a goal, and the ramifications thereof.

Human freedom stems in part from the absence of human nature as a determinative factor. Although various individuals in a given society at a given time will, by their own actions, gravitate toward particular types these types reveal no underlying rigid reality. In particular Wells rejects the idea that human beings are somehow essentially flawed prior to any socialization whatsoever. "The leading principle of the Utopian religion (that is, the religious structure in place after the transition to a utopian society, not the related but distinct religious attitude, referred to above, which precedes and succours the utopian mindset) is the repudiation of the doctrine of original sin; the Utopians hold that man, on the whole is good."[13] Goodness, Wells makes clear, rests on the malleability and trainability of the human character; that is, there is no fundamental defect which renders humanity incapable of transcending itself, whether individually or collectively. Humans are fundamentally good, for Wells, because there is no *a priori* stain on their character, no flaw in the mechanism which vitiates all attempts to eradicate violence and hatred. Human beings have no nature which is unchangeable, and therefore any claim that one thing or another is against human nature proves irrelevant to the project at hand. Thus, for example, to the charge that "Socialism is against human nature," he calmly replies that "it is absolutely true." He expands upon the charge gleefully:

> Socialism is against human nature. That is true, and it is equally true of everything else; capitalism is against human nature, Competition is against human nature, cruelty, kindness, religion and doubt, monogamy, polygamy, celibacy, decency, indecency, piety, and sin are all against human nature. The present system in particular against human nature, or what is the policeman for, the soldier, the debt-collector, the judge, the hangman? What means the glass along my neighbour's wall? Human nature is against human nature.[14]

The nature of human beings, if it can be so called, is to be in conflict with whatever defines or constrains them, to be seeking to overcome such definitions and constraints.

It may be argued that this approach fails to account for the essentially destructive character of human beings, as demonstrated throughout history. Exactly what this charge amounts to, or to what it appeals, is not always clear, but it is a common reproach to peaceful utopian projections. George Kateb, for example, although he admits that the concept cannot be categorically defined or defended, insists that "the doctrine of original sin, in one version or another, is the most serious contradiction of utopian optimism.... It would seem that men itch to smash, especially to smash the perfect; to put it as generously as it can be put, they crave excitement, especially forbidden excitement; they cannot be tamed."[15] Alfred Borrello leveled the same sort of charges directly against Wells, who, according to Borrello, failed to see "man as he really is, a creature filled with foibles, torn by dissension, pettiness, and the thousand and one shortcomings which make the extended peace Wells hoped for impossible but more significantly, intolerable."[16]

Here we see a traditional counter argument against utopian thought, one which it must be admitted is often difficult to answer persuasively, given the metaphysical underpinnings on which it frequently rests: that because human beings under present conditions act in a certain way they will continue to do so, and thus any improvement in the human condition is either trivial or illusory. It is impossible to refute claims about the impossibility of attaining utopian conditions, except by attaining them, and one of Wells's (and others') points is that the opportunities for even beginning the process have only very recently themselves been attained, however partially and imperfectly. A few things can be said here, though, which may at least suggest that the charge of ignoring essential flaws in the fundamental human character is rather too glib, and that it does not prove so devastating as might at first appear. One is a factual point: the enormous range of human cultures and behaviors, even within similar material circumstances, known to history and anthropology would suggest that the belief in the malleability of human thought and action is at the very least reasonable. Another is a point of argumentation: any claim about the future behavior of human beings is an inductive one, and therefore cannot be used as an irrefutable proof. This is all Wells needs here. His argument is likewise inductive, but as it concerns probabilities rather than certainties it is at least somewhat less easily rejected on those grounds than the counterclaim, which is a universal. The essentialist must maintain that no possible education can change certain (admittedly often ill-defined) patterns of human behavior; one example to the contrary destroys that case. Wells, on the other hand, need merely establish the possibility. Since human beings brought up under different circumstances appear to behave differently, it is possible that those brought up under circumstances vastly different than any hitherto imagined will behave differently in ways as yet seldom or never possible. Nor is this last claim based entirely on wishful speculations. Bruno Bettelheim made a special point of distinguishing the aggressive behaviors of children raised on Israeli kibbutzes from those in more typical contemporary individualistic societies. "Not once did I observe any physical fighting among kibbutz children," he reports of his investigations into the matter.

> Not once — beyond the age when they push each other down in the playpen — did I see a child pushing another, not to mention hitting with hand or object. This does not occur in the kibbutz. I asked about it repeatedly, and the answer was always the same; while there are disagreements, they never go beyond verbal expression. There are no fights about things like who comes first, or who sits where. Compared with the frequent fighting that seems typical in our society among pre-school and grammar-school children, life in the kibbutz at this age is peaceful indeed.[17]

No single limited experiment could prove or disprove the claims that Wells is making, but the internal interpersonal relations found in such experiments as the kibbutzes at least suggest that it is possible to raise children in ways less conducive to violent behavior than is maintained by supporters of the idea that human beings are essentially and fundamentally flawed. While it may be objected that the eventual collapse of the kibbutz system into something far more competitive and capitalistic disproves the foregoing, I don't see that it does. The kibbutzes were from the start surrounded by a society only marginally supportive at best, and the messages, both in terms of actions and in terms of presentations (advertising, etc.), conducive to self-aggrandizement seen everywhere but on the kibbutz itself would scarcely have been helpful. The point is not that the kibbutzes collapsed, but that they survived for as long as they did under inauspicious circumstances; the real question is what would have happened had they been supported widely and solidly. Without such an experiment, and that on a large scale, dismissing them as evidence seems premature at best. Wells would presumably stress the support that the results of kibbutzim education provide for his challenge to the idea of original sin, not the particular form the education takes.

Finally, it should be noted that the essentialist here is faced with a peculiar problem. If the fundamental flaw in human beings is social, then those who say that changing society can improve the conditions of human existence are right, unless a further claim, that all possible human societies will lead to the same results entirely through structural problems, is made and somehow supported. The likelihood of such support being provided soon (support which requires a deterministic *a priori* assertion about all future states of human existence) does not appear high; it requires knowledge considerably more profound than any presently available. Indeed, the effort to attain such certainty would require a degree of social experimentation even greater than that imagined by Wells; he needs only to find one social structure which is both open-ended and potentially melioristic in order to change the focus of his search, whereas the advocate of the idea that all possible human societies are fundamentally flawed in such a way as to obviate hopes for peace needs to investigate *all* of them. On the other hand, if the flaw is genetic (or in some other way physical), then there is no reason to presume that it cannot be some day corrected through genetic engineering or some such treatment (since it is, by definition, a flaw, there needs to be some other argument than those given for recognizing its existence to demonstrate why this flaw should not be remedied where possible),[18] and thus again no reason to presume that it is unsusceptible to correction. Only if the flaw is presumed to rest on supernatural causes (which is, presumably, what is being done by defenders of the idea of an 'original sin') can its eradication be presumed to be beyond human (that is, natural) achievement. But it is difficult to see what would count as evidence here, since the supernatural does not show itself in natural ways, and thus is beyond understanding by natural means. Natural behaviors cannot be taken as evidence for supernatural functions.[19]

Even on essentialist grounds, it is not clear that we ought not at least attempt to modify the environmental influences on human thought and behavior, since no one will maintain that these influences are without significance. As no conclusive evidence has been given that the fundamental flaw in human beings is genuinely present (and indeed, no such evidence could be given until all possible attempts to modify the human educational and physical environment had been made), to rest objections to the utopian project on such assumptions is at best unhelpful and perhaps even obscurantist. It may be noted, however, that although the idea of "original sin" is necessarily in itself theological, this by no means implies that all views resting on theistic grounds require either the doctrine or that it be taken as excluding a peaceful world-state. Jacques Maritain, for example, whom no one will accuse of being a Wellsian, claimed that "the problem of World Government — I would prefer to say, of a genuinely political organization of the world — is the problem of lasting peace." He saw the attainment of such a condition as difficult but not impossible; his solution included a "senate of wise men," which would "foster in the consciousness of the peoples that great movement of intelligence and will on which depends the genuine and constructive revolution needed by our historical age, the foundation of a world community politically organized."[20]

Wells does not deny that there are very powerful forces militating against any large-scale modifications of human thought and action, or that a portion of those forces stems from internal constraints which may prove quite difficult to eradicate. His description of the Base character type in *A Modern Utopia* should make this clear in any case, as should his powerful statement of precisely the problem that the "original sin" theorist is addressing in *The Croquet Player*: "Man is still what he was. Invincibly bestial, envious, malicious, greedy. Man, Sir, unmasked and disillusioned, is the same fearing, snarling, fighting beast he was a hundred thousand years ago." And so on; the difference is in the response, not the acknowledgement that a problem exists.[21] Wells recognizes that most human beings are locked by social practices and unchallenged personal inclinations into rigid patterns of behavior and belief. This is an aspect of our biological heritage. He acknowledges

> the inveterate disposition of the normal man to accept his immediate circumstances as he finds them and make the best of them for himself. He sticks to the creed he is born to or to the alternative culture that gives him greater comfort. One might write, indeed, not merely the inveterate disposition but the inveterate disposition of every normal living thing. For the ordinary animal the loss of the sense of security releases panic, flight, violence — vehement and usually quite unintelligent efforts to recover the confidence that has slipped away.[22]

This is not a deterministic condition, but it is a very strong one, and one which many human beings will find difficult to overcome.

That this should be the case is unsurprising; until very recently, virtually all human beings lived under relatively severe material constraints. As it is, most human beings are still required to spend a large portion of their time and energy working to obtain the necessities of life (food, shelter, clothing, etc.), or the money to exchange for those necessities. When these constraints are removed, a great amount of free energy, both mental and physical, will require new things upon which to focus. Freedom means nothing if it is not used in a constructive and stimulating manner; the freedom merely to consume mindlessly is no freedom at all, however free the person thinks of themself as being; such a person is in fact not free, but merely the means to another's end — in this case the producers of trivial gew-gaws. Nonetheless, freedom is not something which can simply appear, or be granted; some social controls over individual behaviors will need to remain for a considerable period of time.

Erich Fromm, in a very Wellsian passage, has pointed out the underlying contradictions in the psychological underpinnings of modern consumer-industrial society. Maximal consumption, seen as an end in itself, leads only to a ceaseless scrabble for position, with the corollary that classes, and class conflicts, will inevitably come into being. "As long as everybody wants to have more, there must be formations of classes, there must be class war, and, in global terms, there must be international war. *Greed and peace preclude each other.*"[23] The orientation toward consumption, which Fromm calls the "having mode" of existence, generates inequalities, and these generate resentment, which in turn generates violence on the parts of both those seeking to protect their possessions and those seeking to acquire them or their associated power.

> The having mode of existence, the attitude centered on property and profit, necessarily produces the desire — indeed the need — for power. To control other living human beings we need to use power to break their resistance. To maintain control over private property we need to use power to protect it from those who would take it from us because they, like us, can never have enough; the desire to have private property produces the desire to use violence in order to rob others in overt or covert ways.[24]

As has long been demonstrated, this structure of human social relations further generates ideological structures (as well as additional social structures based thereon) which serve to justify and entrench present practices and attitudes.

> The growing person is forced to give up most of his or her autonomous, genuine desires and interests, and his or her own will, and to adopt a will and desires and feelings that are not autonomous but superimposed by the social patterns of thought and feeling. Society, and the family as its psychosocial agent, has to solve a difficult problem: *How to break a person's will without his being aware of it?* Yet by a complicated process of indoctrination, rewards, punishments, and fitting ideology, it solves this

task by and large so well that most people believe they are following their own will and are unaware that their will itself is conditioned and manipulated.[25]

There is a vital, and unavoidable, tension here. Compare Fromm's concerns with Sarnac's comments on education quoted earlier ("We are trained from earliest childhood in the world to be tolerant and understanding of others and to be wary and disciplined with our own wayward impulses, we are given from the first a clear knowledge of our entangled nature [....] In this world we breathe mercy with our first fluttering gasp. In this world we are so taught and trained to think of others that their pain is ours").[26] The two sound similar, yet their goals, and therefore the means used to attain those goals, are diametrically opposed. Education is, *and must be*, a form of indoctrination; even the choices of subject or methods of teaching and testing send clear messages to the pupils regarding what is important, what is not, and how individuals should interact. The question is not whether we should indoctrinate students, but what we choose to require and to apply as part of that process, whether we focus on our shared humanity or on individuals in an imagined and impossible isolation from each other's needs and activities. Wells and Fromm have called our attention to the inescapable consequences of an education which emphasizes competition, possessions, and the acquisition of power over others: societies filled with resentment, hatred, conflict, and destruction. Some social control is necessary, lest chaos result, but where freedom is desired the need is to minimize the intrusiveness and self-contradictory qualities of that control. Utopia requires freedom, but a freedom which is not based on inherently destructive competitiveness. Freedom displays its true character in the acts and relations of the individual life. Freedom for one requires equal freedoms for all.

In accordance with this overall approach to freedom, Wells sees political and social controls are part of the shift away from the need for any sort of state at all, and as such subject to change. While in effect, however, each set is of very great importance indeed. In fact, as we have seen, many controls never vanish at all, but become such a part of the social structure as to be internalized; "we are trained so subtly that we scarcely know we are trained," remarks Sarnac, a proposition which his listeners find utterly unexceptionable.[27] Training and social interaction amount to much the same thing; we learn both how to behave as individuals and how to exist as citizens within a social structure simultaneously. Missing this point has led to misconceptions of Wells's view of the freedom of the individual; he is wrongly taken as asserting that the utopian person is free altogether of socially determined beliefs, attitudes, and character traits. When Christopher

Caudwell, for example, claims that Wells, among others, supposes "that man is more free, more at liberty, the more he is free from the pressure of culture, consciousness, and social organisation,"[28] he is quite wrong. It is the *character* of these things which makes the individual more or less free, according to Wells, not simply their presence or absence. Caudwell was a Marxist, and like most such, disliked Wells intensely because of his denial of the necessity of a transformative working-class revolution, a revolution which requires deterministic laws of the very sort Wells is most at pains to reject. To Caudwell any proposed freedom from the putative class struggle is dubious, and he sees discussions thereof as ignoring underlying economic realities. In another attack on Wells, Caudwell claims that Wells "assumes that the relation between mind and environment is perfectly fluid, that the mind can make of the environment anything it pleases."[29] Clearly he is wrong. Wells regularly rejects claims of the sort, as, for example, in *The Science of Life*, where Wells explains why he is rejecting Jung's "very questionable distinction" of *anima* and *animus* along sexual lines: "The persona *imposed upon* the average woman is, by tradition, *social and economic conditions* and physiological necessities, different in its nature from that of the average man."[30] Wells sees the connections, but he sees no evidence that they are inescapable. He does not repudiate the influence of class, but he recognizes that it is only one among many, often conflicting, forces which help shape the individual.[31]

For Wells, the freedom of the individual expands as the utopian process develops. In the early stages, certain freedoms are considerably constrained and others considerably extended; in the later stages, all freedoms are virtually unrestricted, save by the social awareness of the individual concerned. This latter clause, though, covers a very strong depth of communal integration. Nor is it unrestricted; "there is no such thing as absolute freedom," Wells reminds us; "Limitless freedom, anarchy, would be a world of chaotic conduct, ruled only by impulse, a jungle life. All freedom in any society is conditional; it is a compromise;" it requires some form of law.[32]

The laws, for Wells, must in themselves be based on some clearly articulable purposes, and must vanish when those purposes no longer require them. He does not discuss law qua law much in his works, but it is safe to assume that all laws are to be considered provisional. Only a very few principles are to be considered foundational; Wells mentions at one point "the Five Principles of Liberty, without which civilization is impossible."[33] The principles are a distillation of his social concerns; they are comprised of privacy, free movement, "Unlimited Knowledge" (what we might call a right to education and information), honesty, and "Free Discussion and Criticism." In any case, the nature of necessary laws, even those stemming from the five principles, will vary according to the stages of the utopian process.

I have been concentrating on the earlier stages in the Wellsian utopian process, as they provide more detailed glimpses of his expectations relative to the present conditions of humanity than the later stages. Those later stages, though, must be acknowledged, as they demonstrate clearly the expansion of human freedom Wells sought. He was quite clear on the fact that governmental structures, or even politically powerful persons, which attempted to limit or stop the expansion of human freedom would have to go. Thus, for example, Rud Whitlow, the dictator in *The Holy Terror*, is killed by his doctor in order that what is good in the recreation of society over which he had presided will not be crushed by his megalomania; there being no obvious successor, a form of council emerges, the strong implication being that the conditions are such as to render the idea of a single leader otiose. A similar process, though more complex, leads to the dissolution of the ruling council in *The Shape of Things to Come*. The most dramatic example is found in *Men Like Gods*, where the social structure and the ruling structure are identical:

> Utopia has no parliament, no politics, no private wealth, no business competition, no police nor prisons, no lunatics, no defectives nor cripples, and it has none of these things because it has schools and teachers who are all that schools and teachers can be. Politics, trade and competition are the methods of adjustment of a crude society. Such methods of adjustment have been laid aside in Utopia for more than a thousand years. There is no rule nor government needed by adult Utopians because all the rule and government they need they have had in childhood and youth.
> Said Lion: "*Our education is our government.*"[34]

I have already examined the role of education; the exigencies of laying out a discussion may have suggested falsely that education is somehow an overlay on the proper functioning of society, or a fragmentary part thereof. It should now be clear that, in the Wellsian utopia, as in a well-written novel, each element is at once distinct from and inextricably part of the rest. Society and its educational structures eventually meld into one entity; governance becomes collective so that individuals may act freely, secure from preventable need or dominance.

Here we see two more answers, brief but decisive, to different components of the charge that the Wellsian system is inherently unfree, or perhaps even totalitarian. While it must be acknowledged that there are possibilities for abuse of the structures described, and risks in the process of establishing the basic conditions for the utopian process, it is clear that Wells has made a number of serious attempts to circumvent these. Nonetheless, the charge is inescapable. In order to attain any particular societal structure described in advance, some degree of control over those opposed, or even merely indifferent, to the system proposed is necessary. This is an unavoidable condition of all political change. To elect a particular party as the government in New York or North Carolina, say, would mean forcing a number of people with beliefs opposed to those of the party in question (even if the beliefs, as is increasingly the case, have more to do with the means to a given end than the end itself) out of power; it entails as well overcoming and rendering nugatory the votes of at least a portion of those who did not vote for the winning party's candidates. That this is done peacefully is irrelevant; that fact shows only that the people who live under the system have accepted it *de facto*, not even that they wouldn't exchange it for another could they do so without too much effort on their part. Such an electoral system is not a natural fact. It had to be envisioned, created, and put into place, invariably over the objections, often strident, of individuals advocating alternative systems.

Given that the political situation is as described, the best possibilities for avoiding abuses are ones which reject the necessity of force and which provide as much leeway as possible within themselves for self-correction and modification. This is more likely to be the case within a system considered as an infinite process than within a teleological one. Where the Truth about optimal human relations can be known once and for all, then those who know it have at least some justification for imposing a system which will attain those relations. If enough power is involved, whether their putative knowledge is genuine becomes irrelevant, as all that matters is their power to enforce, or their opponents' power to resist, the imposed system. Where this Truth cannot be known, where human relations are always a matter of experimentation, where only what has been shown not to work is excluded completely, there lies much less of a risk of dictatorship or stagnation.

Conversely, where the boundaries of the individual consciousness are recognized as innately and indefinitely flexible, there will be less temptation to demand a narrow and cramping specialization of 'careers' among individuals. Ironically, given Wells's emphasis upon the paramount importance of the individual, many writers have accused Wells of a desire for an undue specialization of individuals. As the Marxist A.L. Morton has put the charge, "Wells accepted Plato's concept of a specialized society, in which everyone does perfectly the one job for which he is fitted by nature and training, a society therefore of degree."³⁵ He has been misled by a careless reading of a passage in the satirical novel *The First Men in the Moon*. Nor is it only Marxists who do this. The same is true of the English philosopher Bernard Bosanquet, who comments, regarding the same novel, on the "limitation of the self to a single function" which the Selenites practice. Bosanquet is led by this "to suspect him [Wells] of a pessimistic view of progress, due to a failure in appreciating the relation of individual to universal for an intelligent being."³⁶ Bosanquet passes over the question on his way to another point; Morton considers it worth refuting in detail, and it is here that the extent of his (and Bosanquet's) misunderstanding becomes clear. Morton quotes, with silent emendations, a passage from the novel concerning the specialized breeding undergone by the Selenites; I give Wells's text:

> "In the moon," says Cavor, "every citizen knows his place. He is born to that place, and the elaborate discipline of training and education and surgery he undergoes fits him at last so completely to it that he has neither ideas nor organs for any purpose beyond it. 'Why should he?' Phi-oo would ask. If, for example, a Selenite is destined to be a mathematician, his teachers and trainers set out at once to that end. They check any incipient disposition to other pursuits, they encourage his mathematical bias with a perfect psychological skill. His brain grows, or at least the mathematical faculties of his brain grow, and the rest of him only so much as is necessary to sustain this essential part of him."³⁷

Morton claims of this description that it merely carries "to its logical extreme what is implicit in all Wells' thought, and it is a logic which leads us to the kind of world shown in Huxley's *Brave New World* or Joseph O'Neill's *Land Under England*."³⁸ He and Bosanquet, who is almost certainly also reacting to this passage and others closely linked to it, have missed Wells's satirical purpose. Only a few pages later Cavor, whose narration is being reported, remarks on seeing "a number of young Selenites confined in jars from which only the fore-limbs protruded, who were being compressed to become machine-minders of a special sort." Cavor, something of a caricature of the detached scientific man, reacts unfavorably: "It is quite unreasonable, I know, but such glimpses of the educational methods of these beings affect me disagreeably." He concludes, however, that "it is really in the end a far more humane proceeding than our earthly method of leaving children to grow into human beings, and then making machines of them."³⁹ In case the satirical point is missed, Cavor presently makes a second comment to the same effect; "To drug the worker one does not want and toss him aside is surely far better than to expel him from his factory to wander starving in the streets."⁴⁰

The point is not simply that certain authors have misread Wells. The point is that in order to write a satire, one must be satirizing some thing or person or situation. In understanding what the object of a given satire is, we can gain a glimpse of how the satirist thinks things ought not to be, if not necessarily what should take their place. Here it is clear that Wells is satirizing specialization of all sorts, whether it be cold scientific detachment from moral considerations or the forcing of independent human beings into mindless and degrading jobs. Wells's sympathy is clearly for the individual, not for the system he describes.

The emphasis on freedom has consequences for smaller social structures within society as a whole, as well as individual behaviors. Earlier I examined some foundational restrictions on the ways in which individuals gain power over other individuals; here I will examine some of the ways in which individuals express their own freedom from certain types of social structures. Describing aspects of the daily life in a Wellsian utopia is something of a problem, as any such descriptions hazard being taken as a claim about the conditions of life in *all* Wellsian utopias rather than just the one at hand, and therefore a claim about some essential quality in human life. What may be offered instead of a firm description will be a brief series of snapshots, preferably contradictory, of various points along the way, snapshots which will serve to limn the constantly changing structure and relations within the Wellsian utopian process. The fact that this is necessary, however, may be taken as one element in the process itself. Wells was quick to deny that his particular visions had more than evocative power; "It will not be like *my* dream, the world that is coming."[41] It will be, it must be if Wells is right, something vastly larger and finer and more complex. It will be a composite of all the greater dreams of humanity itself.

Freedom requires an ability to make use thereof. In utopia the first concern is that one be functioning at or near the peak of one's physical and mental ability at all times. "The general effect of a Utopian population is vigour. Everyone one meets seems to be not only in good health but in training; one rarely meets fat people, bald people, or bent or grey ... the whole effect of a crowd is livelier or more invigorating than on earth."[42] Insuring that everyone knows their task of the moment and does it properly is in Wells the responsibility of the individuals themselves; collectively they determine what is necessary for society to function, and collectively they assure its production. Everyone contributes to the production of necessities, after which they are guaranteed an annual income, or its equivalent, as a return for their work. "The total life product of a worker," Wells suggested, "the money earned during the working years, should be equivalent to all that worker's expenditure and all the expenditure upon that worker, including the overhead charges for directorate and government, from the cradle to the grave. If it is less, he [or presumably she] is a parasite; if it is more, he is being robbed and is carrying nonproductive social elements upon his shoulders that he ought not to carry."[43] As automation reduces the amount of actual human labor needed to produce the necessities of life, the amount of socially required labor, not large to begin with, diminishes tremendously. This idea has a long pedigree; in 1516, Thomas More thought six hours of shared work a day ample to provide all of the necessities; the Utopians, he wrote,

> don't wear people out, though, by keeping them hard at work from early morning till late at night, like cart-horses. That's just slavery — and yet that's what life is like for the working classes nearly everywhere else in the world. In Utopia they have a six-hour working day — three hours in the morning, them lunch — then a two-hour break — then three more hours in the afternoon, followed by supper.[44]

Nor is there "a shortage of essential goods," as someone from the outside might fear, which can be understood "if you reckon up how large a proportion of the population in other countries is totally unemployed."

> First you have practically all the women — that gives you nearly fifty per cent for a start. And in countries where the women *do* work, the men tend to lounge about instead. Then there are all the priests, and members of so-called religious orders — how much work do they do? Add all the rich, especially the landowners, popularly known as nobles and gentlemen [....] When you've counted them up, you'll be surprised how few people actually produce what the human race consumes.[45]

Wells does not provide the same level of supportive detail, but the point remains of extreme importance; the effect of a guaranteed annual income would be a tremendous freeing of individuals from external controls; where we are not directly dependent upon proceeds drawn from the profit of others for our necessities, whether directly or indirectly, we have both much more time and much more mental energy to call our own. Again the touchstone is individual freedom, as Wells seeks to lessen the degree of control impersonal social forces have over human beings.[46]

With the impact of impersonal forces removed or lessened, personal choices become much freer; we are more and more able to determine for ourselves who and what we wish to become. The result, as Wells saw it, would be a great awakening of interest in each other as genuinely productive beings, ones free to come and go, think and create, as they please. "When we have had enough of our own work for a time we fly off— or walk around the corner— to see what other people are doing."[47] The traveler is largely free of restrictions: no national boundaries and customs agents hinder her or his passage from place to place. She or he takes little save things of purely personal interest (e.g. "something to read or a specimen ... to show"). "Whatever else he is likely to want on his way he will find on his way. He needs no other possessions because his possessions are everywhere."[48] The traveler is genuinely a traveler, not a tourist desperately seeking diversion to dress up what is experienced as an otherwise mediocre existence.

The improvement of education and the expansion of freedom from various external forces will release a great wave of creativity. "It seems inevitable," Wells wrote,

> that as man conquers the three major problems that at present confront him, as he escapes from the suicidal obsession of warfare, the plain danger of overpopulation and the perplexities of economic strangulation, his released energy, his ever increasing free energy, will find its satisfactions very largely in immense artistic undertakings. No doubt it will also flow into the service of science, but though science illuminates, its main product is power— and it is art alone which can find uses for power.

Wells offers a variety of hints as to the forms he expects, but wisely refrains from prescribing the details of this. He speculates on the efflorescence of architecture[49] and music, "the primary arts," and a return to oral traditions in poetry and literature, then declines to go further; "But it is not for us to attempt a prophecy of the coming forms of art. It is absurd to suppose that all we now call art, the masterpieces, the supreme attainments, is anything more than an intimation of what the surplus energy of mankind may presently achieve."[50] Wells's stance is clear: it is all but self-evident that our present society has prevented many people from expressing themselves aesthetically at all, and prevented many others from developing anything which could remotely be called a strong aesthetic appreciation of even such artistic opportunities as might be available to them. Nor is Wells's position without broader plausibility on historical grounds. As he noted, "Unless we are to suppose that spontaneous outbreaks of super-men have occurred in the past, it is reasonable to conclude that the Athens of Pericles, the Florence of the Medici, Elizabethan England, the great deeds of Asoka, the Tang and Ming periods in art, are but samples of what a whole world of sustained security would yield continuously and cumulatively."[51]

Some further extrapolations can be made. In a Wellsian world, tragedy, at least as presently understood, will likely no longer be written, for example, and indeed might eventually come to be scarcely comprehensible. As the novelist Eva Figes pointed out,

> Tragedy depends, not on crime and punishment, but on a justification of the sum total of human suffering through some form of inner necessity, and this necessity in turn implies some sort of order that runs through all things, cosmic laws of cause and effect that determine human destiny and which man must attempt to understand in order to avoid disaster. It is by breaking such cosmic laws, not merely human ones, that man meets a tragic fate ... there is a strong suggestion that sticking to one's own humble station in life, knowing one's place, and conformity may protect one from tragedy.[52]

For Wells, no station within the free society of the future is humble, or rather all are equally so; one's place is, or ought to be, open to one to define; and conformity, in a world where all are self-consciously free, has little meaning. Tragedy based on ideas now traditional will eventually cease to have either relevance or resonance, and thus will vanish. Where original sin (or whatever one wishes to call it) is repudiated, eventually so too is tragedy. Comedy, too, will change: "We cannot understand, for instance, the joy our ancestors found in the little blunders and misconceptions of ill-educated people. But then they also laughed at the cripples who still abounded in the world."[53]

Similarly, fiction as a whole will take on new characteristics, and diminish in importance as a commercial publishing phenomenon. Wells was even "disposed to question whether the Novel will have any great importance in the intellectual life of the future," because he expected that it would quite likely "be replaced by more searching and outspoken biography and autobiography."[54] Bestsellers, as we think of them, will cease altogether. Stories will still be told, and will still circulate widely, but their focus and function will be quite different than the focus and function of the average novel written today. Nor does this contradict his previous emphasis on the role of the novel, which refers to an earlier stage in the utopian process. Note that Wells does not reject the continued importance of narrative structures, but merely questions the continued significance of one particular form thereof. His emphasis on the new importance of autobiography is again echoed by Sartre, who speculated that "what spoils relations among people is that each keeps something hidden from the other, holds something secret...." He imagined the day "when two men [sic] will no longer have secrets from each other, because no one will have any more secrets from anyone, because subjective life, as well as objective life, will be completely offered up, given." For the present such honesty can be attained most consistently within the narrative conventions and possibilities of the novel, of writing in general. "But I think that later," he said, "people will talk about themselves more and more, and it will bring about a great change ... a real revolution."⁵⁵ Clearly autobiography, if it were truly honest in a way seldom achieved, would be a superb means of conveying alternative ways of being in the world. Equally clearly, as long as autobiography is limited largely to the self-justifications of the rich and powerful such demonstrations have little meaning or value to the majority of the world's population.

Whatever the means of conveying ideas regarding life and the development of personality, Wells considered it vital that they be freely available to all, both as regards production and distribution.

> Each utopian citizen could get what he had to say printed and distributed to the news rooms. There it was read or neglected as the visitors chanced to approve of it or not. Often if they liked what they read they would carry off a copy with them.... The librarians noted what books and papers were read and taken away, and these they replaced with fresh copies. The piles that went unread were presently reduced to one or two copies and the rest went back to the pulping mills.⁵⁶

There is an obvious prefiguration of, and connection to, the possibilities inherent in the internet here, though the internet is not yet accessible to all. Indeed, proposals to make internet access freely available are, for obvious reasons, opposed by authoritarians of all stripes, for the more widely available the internet becomes the greater become also the possibilities of spreading information, or suggesting actions, subversive of the status quo. Wells would probably have relished the potential of the internet, looking forward to the day when everyone had easy access to a free and rapid link, and when the plethora of trivial chat groups had given way to an intelligent use of the technology.

One reason that the stories from the past will come to have little more than antiquarian interest is that the structure of human relations will have changed to a large degree. The jealousies and tensions which motivate so much of current literature will have vanished. One of the central foci of human relations, the nuclear family, will no longer be the heart of growth, education, and ambition. "The family can remain only as a biological fact," Wells asserted, repudiating his own earlier neutrality on the subject;

> Its economic and educational autonomy are inevitably doomed. The modern state is bound to be the ultimate guardian of all children and it must assist, replace, or subordinate the parent as supporter, guardian and

educator; it must release all human beings from the obligation of mutual proprietorship, and it must refuse absolutely to recognize or enforce any kind of sexual ownership.[57]

The family is the initial source of a variety of later conflicts, because the family establishes, early on, a variety of possessive behavioral structures. The history of vendettas, feuds, dynastic quarrels (both of the powerful and the humble), jealousies again, and endless maladjustments is directly related to the hierarchical structure of the family. Loyalties are demanded that have no basis in anything but a biological connection, and inevitably those loyalties are carried over into politics. The traditional authoritarian structure of the family recurs within the tribe, and new loyalties are formed; likewise into the era of nation-states.

In this Wells and Plato are in general agreement; indeed, it is quite possible that one of the roots of Wells's position is found in *Republic*. There Plato, considering that nothing is "worse for a state than to be split and fragmented," or "better than cohesion and unity,"[58] seeks to give that unity a firm base by encouraging the citizenry to think of themselves as members of one individual body. This can be attained by limiting the attitudes which provoke divisiveness, such as the desire for private property and sexual jealousy. Accordingly, "our men and women Guardians should be forbidden by law to live together in separate households, and all the women should be common to all the men; similarly, children should be held in common, and no parent should know its child, or child its parent."[59] Since the guardians are at one and the same time fellow-citizens and rulers, it is necessary that their attitude be even more communal, if possible, than that of the other citizens, lest tyranny on the one hand result, or resentment on the other. "Our citizens, then," says Socrates, "are devoted to a common interest, which they call *my own*; and in consequence entirely share each other's feelings of joy and sorrow."[60] These shared feelings stem in part from the fact that there are no families (at least at the guardian level); "There won't in fact be any of the quarrels which are caused by having money or children or family."[61]

This, in turn, stems from the fact that the sexual life of the guardians, which for Plato overlaps to a high degree with family life, is likewise under the supervision of the state. Sexuality in *Republic* is, therefore, like much else, strictly regulated; although the result of the actual regulations might appear promiscuous to some, it is not. The purpose is eugenic; "if we're to have a real pedigree herd [of citizens, we must] mate the best of our men with the best of our women as often as possible, and the inferior men with the inferior women as seldom as possible."[62] As Glaucon points out, "Sex is perhaps more effective than mathematics when it comes to persuading or driving the common man to do anything;"[63] Socrates plans to use this to keep the guardians both personally happy and happy to submit to the range of rituals intended to give mating a formal and state-sanctioned seriousness. These restrictions apply during the prime breeding years; after that, their duty done, the citizens can be left "free to mate as they please."[64]

Wells, as we might by now expect, prefers to emphasize the freedoms of love. "In Utopia there are no bonds."[65] Because the utopian framework is one of freedom, its citizens recognize no necessity to maintain formal relations of any sort. "In Utopia there was no compulsion for men and women to go about in indissoluble pairs. For most Utopians that would be inconvenient. Very often men and women, whose work brought them closely together, were lovers and kept very much together.... But they were not obliged to do that."[66] For Wells, relationships maintained through state authority are just as false as ones created by state authority; in both cases they are unnatural.

This is the basis for Wells's writing on sexual freedom; one of the chief problems he recognized in contemporary life was sexual jealousy and possessiveness. Sarnac, in *The Dream*, comparing his life in the far future to ours, comments that "nowadays sex is so simple.... Love is the link and flower of our choicest friendships."[67] Judging from the context, Wells probably is referring to sexual love here, although this is not entirely certain; he is not always as clear in his use of the word love as might be asked, but in general he took sex to be merely one expression among many, an expression lent at times a certain urgency by biological forces, of the deeper feeling that is love. Love, in its proper sense, is a vital component within the utopian world and its inhabitants; as William Burroughs Steele realized,

> Love is personal always; inalterably preferential; it is an intensification of personality in ourselves and in our Lovers. It is the qualification, the corrective, of religious universalism. By religion we become Man, by love we remain individual, and as our religion rises and widens to the world community and the starry mind, so the subtlety of our appreciation of the individual difference in ourselves and others must intensify to keep pace with it.[68]

Here is the final and decisive repudiation of Hayekian, or any other traditional free-market economics, which allows no place for love and concern for the individual as a unique person. Yet here also is the reason why there can be no state or social controls on the mutual expression of love, save only where that expression threatens the freedoms of others. Love is the powerful counterbalance to the necessary submersion of the individual in the collective political environment, as art is to the social. Love serves to focus the unique elements within the personality, to heighten them, to bring them to the fore.

Yet by its very nature, love is interpersonal; one cannot love in isolation. Once the taboos which now encircle love are removed, and once education has made possible individuals less crippled by jealousy, possessiveness, and the hatreds which stem therefrom, the individual expressions of that love will take on a variety of forms now scarcely imaginable, among which sex will take its proper place as but one among many.

In this we see, I think, a distinct superiority of the Wellsian view to the Platonic world-view, and by extension the superiority of evolutionary views to the teleological world-views which have been derived, however silently, from Plato. For Plato, at least in *Republic* (and arguably even in *Symposium*), love is but a means to an end, whether it be procreation or sexual pleasure or as the first step up the ladder to a love of true beauty. As a result, the expressions of love fall under the purview of those who know best the ends desired: the philosopher-kings; those expressions become tools to be used, and the lovers become objects for manipulation by the state. Plato is led to equate love with, on the one hand, sexual desire, and on the other with a pure appreciation of the most abstract qualities: good, beauty, justice. Neither of these is satisfactory; the one is too mechanistic, too animalistic, too simple, while the other rests on the acceptance of a metaphysical scheme which has not, to say the least, had its truth demonstrated convincingly. Nor is it clear that the vision experienced by the philosophers is available to every other person, and those individuals are thus left having to surrender their own love at the behest of people who, by definition, they cannot understand in the service of goals they likewise can comprehend only dimly, and may not share.

On the Wellsian account, by contrast, love is made a central element in a burgeoning system of human freedoms. Love guarantees that we remain, even as we change, still recognizably human — not in some biological sense, for that may, and indeed must, change in the millennia ahead, but in the emotional sense which underlies the utopian urge to begin with, the concern for the improvement of human life and opportunity. Instead of being a means to the utopian end, love, together with art, is the meaning of the utopian process. Where there is no end, no goal, no telos save the increase of human freedom and creativity, then there is no temptation to use these very things merely as tools. True love truly expressed is a foundation, not a superstructure; its necessity cannot be argued for but can only be shown, within a larger context which strengthens it and gives it meaning. This context can be provided, I think, by the Wellsian system.

But love goes further, and in ways of profound significance for the very possibility of inaugurating and sustaining the progressive self-transcendence without which utopia is impossible. Love confronts death, and it is love, if it is anything at all, which can defeat death, at least in its present relation to human being. Here, then, I turn to the question which underlies everything which has preceded: how can the utopian ideal in its wholeness within the Darwinian natural universe be justified? This, though, requires a separate chapter.

5

The Problem of Death

Recognition that overcoming in some manner the fear of personal death is a necessity for utopian existence appears with the utopian idea itself. As part of the training for the guardians in the just city, Plato requires strict controls on the descriptions of the afterlife. If the guardians are to be brave, they need to feel that death holds no terrors; "Will anyone who in his heart fears death ever be brave?" Socrates asks, and it is clear the expected answer is no.[1] The same, at a deeper level, holds true for the philosophers, who "won't think death anything to be afraid of," because "mean and cowardly natures can't really have anything to do with philosophy."[2] Where the goal of life is pure knowledge, then anything, including bodily existence, which interferes with attaining that goal is something the mind must learn to set aside. Plato does not discuss death to any further great extent in *Republic*. Rather, it is in the *Phaedo* where the metaphysical underpinnings of Plato's position are made clearest. In the latter dialogue, Socrates admits that

> If I did not expect to enter the company, first, of other wise and good gods, and secondly of men now dead who are better than those who are in this world now, it is true that I should be wrong in not grieving at death.... I have a firm hope that there is something in store for those who have died, and, as we have been told for many years, something much better for the good than for the wicked.[3]

He goes on to say, in one of the more famous formulations from the Platonic canon, that "those who really apply themselves in the right way to philosophy are directly and of their own accord preparing themselves for dying and death."[4]

The importance of this to the attitude of the ordinary appetitive citizen of the just city is a matter of debate. The exact nature of the soul remains unclear,[5] and one might argue that the different classes of citizens have different types of souls. In such a case, the implications for the less philosophical souls, and their bodily counterparts, will be different than would be the case should the content and character of every person's soul be essentially similar. Nonetheless, it may be said that, at least at the level of the philosophers, the purpose of the individual's life lies beyond life itself.

Something similar, although with a different justification, is found in More's *Utopia*. Here human happiness consists in pleasure (but only of the higher sort), a claim justified by appeal to religious grounds:

> The first principle is that every soul is immortal, and was created by a kind God, Who meant it to be happy. The second is that we shall be rewarded or punished in the next world for our good or bad behaviour in this one.... For what's the sense of struggling to be virtuous, denying yourself the pleasant things of life, and deliberately making yourself uncomfortable, if there's nothing to gain by it? And what *can* you hope to gain by it, if you receive no compensation after death for a thoroughly unpleasant, that is, a thoroughly miserable life?[6]

That is again to say that the justification for *this* life lies in something beyond it, something for which there is little evidence but pious hope, a pious hope unavailable to the naturalistic evolutionary utopian.

Recognition of this fact has led many philosophers to make a focus on death a central component of their views regarding the proper attitude toward life. Miguel de Unamuno's *Tragic Sense of Life* is probably the most famous of these approaches. "This thought that I must die and the enigma of what will come after death is the very palpitation of my consciousness," he writes,[7] rejecting attempts to dismiss the matter as being of no concern. He rejects likewise "arguments demonstrating the absurdity of the belief in the immortality of the soul"; these are not refuted, but rather excoriated for their vacuity in the face of what he perceives as a profound human need; "these arguments fail to make any impression upon me, for they are reasons and nothing more than reasons, and it is not with reasons that the heart is appeased." He adds, "I do not want to die — no; I neither want to die nor do I even want to want to die; I want to live for ever and ever and ever."[8]

Similarly, Martin Heidegger emphasizes the role of our anticipation of death in making us who we are; "death reveals itself as that *possibility which is one's ownmost, which is non-relational, and which is not to be outstripped.*"[9] An authentic response to our impending death is at once an acknowledgement of its unavoidability and a recognition that it is at death that we are defined, summed up, and fixed, as was never possible in life. In envisioning this we envision our Being — who we really are. "Anticipation utterly individualizes Dasein, and allows it, in this individualization of itself, to become the totality of its potentiality-for-Being."[10] It is death which brings the self most sharply into focus, as it is in anticipating that which we may never be that we truly discover what we are and what we desire (as opposed to what we un-self-questioningly accept as a superficial account of our character and potentialities. Yet this definition is created, indeed is demanded, by virtue of the fact that the possibility of death, properly understood, is "the possibility of the impossibility of any existence at all."[11] Heidegger insists that we confront the fact that all personal possibility will cease, and that we live accordingly, but he offers nothing beyond anxiety as a response. Utopianism demands more; there is in Heidegger, and in Unamuno, little which carries us beyond the present of the self as conventionally defined and experienced, nothing to give fire and force to a utopian vision.

This should come as no surprise; views of death such as these are too personal, too grounded in a conception of a centralized unified ego to encourage transcending such an ego. Yet it is such a transcendence which will be necessary if an evolutionary utopian project is to become the dominant force in human social and political structures. Nonetheless, there are elements here which, properly modified, suggest already one possible answer to the conundrum of personal death.

Wells's attitude toward personal death is implicit in all that has been examined in the preceding chapters. It begins with the recognition of the ultimate hegemony of natural processes. Death is the inescapable conclusion of human life, and with death the individual ceases once and for all. There are no safety hatches, no escape clauses, and no extensions. "I do not believe I have any personal immortality," wrote Wells, adding that "That distresses me not at all. Immortality would distress and perplex me.... I cannot respect, I cannot believe in a God who is always going about with me."[12] Immortality in the conventional sense, as an infinite continuation of a particular ego, would render human existence on the earth a mockery; nothing which could be done here would have any possibility of value under the light of eternal life; the desire for such a thing is really a devaluation of everything which is most human, and most important. Actions have meaning within a particular context; in an eternal life there would eventually be no context at all. Wells, like Plato, finds the fear of death to be emotionally and personally debilitating; his utopias are filled with suggestions that the people of the utopian future no longer regard their individual deaths as anything to be greatly feared or regretted. In *Men Like Gods*, for example, Mr. Barnstaple, a representative of our world, realizes his connection with utopian thought in at least one fashion: his, and their, attitudes toward death. Apropos of the death by drowning of two children and their father, Barnstaple reflects on the irremediable situation: "To him as to Utopia it seemed rather an occasion for gladness than sorrow that her man and her children had met death fearlessly. They were dead; a brave stark death; the waters still glittered and the sun still shone." *The Dream* makes the point even more explicitly: "Sudden death there is still in the world [of a utopian future], a bright adventure — that lightning yesterday might have killed all or any of us, but such death is a rare thing and a clean thing.... And one death does not devastate a dozen or more lives as deaths often did in the old days."[13] Unlike Plato, though, Wells finds a fixation on personal immortality to be equally debilitating. Worrying about what comes after death is at best unproductive and at worst destructive of the individual's mental life. Wells sees the best way to overcome the fear of personal death as lying in a direct confrontation with, and acknowledgement of, its inevitability.

For Wells, death is a random event in a random world. It comes, and there is nothing to be done about the fact (that it can be postponed by advances in medicine is irrelevant; on the scale of evolution it makes no difference whether we live seventy or seventy times seventy years). Death challenges all of our meanings, undercuts all of our purposes. Throughout his novels and other writings Wells emphasizes this juxtaposition. Many of his characters are shown formulating plans, developing hopes, entering into projects, only to meet with sudden deaths, abrupt and meaningless. William Burroughs Steele in *The Anatomy of Frustration* accidentally poisons himself; William Clissold dies in an automobile accident (although, back broken, he "lived, pointlessly and irrationally, for some time" after the accident)[14]; William Porphyry Benham in *The Research Magnificent* is shot in the course of a civil disturbance; Karenin in *The World Set Free* dies from an unexpected detached blood clot after a "successful" operation; the list could be extended considerably. Even the garrulously cheerful Uncle in Wells's first collection of humorous topical essay-stories met an "abrupt extinction [when] the cares of the world suddenly sprang upon and choked him."[15] Time and again, Wells confronts his characters, and his readers, with the reminders that the world moves in a manner completely indifferent to, and scarcely connected with, human aspirations. The message of *The Time Machine*— that no life escapes extinction — is brought down to the individual level, so as to make the difficulty of the utopian life manifest.

Another aspect of what has already been discussed is relevant here as well, though; with it the nature and significance of personal death take on an entirely new coloration. It will be recalled that in the Wellsian conception, the personality is "a collection of mutually replaceable individual systems held together in a common habitation. One ascends; another fades before it."[16] The ego is not something fixed and definite, but rather "a serviceable synthetic illusion of continuity that holds the individual behavior together."[17] This already open-ended definition turns out to be expandable to an even greater degree than may at first appear. Personality, in its self-conceptualization, relies upon memory. Even in the most focused of personalities, however, there is much that is gone without hope of recollection, much which is simultaneously nothing, as if it never existed, and something which is present as a no longer conscious influence, a building block of individual being long buried under later accretions. In this sense, then, there is much in a given persona which is already dead: that is, gone beyond recall or resurrection. There may be, so to speak, fossils within various aspects of a given set of behaviour systems which can be excavated, but these remain fossils; were they living components of the personality, they would not need excavation.

These considerations extend further. If an individual personality is but a fragment, even if a large one, of a greater set of experiences, attitudes, memories now lost, goals now forgotten, and states of being now transcended, it must be argued that any such personality contains within its causal background (that is, within the set of reasons why it is *this* way and not some other way) much which is now external to it, much which would appear alien, or even hostile, to its present state. Who I am at any given moment is contingent on my having been things which I no longer know or believe, some of which I would in my present state of being modify substantially or even reject wholly. In addition, many of those things are, or were, themselves primarily external to me: the books I read, the music I hear, the conversations I have. All these, indisputably in some measure a part of who I am at any given moment, are things which, at least initially, I did not wholly choose to create and shape. I am who I am, then, to a degree because I am who I was not, and because of causes partly or wholly beyond the control of who I was then.

The next step is suggested by the foregoing. In devising plans for the future, my present state of being often takes into account a quite different state of being which I still accept as somehow "mine." Similarly, on the evidence of photographs, say, or testimony from other persons I may accept, and even enjoy and cultivate, another aspect of a being, no longer extant in itself, with which I have no direct contact in memory, a being which is therefore, to all intents and purposes, not "me."[18] That this is so can be realized by imagining the quite plausible circumstance that the story I have accepted as applying to my earlier self turns out to be not about that person at all. It is quite possible that any number of such stories, self-told or told by others, could upon consideration turn out to be impossible to confirm or deny with certainty. This, though, does not suggest that it is in the least bit impossible for them to form an important part of "who I am" at some later point. What is happening is clear: the memory based narrative structure which gives focus to my present self-conception is expanding imaginatively to take into itself other beings only vaguely linked thereto. It is choosing (and thus the I of the moment may say that I am choosing) to become something fuller and more complexly imbricated within the world which surrounds, and will surround, it. Yet since that world as a coherent meaningful whole is at least in part created by the narrative structure I adopt, I am choosing to recreate the world as I recreate myself.

This re-creation in turn allows me to redefine myself so as to include things physically and mentally external to what appears as the direct stream of relation; that is, I can extend my "self" not only backward and forward in conceptual time, but outward in conceptual space — "conceptual" because it is clear that I cannot actually extend myself backward temporally as a physical object in relation to the external world; I can only live in an eternal "now" in the strict physical sense. But this merely serves to demonstrate the vital importance of the conceptual self in every project of any importance; very few people live in an eternal "now" in the mental sense.[19] I can, as in practice many do with friends and lovers and even strangers, include aspects of others contemporary with me within my concept of my "self," and then again aspects of others before or after me in such a conception. I connect with others in a way which, both intentionally and unintentionally, reshapes who I am. As Wells expressed it, "The way creatures *contact* one another can change." He explains in a passage rife with extensive implications:

> How does a dog contact its fellows? Touch, not very accurate achromatic sight, rich abundant smell, sex as a transient storm; what else is there that reaches from dog to dog? Our contacts are fuller than that. And they are becoming subtler and more abundant. Ages ago man began to elaborate life by using definite words. Also he began to clothe and elaborate love. He became more companionable. By words especially. Lovers talk and weave a thousand fancies. Words become the mechanism of a vast abundance of suggestion and enrichment. We smell each other's minds in conversation. And man's eyes also become more exact. We see with a new precision and discover beauty. We harmonize.... We love the mind that speaks to us in music, we find beauty in pictures, we respond to the wisdom or to the caress in a poem. We love the woman Leonardo loved and writers who were bodily dead centuries ago live on to stir us. Our contacts stretch out more and more beyond the here and now.[20]

If it is true that someone who we are no longer, and can no longer remember being, can nonetheless come to be again important to who we are, if it is true that someone we are not yet, and who therefore does not exist and may in fact never come to exist, can influence the actions we take, and if it is true that each of these beings can come to be included in our self-conception, then it must be possible for beings quite external to us to become important thus as well.

But there is no necessary limitation on the scope of this process; while we have self-consciousness at all we can strive toward expanding that self-consciousness so as to include ever more. As a result, the particular focal point grows less important; such a process, following the lead of biological understandings, "consists essentially in diminishing the importance of the individual and developing the realisation of the species, as if it were a kind of super-individual, maintaining itself against the outer universe by the birth and death of its constituent individuals."[21] If we can deem someone who we are not (whether because that person no longer exists or because that person does not yet exist is irrelevant) as worthy of inclusion in our self-conception, then we can deem, at the very least, aspects of others, even unto the whole of the human species, as worthy of inclusion in our conception of self. Wells in fact goes still further along the line I am pursuing here, in that he suggests the possibility of a "Mind of the Race" (the human species),

> something more extensive than individual wills and individual processes of reasoning in mankind, a body of thought, a trend of ideas and purposes, a thing made up of the synthesis of all the individual instances, something more than their algebraic sum, losing the old as they fall out, taking up the young, a common Mind expressing the species —[22]

How seriously Wells himself took this is unclear. I have been treating it as a metaphor for the growing acceptance of the world state and the growing network of intersubjective connections, but others, such as the Jesuit palaeontologist, priest, and philosopher Pierre Teilhard de Chardin, took it, under a theistic guise, very seriously indeed. See, for example, his comments on "that very good and very bad book, Wells's *God, the Invisible King*." Teilhard found the book quite compelling; "in spite of the 'impieties' it's littered with, I found a strange kinship with my own aspirations." He makes a final comment, an even stronger endorsement of Wells's soon-to-be-self-repudiated achievement: "you couldn't, I think, imagine a more touching call towards some divine *immediacy*."[23] Teilhard's later cosmological system is in fact hyper–Wellsian, save in its attachment to a specifically Christian divinity.

What is the "I"? It can be only the sum of influences and intentions, known and unknown, present at any given moment within a single apparent self-consciousness. Yet both the influences and intentions can encompass persons, things, and situations quite beyond that self-consciousness. There is thus no essential reason to limit the interest of the "I" as now constituted to just those aspects of it which are linked consciously to its own self-awareness at any given moment. There is likewise no reason to restrict one's idea of death to the cessation of the particular consciousness of a given moment or series of moments; if one's self-conception has expanded to include aspects of the process of human development not presently available to one's consciousness, then the survival of the process is, in a very real sense, the survival of an aspect of one's self, even if it happens to be an aspect not self-conscious. The more we limit ourselves, the more we have to lose; the more we include, the more there is to survive the loss of any single aspect of our self-definition. The attempt to limit a self to its immediate awareness is counterproductive and stultifying. "Everyday affairs and whatever is made an everyday affair, are transactions of the ostensible self, the being of habits interests, usage. Temper, vanity, hasty reaction to imitation, personal feeling, are their substance," Wells points out. He expands the charge to indicate the sort of self-transcendence demanded by our very existence.

> No man can abolish his immediate self and specialize in the depths; if he attempt that, he simply turns himself into something a little less than the common man. He may have an immense hinterland, but that does not absolve him from a frontage. That is the essential error of the specialist philosopher, the specialist teacher, the specialist publicist. They repudiate frontage; claim to be pure hinterland.... A human being who is a philosopher in the first place, a teacher in the first place, or a statesman in the first place, is thereby and inevitably, though he bring God-like gifts to the pretence — a quack.[24]

What we are at any given moment in our self-awareness can never be taken as the whole, as there is always more than that of which we are aware. In romantic love or, especially, friendship love our self-conception enlarges to include the needs, desires, and self-conception of the other (and theirs bends to include ours); in social self-transcendence we apply the same attitude to other states of being outside our conventional self. It is not the same as love, but neither is it wholly dissimilar.

This is not an unprecedented way of viewing these matters. In fact, something similar to what I am describing here can be found in the philosopher Anselm Feuerbach. In his *Thoughts on Death and Immortality*, he describes life in terms surprisingly relevant here; the life of each person, he admonishes his readers,

> is the uninterrupted process of canceling the boundary between you and others and therefore canceling your personal being and with it your personhood. In death, the result of this process, those boundaries for the cancellation of which you have worked in and by Spirit throughout your entire life completely disappear. The last word you speak is death, in which you totally express yourself and impart yourself to others.[25]

Wells would not accept the metaphysical underpinnings of Feuerbach's claim, but the claim itself connects solidly with his overall position. For both authors, the process is grounded in love; we transcend our self-identity in loving;

> In loving, I love myself in another, I locate myself, my essence, not in myself, but in the object that I love. I bind my being to the being of another; I exist only in, with, and for another. If I am not in love, I exist only for myself. But when I am in love, I posit myself for another; I no longer possess my own being, my being-for-self; the being of the other is my being.[26]

The chief distinction is that for Feuerbach love is evidently an attachment, although not necessarily purely sexual or romantic, to one other person, whereas for Wells love can come to be attached to an indeterminate number of other beings, and through them to the idea of humanity as a whole. Yet it is not divorced entirely from the sexual, which is a biological base whence stem a variety of human urges and feelings. As Wells draws the portrait, the "Lover-Shadow" emerges as something which, although grounded therein, expands upon both the sexual and the social; "in every human mind, possibly from an extremely early age," Wells writes,

> there exists a continually growing and continually more subtle complex of expectation and hope; an aggregation of lovely and exciting thoughts; conceptions of encounter and reaction picked up from observation, descriptions, drama; reveries of sensuous delights and ecstasies; reveries of understanding and reciprocity; which I will call the Lover-Shadow. I think it is primarily sexual and then social — I mean sexual in origin, because I do not see how a living creature could ever be anything but self-centred except through the development of sexual, family and group mental systems. I think it is almost as essential in our lives as our self consciousness. It is *other* consciousness.[27]

Love requires an external object, yet no particular object corresponds with all the needs and desires in the multifold individual consciousness. The person thus has the opportunity to move beyond pure self-love and its all too frequent concomitant, love of those who, or that which, merely echoes and reinforces the dominant aspects of the person concerned. Such love requires an effort (we do not "fall in love" with the idea of humanity), but the effort is ours to make. Again, the model is the novelist, who must feel some empathy with her or his characters in order to make them live for the reader; the greater the compassion, the more profoundly the character lives, despite never having truly lived at all, in a physical sense.

As always, though, there is no compulsion available here. Just as we cannot be forced to love, we cannot be forced to transcend our isolated individual existence. What is presented to us, then, is, as always in Wells, a choice. "After all," he writes,

> the present writer has no compelling argument to convince the reader that he should not be cruel or mean or cowardly. Such things are also in his own make-up in a large measure, but none the less he hates and fights against them with all his strength. He would rather our species ended its story in dignity, kindliness and generosity, and not like drunken cowards in a daze or poisoned rats in a sack. But this is a matter of individual predilection for everyone to decide for himself.[28]

Wells admits, as he has admitted, and even insisted, all along, the fact that no argument can persuade those whose fundamental choices are radically different to make those choices afresh. No argument can make someone love another, or even to deem them as worthy of being loved, in the absence of a prior commitment to a self-conception as a person who loves. Arguments are persuasive to the degree that they appeal to principles already shared by the proponent and opponent of that over which the argument is taking place; where fundamental principles are not shared, no argument can result in their being shared, as it is to those principles that the argument appeals for its force in the first place. Some other means of persuasion is required, some other avenue toward mutual understanding and compassion. Specifically, where the subject of concern is the future of human society, and where the medium of discussion is utopian speculation, what is needed is an act of imagination, indeed of love, on the part of the reader, a choice to enter into the mind and heart of the other. Once this choice is made (and it is the primary aim of the whole of the Wellsian canon to invoke and to assist in the process of becoming the sort of person to whom such a choice comes, if not easily, at least more easily than is so often now the case), it becomes a viable hope, but always never more than a hope, not a necessity, that the recognition will lead, through its will to establish a secure base for its own fulfillment, to a recognition of communality. That is, our personal meanings require social supports to truly be meaningful at all; our existence as human beings requires the existence of humanity. To the degree that humanity is no more than an atomistic collection of individuals, we among those individuals will find self-transcendence difficult, and true coherence of personality an impossibility.

As we have seen again and again, the importance of imagination, of the act of mental creation, in the Wellsian vision cannot be overstated. Wells inverts Plato; it is the poets (novelists) who can envision reality most truly, because it is they who recognize most clearly that, where human beings are concerned, reality is change. "Will there be any *finality* in your success?" asks "that human blight, Mr. Chamble Pewter," in Wells's last novel. "None whatever, is the answer. Why should there be?"²⁹ To envision the end, the final point — there truly is the envisioning of death, once and for all. Humanity makes, or at least has the capacity to make, its own telos from its own situation, and the situation of humanity is forever changing.

This provides the basis for an answer to another challenge to Wells which I have deliberately left unaddressed until now: if there is no point at which it may be said that utopia has been truly reached, why aren't we in a utopia now? The response is that the question itself, the demand for a final answer, makes sense only from within a given perspective, that it assumes the truth of that perspective, that it thus needs to be expanded. What, Wells would ask, counts as a utopia for you, the questioner? If you can give an answer, and if your answer coincides with society as it now exists in all its particulars, then we *are* in utopia now — for you. From that perspective, from the limited points of view of many in the past, we have reached utopia because all of your, and their, desires have been addressed, all of your, and their, wants satisfied. This proves only the lack of imagination, and of compassion, endemic to so many individuals over the course of human history, individuals for whom the boundaries of their personal experience marked the limits of human knowledge and hope. In short, they could not see beyond their own being to the external world that is always becoming. To be satisfied with the world as it is, as it is at any point, is to be satisfied with the sorrows, the losses, the hungers and the dissatisfactions of the whole of humanity at that point and ever after. Only when the imaginative leap, the leap of human sympathy (mutual charity), into the unimaginable future is taken, can the individual understand that no satisfaction is possible until all are satisfied, and that the very conditions which allow us to strive for satisfaction as individuals are the conditions which prevent us from ever reaching that satisfaction. Satisfaction can only come about under conditions of freedom, and the boundaries of freedom are infinite.

Except for another death, this time of the species and of its descendants, of the world and of its universe. Again we face, but now at the level not of the individual but of the collective energies of all possible thought and effort, "the undiscovered country from whose bourn no traveller returns." It may be possible to transcend the idea of personal death by subsuming the universal, or at any rate elements thereof, in the individual — but is there not, the question echoes, a terminus to the process, a point beyond which there can be no passage?

It remains a fact of human existence that individuals die, that species die, that worlds die. Many more persons have died than are now alive; many more species have become extinct than remain. It is an as yet unrefuted probability of a very high order that all species and the earth upon which they play out their existences, that the solar system and the galaxy in which it rests like an atom within a dust mote adrift amidst the sands of the Sahara, that all the uncounted galaxies and even the expanding universe in which they whirl, will at last cease to exist. There is no visible refuge from the inexorable processes of entropy, and the intellectual inventions which have been proposed from time to time remain, in their multitudes, unconvincing on scientific grounds and eventually unpersuasive on emotional ones.

What does all this imply for utopian life and thought? If the process ends, however far in the future, in the same death to which the isolated individual succumbs so much the more quickly, then what purpose is there in pursuing a utopian dream, or indeed any sort of dream, at all? If there is in the end no transcendence of the whole system of human relations but only dissipation and nullity, of what avail is the effort described above to expand the self so as to include the future being of humans? Consider Walt Whitman's beautiful lines from *Leaves of Grass*:

> I bequeath myself to the dirt to grow from the grass I love,
> If you want me again look for me under your bootsoles.
>
> You will hardly know who I am or what I mean,
> But I shall be good health to you nevertheless,
> And filter and fibre your blood.
>
> Failing to fetch me at first keep encouraged,
> Missing me one place search another,
> I stop somewhere waiting for you.

Where there is nothing left, there is no "where" to wait, or to search, and the processes of nature would seem, eventually, to eradicate all places and all searchers. The image is bleak, and its pull is chilling. As Jean-Paul Sartre, himself assuredly no utopian, commented regarding the tug of this thought,

> I cannot think about the cooling of the sun without fear. I don't mind if my fellowmen forget about me the day after I'm buried. As long as they're alive, I'll haunt them, unnamed, imperceptible, present in every one of them just as the billions of dead who are unknown to me and whom I preserve from annihilation are present in me. But if mankind disappears, it will kill its dead for good.[30]

Mankind — humanity — *will* disappear. The corollary concern, then, is whether any hope for a genuine utopian outlook must disappear as that certainty grows among the citizenry, or whether utopia must in the end rest upon some sort of denial of the natural world.

There certainly appears to be no hope offered at the social level, the biological level, or the level of the universe itself. As Wells has seen, we seem oblivious even to the dangers we could prevent; "in a few decades at most, it will be possible for any small body of desperate men to poison your whole atmosphere, sweep your world bare with infections or blow your planet to pieces," warns the mysterious voice that haunts Camford. "You here will do nothing to anticipate and prevent that."[31] Wells wrote this in 1937. The time before such a possibility becomes all too real a probability is surely almost now upon us, yet still little is done; nationalism combines with ecological hubris to ensure that the environment is rendered ever less likely to continue supporting human life. Thanks to his biological training, Wells directly confronted this idea at the very beginning of his career, as in one of his earliest published articles, the 1893 "On Extinction," where he insisted that "the life that has schemed and struggled and committed itself, the life that has played and lost, comes at last to the pitiless judgment of time, and is slowly and remorselessly annihilated. This is the saddest chapter of biological science — the tragedy of Extinction."[32] Only the capital letter vanishes in Wells's later writings; the awareness remains. "We shall be wiped out as carelessly as we have been made," says Job Huss in Wells's dialogue novel based on the Book of Job; "Your Process is just Chaos; man is the opportunity, the passing opportunity for order in the waste."[33] Writ small in our everyday experience is the larger possibility of worldwide extinction; "If the universe can kill a child unjustly, so it can kill a race or a planet unjustly. If so many lives end tragically, why should not the whole species end tragically?"[34]

Wells concludes his last novel with a restatement of his recognition that utopia cannot be truly envisioned, because the truth about utopia exists only in its flexibility, its impermanence, its readiness to change, its rejection of timidity in the face of uncertainty. "Yet," he writes,

> a vista of innumerable happy generations, an abundance of life at present inconceivable, and at the end, not extinction necessarily, not immortality, but complete uncertainty, is surely sufficient prospect for the present. We are not yet *Homo sapiens*, but when at last our intermingled and selected offspring, carrying on the life that is now in us, when they, who are indeed ourselves, our heredity of body, thought and will, reassembled and enhanced, have established their claim to that title — can we doubt that they will be facing things at present unimaginable, weighing pros and cons altogether beyond our scope? They will see far and wide in an ever-growing light while we see as in a glass darkly. Things

yet unimaginable. They may be good by our current orientation of things; they may be evil. Why should they not be in the nature of our good and much more than our good — "beyond good and evil?"[35]

Properly speaking, the phrase "innumerable happy generations" is inaccurate, since it is a condition of the evolutionary utopian outlook that final happiness is not possible. Nonetheless, there is nothing to prevent people from being much happier, or unhappy for reasons entirely different (and less grounded in material scarcity and its concomitant emotions of greed (in the rich) and desperation (in the poor)) than those now operant, in a later stage of the utopian process. Happiness is contextual, and in a utopian society whatever unhappiness exists is tempered by one's awareness that one is still better off than even the happiest individuals of but a few generations before, and that one is truly free to work toward ever greater joys to come.

For Wells, (e)utopia may or may not be 'good'; it is assuredly, however, not a place which can be found on any map, past, present, or future, at all. Again, Wells's understanding of the function of utopian writing finds an echo in Lukács, although again from a different perspective. "The utopian longing of the soul is a legitimate desire," writes the latter, "worthy of being the centre of a world, only if it is absolutely incapable of being satisfied in the present intellectual state of man, that is to say incapable of being satisfied in any world that can be imagined and given form, whether past, present, or mythical."[36] Wells is usually careful to show that each of his utopias is not capable of satisfying all of its inhabitants, and that something else will eventually be necessary, or to leave the reader dissatisfied, destabilized, uncomfortable with both the current situation and the envisioned future. One is reminded of Oscar Wilde's famous dictum on utopia: "A map of the world that does not include Utopia is not worth even glancing at, for it leaves out the one country at which Humanity is always landing. And when Humanity lands there, it looks out, and, seeing a better country, sets sail. Progress is the realisation of Utopias."[37] Any utopia by its very nature is a place which can be found only in the map of the imagination. And the final act of the imagination is to conquer death, to answer the question death poses concerning meaning by realizing that the question is always already the answer.

For death to subvert meaning, death itself must already have a meaning in itself: at the very least that it is that which subverts meaning, which destroys purpose. But this is to assume that at least one meaning exists outside of the destruction of meaning, which is to say that meaning has not been destroyed. The step which is necessary to escape, not the fact of death as an end to individual consciousness or species being but the threat of death as the destroyer of meaning and purpose, is the step beyond all meaning, including death. Death is nihilation; utopianism is the nihilation of nihilation. Utopianism truly prepares one, not to die but for death itself, by preparing one to escape from all meaning except the meanings which are created, which are chosen. The infinite process reaches toward infinite freedom, which can be attained only when the process itself is no longer the goal of those within it because they have become the process in themselves, because they have transcended the state of mind in which beginning or end makes any difference at all, when they have transcended the need for certainty concerning final answers.

Meaning is something we already choose to a degree, and therefore we can choose not to allow death to undercut meaning, or at least choose to work toward the time and society when such a choice is genuinely possible. By choosing the process over finality, we shut out the putative meaning of death, because death becomes merely another aspect of that which has not yet happened. We tell the story of our lives, and that story continues endlessly, because imagination ceases only when we, or our descendants, cease. And by then we will no longer be concerned with death, because we will no longer be here to experience, or fear, death. As Wittgenstein wrote, "Death is not an event in life: we do not live to experience death."[38] As Wells reminds us, "Our history is just a story in space and time, and to its very last moment it must remain adventure."[39] Indeed, the adventure includes the fact of death. Awareness of individual death can drive us to recreate our individuality so as to transcend ourself and thus our death, save in the now trivial sense of the cessation of one element among many, a cessation which does not occur with, or within, our life. Our history is, in its meaning if not in its facts, an imaginative construct, just as our societies, present and future, are imaginative constructs, and just as we ourselves are imaginative constructs. And just as the meaning of death is an imaginary construct.

Our knowledge of the end of the universe turns out to be only a story we tell ourselves, and from which we draw a particular meaning. But the story, no matter how probable, remains only a story, not a certainty, and we are free to change the meaning we derive therefrom at any time.[40] In Wells's utopian process, there is always the possibility of change, of creation anew, of some new light thrown into a previously dark corner. "For Hope, the redeemer of mankind, there is perpetual resurrection."[41] We know nothing outside of imagination, yet the knowledge opened to us through imagination allows ever greater imaginative recreations of who and what we are. Imagination, even regarding the past, is a permanent inhabitant of the future. The truth of this can be seen in contemplating the specific utopian anticipations of such writers as Plato, More, Bacon, Campanella — and Wells. Such anticipations are often now merely amusing, either because they have come to pass, and we no longer regard them as all but unattainable projections, or because we have passed beyond the need for them, or even the possibility of imagining that we ever thought we could need them. What makes these imaginings useful and important still is the way they invite us to build upon them yet further, to return them to the future they seem to have missed. They have been superseded in fact, but not in imaginative force and evocative power; from them, and others like them, and from our own needs and desires and imaginings we are now engaged in creating our own, someday themselves to be passé and amusing, utopian visions. In all such utopian, or dystopian, imaginings there is an element of uncertainty, unavoidable because necessary; without the uncertainty the utopian vision is merely, at best, a piece of modest urban renewal, and at worst a fixed and recurring nightmare of inhumanity. Without the uncertainty, there is no freedom. To plan fixedly for the future on any but the smallest personal scale requires denying the very thing which makes the future different from the present, or gives planning any moral authority at all: its malleability.

Wells's path leads into a mist: the future. There imagination is unfettered, and fact is subordinate to will. As Romolo Runcini noted of Wells, "He realized that the only creative space in the history of a programmed society is the future; that is, not in a vision obtainable from the present but an event we are all waiting for."[42] The event is not, as in Heidegger, the cessation (death) of a unified ego, but the future itself as imagined and reimagined again and again. It is an event without knowable boundaries, an event which exists within us already as potentiality, and beyond us as an unknowable fact awaiting our determinative choices. What awaits the human species, or its descendants, depends in large measure upon the choices we make now, but the relation of those choices to what the human species will become is something which is, even in principle, only partially knowable. The "final" outcome of our choices is likewise unknowable, but choose we must. The question Wells poses, the last of many, is whether we will choose imagination and life, or fixity and death.

> The impenetrable clouds that bound our life at last in every direction may hide innumerable trials and dangers, but there are no conclusive limitations even in their deepest shadows, and there are times and seasons, there are moods of exaltation — moments, as it were, of revelation — when the whole universe about us seems bright with the presence of as yet unimaginable things.[43]

The task of the utopian process, for Wells, is the continual unveiling of those things as yet unimagined. Our task, within that process, is the discovery and creation of ways to render that unveiling ever more accessible to our compatriots, and to ever widen the circle of those we define as those compatriots. Therein lies as much meaning as anyone could ask.

Chapter Notes

Introduction

1. E.g. the Bishop of Oxford, Samuel ("Soapy Sam") Wilberforce and the noted naturalist Louis Agassiz.

2. Marx, e.g., and the various thinkers and businesspeople loosely subsumed under the rubric "social Darwinists."

3. See, e.g., works such as John Fiske's *Outlines of Cosmic Philosophy* (1874), an important exemplar of the type, to which I shall recur in the final chapter.

4. As, most famously, in his Romanes lecture on evolution and ethics.

5. This has long been recognized as one of Wells's most significant achievements. The noted historians of utopian thought the Manuels, otherwise utterly dismissive of the value of Wells's writings, describe it as "perhaps [his] only great work" (Frank E. and Fritzie P. Manuel, *Utopian Thought in the Western World* [UTW] [Oxford: Basil Blackwell, 1979], p. 775). Jorge Luis Borges is more enthusiastic still. Writing of Wells's early novels in general, he claims that "they tell a story symbolic of processes that are somehow inherent in all human destinies." He later adds, with a specific reference to *The Time Machine* (among others), that he expects of these works of Wells that "they will be incorporated, like the fables of Theseus or Ahasuerus, into the general memory of the species and even transcend the fame of their creator or the extinction of the language in which they were written." See Patrick Parrinder, ed., *H. G. Wells: The Critical Heritage* (London: Routledge and Kegan Paul, 1972), pp. 331, 332.

6. H.G. Wells, *The Time Machine* (London: Dent [Everyman's Library], 1961), pp. 293, 294–295.

7. All quotes p. 303.

8. On this, see any number of recent major writings on the topic. Particularly interesting here are, e.g., Richard Dawkins, *The Blind Watchmaker: Why the evidence of evolution reveals a universe without design* (New York: W.W. Norton, 1986) (Dawkins develops similar ideas more tendentiously and less originally in *The God Delusion* [Boston: Houghton Mifflin, 2006]); Daniel C. Dennett, *Darwin's Dangerous Idea: Evolution and the Meanings of Life* (New York: Simon and Schuster, 1995) (Dennett further takes up the question of scientific answers to apparently religious questions in *Breaking the Spell: Religion as a Natural Phenomenon* [New York: Viking, 2006]); Stephen Jay Gould, *Wonderful Life: The Burgess Shale and the Nature of History* (New York: W.W. Norton, 1989); and Carl Sagan, *Pale Blue Dot: A Vision of the Human Future in Space* (New York: Random House, 1994). This last provides some truly awesome visual supplements to the philosophical message of all these sorts of books. Those who wish to maintain that the purpose of the universe (or Universe) is anthropocentric need to provide a great deal more evidence than hitherto has been seen.

9. *A Modern Utopia* (hereafter MU) (Lincoln: University of Nebraska Press, 1967), pp. 10–11.

10. MU, p. 2.

11. Ralf Dahrendorf, "Out of Utopia: Toward a Reorientation of Sociological Analysis," in George, Kateb, ed., *Utopia* (New

York: Atherton Press, 1971), pp. 103–126, p. 103.

12. Republic 500c (Desmond Lee translation; Paul Shorey has "…things of the eternal and unchanging order … [to which the philosopher endeavors] "to fashion himself in their likeness and assimilate himself to them."

13. Thomas More. *Utopia*, trans. Paul Turner (Harmondsworth: Penguin, 1972), p. 131.

14. There is a real problem with trying to accommodate Wells, or in fact any kind of genuine evolutionary social philosophy, within an academic framework, By the simple fact that you're wrapping it up and presenting it in the form of a book, or even a paper, you're implying that it's all been thought through and can now be shelved until the next dusty scholar comes along in search of a topic. It's inherently false to the subject. That's why so often the really interesting stuff is found in footnotes; the author knows that hostile critics will rip them apart for appearing even remotely inconsistent in the text itself, but that most of the critics don't care about what appears in the footnotes, if they even read them at all. So the authors tuck away the bombshells, and wait for a genuinely engaged reader, one who wants not just to "understand," but to become involved in the eternal process of discovery…. Maybe I take reading too seriously. But it's too much *fun* not to take seriously.

15. See, e.g., H.G. Wells, *Mr. Belloc Objects to "The Outline of History"* (London: Watts, 1926), p. 48, for an explicit rejection of the label "profound and exhaustive philosopher." His autobiography disingenuously claimed, in its subtitle, to be the record of a "very ordinary brain."

16. Zygmunt Bauman, *Modernity and Ambivalence* (Ithaca: Cornell University Press, 1991), pp. 232, 272. Similar sentiments abound in many contemporary thinkers.

17. Quoted in Norman and Jeanne Mackenzie, *H.G. Wells: A Biography* (New York: Simon & Schuster), 1973, p. 430.

18. W. Warren Wagar, *H.G. Wells: Traversing Time* (Middletown, CT: Wesleyan University Press, 2004), p. 277.

19. MU, p. 6.

20. Lewis Mumford, *The Story of Utopias* (New York: Boni and Liveright, 1922), p. 184; Henry Newbolt, *Studies Green and Gray* (London: Thomas Nelson and Sons, 1926), p. 132; obituary notice from Patrick Parrinder, ed., *H.G. Wells: The Critical Heritage* (London: Routledge & Kegan Paul, 1972), pp. 322–323, p. 323; Krishan Kumar, *Utopia and Anti-Utopia in Modern Times* (Oxford: Basil Blackwell, 1987), p. 168.

21. H.G. Wells, *Experiment in Autobiography: Discoveries and Conclusions of a Very Ordinary Brain (Since 1866)* (hereafter EA) (New York: Macmillan, 1934), p. 106.

22. *Ibid.*, p. 141.

23. EA, pp. 106–107; H.G. Wells, *The Outline of History: Being a Plain History of Life and Mankind* (herefter OH) (Garden City, NY: Garden City Publishing Company, 1931), p. 331.

24. EA, p. 141.

25. *Ibid.*, pp. 143, 147.

26. H.G. Wells, *The Future in America* (London: Chapman and Hall, 1906), p. 7.

27. *Ibid.*, p. 5. He is referring to, as he quotes it, "There is no Being but Becoming."

28. See Diels fragment 66, as translated by Kathleen Freeman, *Ancilla to the Pre-Socratic Philosophers* (Cambridge, MA: Harvard University Press, 1977). As V.S. Pritchett famously commented, "There are always fistfights and fires in the early Wells. Above all, there are fires" (V.S. Pritchett, "The Scientific Romances," in Bernard Bergonzi, ed., *H.G. Wells: A Collection of Critical Essays*, pp. 32–38, p. 32).

29. MU, p. 21 (ellipses Wells's). It is not certain whether Wells knew of Plato's strictures against Heraclitus; if he had, he might have made the distinction he did considerably more forcefully, or felt compelled to quarrel more vigorously with Plato. See, e.g., *Cratylus* 411b–c, where Socrates comments on

> modern philosophers, who, in their search after the nature of things, are always getting dizzy from constantly going round and round, and then they imagine that the world is going round and round and moving in all directions. And this appearance, which arises out of their own internal condition, they suppose to be a reality of nature; they think that there is nothing stable or permanent, but only flux and motion, and that the world is always full of every sort of motion and change.

He provides an argument against the idea of continual change at 439e-440. Apart from *Republic*, my citations of Plato are drawn from the translations found in *The Collected Dialogues of Plato, Including the Letters*, ed. Edith Hamilton and Huntington Cairns (Princeton: Princeton University Press, 1989 [Bollingen Series LXXI]). For readers unfamiliar with the practice of Platonic references, I should note that the numbers used in place of page citations (known as Stephanos Numbers) will be found in the same place in any reputable edition of a Platonic work; they allow a comparison of the same material in different translations, which can vary widely.

30. At the Normal School for Science, from 1884–1885.

31. EA, pp. 162–163.

32. Wells would add also the influence of Arthur Schopenhauer, whose vision of the blindly striving Will served as a counterbalance to any temptation to view progress as inevitable. Wells also found Schopenhauer's views on the commonalty of human suffering quite evocative, although he rejected the lessons Schopenhauer drew therefrom. See *Mankind in the Making* (hereafter MM) (New York: Scribner's, 1904), pp. 14–15. The Wellsian vision of evolution owes something to a blend of Darwin-Huxley and Schopenhauer; the Schopenhauerian elements will reappear in the final chapter.

33. MU, p. 5. Not all previous utopians saw their societies as lasting forever, but they did agree on the idea that any change from the ideal state could be only one for the worse.

34. MU, p. 9.

35. *Ibid.*, p. 10. Cf. *Republic* 498d: Socrates comments that "there's no reason to be surprised if we can't convince the majority of people. They have never seen our words come true." What is not yet known is often feared or doubted. (My citations from *Republic* are drawn from *The Republic*, trans. Desmond Lee (Harmondsworth: Penguin, 1967).

36. MU, p. 9.

37. Martha C. Nussbaum, *Love's Knowledge: Essays on Philosophy and Literature* (New York: Oxford University Press, 1992), pp. 7, 19.

38. H.G. Wells, *Apropos of Dolores* (hereafter AD) (New York: Scribner's, 1938), p. 255.

Chapter 1

1. H.G. Wells, *New Worlds for Old* (hereafter NWO) (New York: Macmillan, 1908), p. 209. A similar recognition is found in Plato; Socrates admits, just prior to proposing the idea of the philosopher-kings, that his suggestion is likely to lead to ridicule. Immediately afterward, Glaucon exclaims, "My dear Socrates, if you make pronouncements of that sort, you can't be surprised if a large number of decent people take their coats off, pick up the nearest weapon, and come after you in their shirt sleeves to do something terrible to you" (473e-474a). Eventually, of course, they did.

2. 477a.

3. 533b.

4. 596a. This interpretation of Plato, though controversial, is not without scholarly or textual support (Cf., e.g., *Phaedo* 102b: "it was agreed that the various forms exist, and that the reason why other things are called after the forms is that they participate in the forms"). I shall not take up the controversy; it seems clear that Wells saw Plato as holding this claim in the manner which I have described.

5. 596b.

6. 597c.

7. See 434e *et seq.* for the development of this.

8. 441e. Wells does not disagree with this; for example, in examining the "probability of the establishment of a long world peace," he notes that "what is really being examined here is the power of human reason to prevail over passion — and certain other restraining and qualifying forces" (*What Is Coming? A European Forecast* [New York: Macmillan, 1916], pp. 8, 9.) In fact, as I will show later, it is precisely this dichotomy which renders a philosophical basis for utopia impossible.

9. 442a.

10. 434c.

11. 370a-b. He slips this claim in without demur from any of his interlocutors; yet, as it implies that a balance between social needs and individual aptitudes is already nascent within the body public, it allows him to avoid a potential difficulty in the distribution of jobs and tasks.

12. 370d.

13. *First and Last Things* (hereafter FLT) (New York: Putnam's, 1908), p. 26. See also Edward Tenner, "The Life of Chairs: How *Homo sapiens* became *Homo sedens*—and at what cost" *Harvard Magazine*, January-February 1997, vol. 99, #3, pp. 46–53 for some amusing illustrations of Wells's point.

14. *Social Forces in England and America* (hereafter SFEA) (New York: Harper & Bros., 1914), pp. 228, 230.

15. Max Black, *The Labyrinth of Language* (New York: Mentor, 1968), p. 170.

16. I say "gives focus" because consciousness in itself as a function of the brain is a natural phenomenon like any other, and thus dependent on the "natural world." But what is interesting about consciousness in the context of a discussion of utopia is not its mere facticity but what it does with the experiences and imaginings present within it.

17. H.G. Wells, *Babes in the Darkling Wood* (New York: Alliance, 1940), p. 400.

18. *'42 to '44: A Contemporary Memoir Upon Human Behaviour During the Crisis of World Revolution* (hereafter 42/44) (London: Secker & Warburg, 1944), p. 169.

19. *Ibid.*, p. 170.

20. Cf. Lizzie Borden and O.J. Simpson, who were found innocent in courts of law but not by popular opinion. No one remembers much at all about Borden except the verse concerning her purported deed, and it is likely the same will eventually be true for Simpson. One can already imagine the rhyme of the future:

O.J. Simpson took a knife,
And did a nasty to his wife.
When he saw she'd met her end,
He promptly sliced and diced her friend.

21. H.G. Wells, *The Dream* (hereafter D) (New York: Macmillan, 1924), p. 312.

22. 42/44, p. 171.

23. *Ibid.*, p. 171.

24. *Ibid.*

25. *Ibid.*, p. 172.

26. MU, p. 318.

27. FLT, p. 37. In his short story "The Man Who Could Work Miracles," Wells shows, in an amusing fashion, the devastating consequences of emulating Joshua. Cf. Wordsworth's famous line (from "The Tables Turned"): "We murder to dissect." Wells's connection with the Romantics, particularly Shelley, and the Enlightenment ran deep.

28. H.G. Wells, *Washington and the Riddle of Peace* (New York: Macmillan, 1922), p. 13.

29. H.G. Wells, *Men Like Gods* (hereafter MLG) (London: Cassell, 1923), p. 55.

30. FLT, pp. 21, 27 (ellipses Wells's).

31. MU, pp. 264–265.

32. MU, p. 266.

33. Compare, for example, Wells's loose definition of his classes with Russell's definition, on a similar topic, in *The Principles of Mathematics*: "We agreed to call *man* a class-concept, but *man* does not, in its usual employment, denote anything.... Thus *man* is the class-concept, *men* (the concept) is the concept of the class, and men (the object denoted by the concept *men*) are the class" (London: George Allen and Unwin, 1948), p. 67. It is difficult to imagine Wells writing in this vein or style at all. Nor is it clear that such an approach would allow him to say anything remotely relevant to the concerns of his intended audience. Indeed, it is hard to imagine an analytic utopia, since the very things which make the scope of human life so difficult to portray save at the individual level are those things which make for vagueness in philosophy. As Russell himself remarked, "Vagueness is the rebellion of truth against intellect" (Bertrand Russell, *Fact and Fiction* [London: George Allen and Unwin, 1961]), p. 185.

34. MU, p. 270.

35. All quotes MU, p. 265.

36. All quotes MU, p. 266.

37. Wells, as he freely recognized, was a product of his times; although at his best he foresaw women as sharing equally in the necessary recreation of the future prospects of humanity, his language too seldom reflects this.

38. MU, p. 267.

39. *Ibid.*, p. 268.

40. *Ibid.*, p. 267.

41. All quotations *ibid.*, p. 268.

42. *Ibid.*, pp. 268–269.

43. *Ibid.*, p. 269.

44. H.G. Wells, *The War of the Worlds* (hereafter WW) (New York: Harper and Bros., 1900), p. 259.

45. H.G. Wells, *Star-Begotten: A Biological Fantasia* (New York: Viking, 1937), p. 201.

46. WW, p. 278 (emphasis mine).
47. MM, p. 34.
48. All quotations MU, p.143.
49. *Ibid.*, p. 144.
50. *Ibid.*, p. 147.
51. Both quotations *ibid.*, p. 144.
52. *Ibid.*, p. 145.
53. *Ibid.*, p. 147.
54. *Ibid.*, p. 143. Wells was not entirely consistent regarding capital punishment. In 42/44 he argued that "whatever comes out of this war there must be no killing of Hitler" (p. 129) for he expected such killing to create a martyr around which Naziism would eventually revive. He assumed, incorrectly, that Hitler would be incapable of suicide and would, if not assassinated by the German resistance, be captured; "our proper treatment of him, if we catch him in time, is to certify him and put him away in a not too luxurious asylum for criminal lunatics. And forget about him" (p. 131). Nor did he see any point to executing Goebbels; "Lying is not a capital offense. God help all propagandists everywhere if he is to be killed" (p. 131). Yet Hess, he thought, "ought to have been shot as a spy directly he was caught" (p. 129), and he was utterly unforgiving of the Nazi military and police leaders; "the real criminals, the cold-blooded killers and tormentors, are a different problem altogether. They should be documented now, tried now and shot as they come to hand" (p. 131). His conclusion is typical, apart from his admittedly sanguinary demands regarding war criminals:

> Murder and cruelty can be punished by a considerable amount of shooting "leaders"; those natural-born killers will give less trouble and serve a useful educational purpose if they are put out of the way; works of art can be restored to the collections to which they belong, which are either now in the public domain or marked for ultimate socialization; but a reparation of devastated economic resources at the expense of the devastators is no more possible than a resurrection of the dead. Let the dead past bury its dead. The world commonweal has to recondition the planet with as little vindictiveness as possible [p. 132].

55. STC, p. 422.
56. All quotations STC, p. 423.
57. Glenn Negley and J. Max Patrick, *The Quest for Utopia* (New York: Henry Schuman, 1952), p. 330.
58. Michael Coren, *The Invisible Man: The Life and Liberties of H.G. Wells* (Toronto: Random House, 1993), p. 226. This is probably the most virulent assault on Wells ever written. Coren uses selective quotes, half-truths, and misstatements to create a repulsive caricature of Wells. The main reason for singling this otherwise negligible book out here is that it demonstrates that even recent authors determined to do so, and undeterred by any need for intellectual honesty, will make a case for Wells as a hard core eugenicist. He is not, as what follows will show. Wells, incidentally, responded in advance to the comment about social engineers:

> What are we going to do with all the swarming multitude of unsuitable people who constitute the great majority of mankind? We want peace on earth and good will to all men. That alone precludes the idea of cleaning the slate by a worldwide massacre. Even if it were not—let us use a mild adjective—anti-social, it would be impracticable.... So let us dismiss any anticipation of a clean slate for the Revolution. There will be no clean slate [H.G. Wells, *Phoenix: How to Rebuild the World: A Summary of the Inescapable Conditions of World Reorganization* (Girard, KS: Haldeman-Julius, 1942), p. 32].

The answer, of course, is more and better education. Coren, of course, does not cite this book or show any sign of having read it or virtually any of the others discussed here.

59. MM, p. 37 (emphasis added).
60. *Ibid.*, p. 38.
61. Both quotations *ibid.*
62. H.G. Wells, *The Salvaging of Civilization* (New York: Macmillan, 1921), pp. 142, 143 (emphases Wells's).
63. The passage is from Chesterton's 1905 book *Heretics*. I have quoted it as found in Patrick Parrinder, ed., *H. G. Wells: The Critical Heritage*, p. 103.
64. MM, p. 43.
65. *Ibid.*, p. 68.
66. *Ibid.*, p. 63; the description of the wedding is found in the newspaper article cited by Wells.
67. *The Work, Wealth, and Happiness of Mankind* (hereafter WWH) (Garden City, NY: Doubleday, Doran, 1931), p. 746.

68. *Ibid.* (second quotation, p. 749).
69. *Ibid.*
70. *Ibid.*, p. 270.

Chapter 2

1. H.G. Wells, *The Food of the Gods* (New York: Charles Scribner's Sons, 1924), p. 124. One is reminded of Sherlock Holmes's comment apropos Inspector Gregory: "Were he but gifted with imagination he might rise to great heights in his profession" ("Silver Blaze").

2. Cf. Sartre:
First, the language of the speaker generally dissolves at once in the mind of the listener; what remains is a schema, both conceptual and verbal, that controls *reconstitution* and comprehension. Comprehension will be deeper, the more imprecise the word-for-word reconstitution. Now comprehension is a personal act. If the listener repeats what he has heard, he is merely lending his voice to a transcendent object that is realized through his voice and then flies off toward new tongues. If he *comprehends*, he reshapes the well-worn path *for himself.* In the end, the act is completely his own, although the comprehended reality can be a universal notion [Jean-Paul Sartre, *The Family Idiot*, vol. 1 (Chicago: University of Chicago Press, 1981), pp. 11–12].

3. A.J. Ayer, *The Meaning of Life* (New York: Charles Scribner's Sons, 1990), p. 3.

4. *Ibid.* It is hard to see why people who hold these sorts of views complain when others use emotional rhetoric to persuade ordinary readers that such views are pernicious; on an emotivist view, any presentation which changes someone's ethical stance must perforce be as valid an ethical argument as any other sort of combination of words or images. Bertrand Russell, although wishing "to exclude all value judgments from philosophy," at least admitted his dissatisfaction with the sorts of conclusions which follow from such a course of action, although he did not see any way out of them. (See Paul A. Schilpp, ed., *The Philosophy of Bertrand Russell* [Evanston, IL: Library of Living Philosophers, 1946], pp. 719 (quotation); 724: "I can only say that, while my own opinions as to ethics do not satisfy me, other people's satisfy me still less."

5. *The World Set Free* (New York: E.P. Dutton, 1914), pp. 14–15.

6. *Ibid.*, p. 15.

7. Antony Flew, "Introduction," to *A Dictionary of Philosophy* (London: Pan, 1984), pp. vii–xi, p. viii. As Flew describes it further, philosophy "is characteristically argumentative and essentially directed towards the determination of what logical relations do and do not obtain..." (p. ix). It is, in other words, concerned primarily with validity rather than truth.

8. *Republic* 441e.

9. Richard Kostelanetz, "An ABC of Contemporary Reading," in Richard Kostelanetz, ed., *Esthetics Contemporary*, rev. ed. (Buffalo, NY: Prometheus, 1989), pp. 350–382, p. 356.

10. From a lecture quoted in A.H. Johnson, *Whitehead's Theory of Reality* (New York: Dover, 1962), p. 103.

11. Peter Caws, *Sartre* (London: Routledge & Kegan Paul, 1979), p. 160.

12. It should be acknowledged, as an indication of the problematic nature of rigid disciplinary demarcations, that even those commonly taken as accepting such demarcations may, in one context or another, admit to their deficiency. For example, Bertrand Russell, surely among the most profound and rigorous of analytic and critical philosophers, recognized that his own approach was by no means the only possible one, and that other approaches required other means than logical analysis by which to reach a sympathetic critical understanding. "Apart from the attempt to understand the world," he wrote, apropos of George Santayana's philosophical style,
philosophy has other functions to fulfill. It can enlarge the imagination by the construction of a cosmic epic, or it can suggest a way of life less wayward and accidental than that of the unreflective. A philosopher who attempts either of these tasks must be judged by a standard of values, aesthetic or ethical, rather than by intellectual correctness ["The Philosophy of Santayana," in Paul Arthur Schilpp, ed., *The Philosophy of George Santayana* (New York: Tudor, 1951), pp. 453–474, p. 453.]

Despite this testimony from a reputable figure, it is safe to anticipate that attempts to perform the tasks described by him are, at least within the dominant academic tradition, more commonly considered acceptable when performed by novelists than when performed by professional philosophers.

13. Timothy Findley, *Headhunter* (Toronto: Harper, 1997), p. 296.

14. Marcuse, *op. cit.*, p. 54.

15. Hannah Arendt, *The Human Condition* (Chicago: University of Chicago Press, 1998), p. 192.

16. *Ibid.*

17. *Ibid.*

18. Northrop Frye, "Varieties of Literary Utopias," in Frank Manuel, ed., *Utopias and Utopian Thought: A Timely Appraisal* (Boston: Beacon Press, 1971), pp. 25–49, p. 25.

19. William H. Gass, *Fiction and the Figures of Life* (New York: Vintage, 1972), p. 18.

20. H.G. Wells, *The Nose and the Other Uncollected Short Stories of H.G. Wells* (London: Athlone Press, 1984), pp. 62–63.

21. H.G. Wells, *The Anatomy of Frustration: A Modern Synthesis* (hereafter AF) (New York: Macmillan, 1936), p. 204.

22. *World Brain* (Garden City, NY: Doubleday, Doran, 1938), p. xi.

23. *Ibid.*, pp. x–xi, xi.

24. Michael Draper, *H.G. Wells* (New York: St. Martin's, 1988), p. 115.

25. George Santayana, *Interpretations of Poetry and Religion* (New York: Harper and Bros., 1957), pp. viii–ix.

26. AD, p. 278.

27. *World Encyclopedia* (n.p.: Folcroft Library Editions, 1973), p. 2.

28. Wilbur Marshall Urban, *Language and Reality: The Philosophy of Language and the Principles of Symbolism* (London: George Allen & Unwin, 1951), p. 494.

29. *Babes in the Darkling Wood* (New York: Alliance, 1940), p. x. Presumably he would still recognize the short story as a more or less distinct entity; "A short story is, or should be, a simple thing; it aims at producing one single, vivid effect; it has to seize the attention at the outset, and never relaxing, gather it together more and more until the climax is reached. The limits of the human capacity to attend closely therefore set a limit to it; it must explode and finish before interruption occurs or fatigue sets in" (SFEA, p. 178). During the development of a utopian society attention spans, and thus presumably short stories, will likely grow longer. But the point at hand is not the classifications of literary forms but what one is to expect of them, and to do with them.

30. Jean-Paul Sartre, *Life/Situations* (New York: Pantheon, 1977), p. 112.

31. SFEA, p. 173.

32. *Ibid.*, p. 185.

33. Georg Lukács, *The Theory of the Novel* (Cambridge, MA: MIT Press, 1990), Tr. Anna Bostock; originally completed in 1915, though not published until 1920, pp. 72, 73.

34. MM, p. 291.

35. SFEA, p. 189.

36. See, e.g., Herbert Marcuse, *An Essay on Liberation* or any of a number of works by Erich Fromm for examples of this.

37. SFEA, p. 190.

38. *Ibid.*, p. 195. As Martin Buber remarked of the urge to create utopias, "What is at work here is the longing for that *rightness* which, in religious or philosophical vision, is experienced as revelation or idea, and which of its very nature cannot be realized in the individual, but only in human community" (*Paths in Utopia* [New York: Collier, 1988], p. 7).

39. SFEA, p. 195.

40. Alan Wykes, *H.G. Wells in the Cinema* (London: Jupiter, 1977), p. 20.

41. H.G. Wells, *The King Who Was a King: An Uncollected Novel* (Garden City, NY: Doubleday, Doran, 1929), p. 13.

42. *Ibid.*, p. 3.

43. *The Salvaging of Civilization*, p. 163.

44. H.G. Wells, *H.G. Wells's Literary Criticism*, ed. Patrick Parrinder and Robert M. Philmus (Sussex: Harvester, 1980), pp. 249–250. Interestingly enough, the renowned British documentarian John Grierson thought, apropos Well's published script for the film, that "a film description has many advantages over plain narrative. Events, characterizations and the argument of the drama are whipped into a running shape more precisely and with less meandering than the narrative form permits" *Grierson on Documentary*, ed. Forsyth Hardy (London: Collins, 1946), pp. 59–60. Grierson appears never to have read any of Wells's more discursive novels, in which it is precisely that meandering

which gives the necessary illusion of verisimilitude.

45. Marcuse, *op. cit.*, p. 9.

46. Karl Mannheim, *Ideology and Utopia* (New York: Harvest, n.d.), p. 192. His use of the term includes both dystopias (worlds gone wrong) and anti-utopias (imagined worlds intended to demonstrate the impossibility of utopianism), but the difference is irrelevant here.

47. FLT, p. 44.

48. 42/44, p. 172 (emphases Wells's).

49. Mark Turner, *The Literary Mind: The Origins of Thought and Language* (New York: Oxford University Press, 1998), p. 25. Corresponding claims can be found in Daniel Dennett as well as others similarly free of utopian interests.

50. Nussbaum, *op. cit.*, p. 367.

51. EA, p. 532.

52. Robin Morgan, *The Anatomy of Freedom: Feminism, Physics, and Global Politics* (Garden City, NY: Anchor Press/Doubleday, 1982), p. 318.

53. AD, p. 284; final ellipses Wells's.

54. Urban, *op. cit.*, p. 491. According to Urban, "A symbol is always a form of re-presentation, not of presentation. Some duality between the intuition and the concept, between the idea and the intuition which stands for it, is necessary for the symbolic relation to exist" (*ibid.*, p. 469; he adds, "to be a symbol it must contain both truth and fiction" [p. 471]). A similar point is made by Martha Nussbaum; "Life is never simply *presented* by a text; it is always *represented as* something" (Nussbaum, *op. cit.*, p. 5). In the context of the Wellsian evolutionary utopian view, it is worth remembering the Chorus Mysticus from Goethe's *Faust*:

"Things that are transient
As symbols appear"
[or]
"All earth comprises
Is symbol alone"

(The first translation is that of W.H. Van Der Smissen [London: Dent, 1926]; the second is George Madison Priest [New York: Covici-Friede, 1932]. Wells does not share Goethe's Platonism, but in both cases the purpose of that which is is to point toward that which can become.)

55. Marcuse, *op. cit.*, pp. 32–33.

56. D, p. 33.

57. EA, p. 410.

58. *Ibid.*, p. 414.

59. H.G. Wells, *Early Writings in Science and Science Fiction*, ed. Robert M. Philmus and David Y. Hughes (Berkeley: University of California Press, 1975), p. 228.

60. 42/44, p. 7.

61. SFEA, p. 175.

62. *Ibid.*, p. 8.

63. Laurence Sterne, *The Life and Opinions of Tristram Shandy, Gentleman* (n.p.: Books Incorporated, 1942), p. 84 (Book II, Chapter 11).

64. AF, p. 180.

65. George Santayana, *Three Philosophical Poets: Lucretius, Dante, Goethe* (Cambridge, MA: Harvard University Press, 1945), p. 3.

66. Immanuel Kant, *Perpetual Peace and Other Essays*, trans. Ted Humphrey (Indianapolis: Hackett, 1988), p. 41.

67. R.H.S. Crossman, "Plato and the Perfect State," in Thomas Landon Thorson, ed., *Plato: Totalitarian or Democrat?* (Englewood Cliffs, NJ: Prentice-Hall, 1963), pp. 15–40, p. 39.

68. Cf. A.L. Morton's comments on *1984*. "What Orwell does with great skill," Morton writes, "is to play upon the lowest fears and prejudices engendered by bourgeois society in dissolution. His object is not to argue a case but to induce an irrational conviction in the minds of his readers that any attempt to realise socialism must lead to a world of corruption, torture and insecurity" (A.L. Morton, *The English Utopia* [London: Lawrence & Wishart, 1952], p. 212). We may quarrel with Morton's view of Orwell, but it is not entirely inaccurate as regarding Orwell's method. No factual work had as devastating an influence on the popular view of state socialism until Aleksandr Solzhenitsyn's *The Gulag Archipelago*—and Solzhenitsyn is a far greater writer than Orwell.

69. David Hume, *A Treatise of Human Nature* (Oxford: Clarendon Press, 1983), p. 415 (Bk. II, Pt. III, Sect. III).

70. Which is, in fact, the case with *A Modern Utopia* and the Wellsian vision in general, against which Huxley was reacting; Wells's vision was tremendously influential in its time.

71. My claims here may have slightly less force in regard to a modern phenomenon: the serial utopia, of which the most prominent

example is surely the aforementioned *Star Trek* and its many spin-offs. Hundreds of television episodes and several theatrical motion pictures (not to mention hundreds more more-or-less related books and comics) have presented a world view which is detailed enough to seem at least vaguely real, and vague and inconsistent enough to allow the viewer to supply details which seem appropriate within her or his own moral view. The chief advantage of such a utopian vision is that it removes any real need for the viewer to think about its practical aspects, since the impression given is that this is *what will happen*. There are surely those who fully expect that somewhere out there we will encounter Klingons in centuries to come. The *Star Trek* universe, in its hypnotic popularity, is deterministic; the viewer need only wait, so to speak, for utopia to arrive. No one seems ever to have had to do anything, save make the requisite technological advances in a timely fashion, for the attainment of the desired result. In fact, sometimes the suggestion is made that those advances are given to the present by the future, a future which is based on the fact of those advances having been made in the first place (Cf. the film *Star Trek IV: The Return Home*).

72. All quotes from EA, pp. 575, 575–576, 578. Even within this mental digression, Wells's use for the religious spirit is appropriately atheistic in character, and includes within it an explanation of the need for deities (see above). Since the purpose of the discussion here is to develop the main line of Wells's thought, disavowed dead ends need be examined only to understand why they were taken in the first place, and how utopians may avoid taking them in the future. These errors have their value; as T.S. Eliot remarked, "It is, after all, worth while exploring a blind alley, if only to discover that it *is* blind" ("Introduction" to Joseph Pieper, *Leisure: The Basis of Culture* [New York: Mentor, 1963], p. 12.) Regarding this particular aspect of Wells's thought, though, it is not a value I see any need to expand upon in detail. Traditional theism is at heart merely another form of teleological utopianism, albeit one in which human actions have little relevance to the utopia itself (heaven, paradise, etc.).

73. MM, p. 14.

74. *Ibid.*, p. 15 (ellipses mine).

75. *The Open Conspiracy* (hereafter OC) (Garden City, NY: Doubleday, Doran, 1928), p. 2. Cf. Annette Baier: "Atheism undermines a solitary thinker's single-handed cognitive ambitions, as it can undermine his expectation that unilateral virtue will bring happiness" (*Postures of the Mind: Essays on Mind and Morals* [Minneapolis: University of Minnesota Press, 1985], p. 292). As Baier indicates, theism has been a traditional form of social glue; even if *my* virtue goes unrecognized socially, the feeling underlying theism implies, I can rest assured that such recognition will nonetheless be vouchsafed to me at some future point; it is therefore worthwhile to be virtuous even if alone. This attitude will again be seen, in a new context and bearing greater weight, in the final chapter.

76. *Ibid.*, p. 3.

77. *Ibid.*, p. 10.

78. *Ibid.*, p. 19.

79. The phrase here should be "will become," as there is no reasonable doubt that in another million or ten million years humanity will be something altogether different from whatever we can imagine now. I say "may become," though, because I wish to avoid any possible misinterpretation of Wells as implying a deterministic outcome along teleological lines.

80. *Ibid.*, p. 18.

81. *Ibid.*

82. *The Discovery of the Future*, London, Jonathan Cape, 1925, p. 46.

83. *Ibid.*, p. 48.

84. *Ibid.*, pp. 48, 49.

85. EA, p. 562, e.g. In *New Worlds For Old*, Wells does acknowledge Marx's contributions to economic understanding, but then and always he remained opposed to the dogmatic Marxist insistence upon the inevitability of a single transformative revolution.

86. OH, p. 1158.

87. H.G. Wells, *The World of William Clissold* (hereafter WWC). New York: George H. Doran Co., 1926,, p. 64.

88. *The Happy Turning: A Dream of Life*. London: Heinemann, 1945, p. 13; *All Aboard for Ararat*. London: Secker and Warburg, 1940, p. 10. One is reminded of the film *Monty Python and the Holy Grail*.

89. Citations here reveal an interesting

fact. Most American readers will have access to *The Fate of Man: An unemotional Statement of the Things that are happening to him now, and of the immediate Possibilities confronting him* (hereafter FM) (New York: Alliance, 1939), which appears to be a retitled version of the English *The Fate of Homo Sapiens* (hereafter FHS) (London: Secker and Warburg, 1939). The two, though, are not identical, so I shall cite from both to facilitate finding the quotations. The first quotation is found in FHS, p. 128; FM p. 103; the second is found in FHS, p. 129, but not in FM; the third comes from FHS p. 133, FM, p. 106; the last from FHS p. 140, FM, p. 110.

90. H.G. Wells, *Crux Ansata* (New York: Agora, 1944), pp. 123, 8, 132. This work, which also called into question the strength of the Allied commitment to defeating the Axis, was too controversial to be published in England during Wells's lifetime. The charge against Pius XII is not Wells's alone, nor will it go away, as the ongoing controversy over John Cornwell's *Hitler's Pope: The Secret History of Pius XII* (New York: Viking, 1999) demonstrates. Here, by the way, we find an ironic illustration of the distinction between fact and value: the *facts* regarding the actions of Pius XII are largely at the disposal of historians and writers; the *motives* underlying those actions remain largely a mystery subject to widely varied interpretations, interpretations themselves grounded in disparate moral outlooks. The controversy stems from the impossibility of fully reconciling these two situations; in itself it is not subject to correction through the acquisition of further facts.

91. *Crux Ansata*, p. 143.

92. FHS, p. 141; FM, pp. 110–111.

93. FHS, p. 128; FM, p. 103.

94. Isaiah 9, 19–20; 9; 15–16, King James Version. I have quoted from Isaiah because of Wells's reference to it, but even more violent diatribes may be found in Leviticus. Whatever the early prophets were, they were not subtle.

95. FHS, p. 324; FM, p. 258.

96. OH, p. 739.

97. H.G. Wells, Julian Huxley, and G.P. Wells *The Science of Life* (hereafter SL) (New York: Literary Guild, 1934), p. 1466.

98. D, pp. 249, 257.

99. 42/44, p. 173.

100. H.G. Wells, *World Brain* (hereafter WB) (Garden City, NY: Doubleday, Doran, 1938), p. 101.

101. My source for many of these ideas comes from his Presidential Address to the Educational Science Section of the British Association for the Advancement of Science.

102. WB, p.103; MU, pp. 280–281.

103. See the diagram in WB, pp. 106–107 (reprinted in 42/44, p. 168) for the organization of this.

104. WB, p. 108.

105. *Ibid.*, p. 109.

106. *Ibid.*, p. 110.

107. H.G. Wells, *The Shape of Things to Come* (hereafter STC) (New York: Macmillan, 1934), pp. 364–365. Cf. Plato, *Laws*, 798a–b: "When men have been brought up under any system of laws and that system has, by some happy providence, persisted unchanged for long ages, so that no one remembers or has ever heard of a time when things were otherwise than as they are, the whole soul is filled with reverence and afraid to make any innovation on what was once established. A lawgiver, then, must contrive one device or another to secure this advantage for his community...."

108. H.G. Wells, *Travels of a Republican Radical in Search of Hot Water* (Harmondsworth: Penguin, 1939), p. 99.

109. WB, p. 111.

110. *Ibid.*, pp. 111–112.

111. As Socrates notes, e.g., "If we are to persuade them that no citizen has ever quarrelled with any other, because it is sinful, our old men and women must tell children stories with this end in view from the first, and we must compel our poets to tell them similar stories when they grow up" (*Republic* 378c–d).

112. WB, p. 142. Cf. Eva Figes, *Tragedy and Social Evolution*, who notes that "history represents one form of collective identity. Whether that history has any basis in fact is irrelevant so long as the community has some belief in it.... One could almost say that it is difficult to imagine a collective identity at all without a sense of history, of something having once happened. Most religions are based on it" (New York: Persea, 1990, p. 31).

113. This seems unlikely, given *Republic* 465a: "If one man is angry with another, he can take it out of him on the spot, and will be less likely to pursue the quarrel further." Once more there is an ambiguity about how

far we are to take these proposals as having any connection to the lives of the artisans. Perhaps the angry action to which he refers is to be thought of as taking place inside the guardians' encampment, where presumably the artisans would not be allowed.

114. I say inevitable because Plato acknowledges the fact: "since all created things must decay, even a social order of this kind cannot last for all time, but will decline" (546a). The question, then, is whether the decay can occur only in the way Plato specifies or in other ways as well.

115. STC, p. 35.

116. H.G. Wells, *The Story of a Great Schoolmaster* (New York: Macmillan, 1924), p. 34.

117. WWC, p. 627.

118. STC, p. 375. This is from the aphorisms of Ariston Theotocopulos, the artist who figures, much more simplistically than in the novel, as the leader of the opposition in the film version. In the novel Wells makes his sympathy with Theotocopulos's views quite evident; "So they were thinking in 2046," the future historian comments. "Have we really got very much further to-day?" (*ibid*).

119. *Joan and Peter* (New York: Macmillan, 1918), p. 257.

120. WWC, p. 656.

121. WB, p. 128. His emphasis.

122. *Ibid*., p. 124.

123. WWC, pp. 165–166.

124. This criticism turns up in some rather odd places. H.R. Haldeman recounts a comment by Richard Nixon apropos of an unnamed book by Wells: "Wells has the feeling that the solution to all problems is education for everyone, and that's a terrible idea, especially for women, says the P" (*The Haldeman Diaries: Inside the Nixon White House* [New York: G.P. Putnam's Sons, 1994], p. 397). Further comment would be supererogatory.

125. Quoted in Brian Murray, *H.G. Wells* (New York: Continuum, 1990), p. 64. Murray evidently agrees with Mencken's comments.

126. W. Warren Wagar, "Science and the World State: Education as Utopia in the Prophetic Vision of H.G. Wells," in Parrinder and Rolfe, eds., *op. cit*., pp. 40–53, pp. 42, 43–44. Wagar's concerns appear to have diminished considerably in subsequent years, as may be seen in his last book on Wells, the aforementioned *H.G. Wells: Traversing Time*. Here he describes *The Shape of Things to Come* as "one of the greatest utopias ever written, not only because of its formal utopography but also, and more so in my judgment, because Wells found the courage to imagine the labors that might be required from year to year to attain his promised land" (p. 217). Wagar also argues that Leon Stover (of whom more below) goes "much too far" in his condemnation of supposed fascistic elements in Wells's thought (p. 74).

127. Parrinder and Rolfe, p. 44.

128. *Ibid*., p. 52. It is worth noting that Wagar nowhere justifies his assumption that democracy is in fact the form of political structure best suited to attaining utopia. Oddly enough, both Plato's and Wells's concerns regarding democracy met in the analytical philosopher C.D. Broad. As a young man, Broad read Wells's writings extensively; Broad's childhood Christianity disappeared partly under the influence of *Anticipations* and *Mankind in the Making*, which he read with "great admiration." Soon afterwards, Broad read Plato's *Republic* which, as did Wells at a similar age, he found extremely powerful, particularly in its attitude toward democracy. "My scepticism about parliamentary democracy was further strengthened," Broad wrote later, "by the very critical attitude which Wells took towards it in his social and political writings" (Paul Arthur Schilpp, ed., *The Philosophy of C.D. Broad* [New York: Library of Living Philosophers, 1959], pp. 43, 46). Broad, being a philosopher in the critical tradition, could offer no way forward; Wells offered many such ways.

129. Leon Stover, *The Prophetic Soul: A Reading of H.G. Wells's Things to Come* (Jefferson, NC: McFarland, 1987).

130. *Ibid*., p. 67.

131. *Ibid*., p. 12.

132. *Ibid*., p. 57 (footnote).

133. *Ibid*., p. 56.

134. *Ibid*., p. 74.

135. These criticisms are similar in content, albeit in a different context, to those regarding Wells's rejection of private property, which rejection I shall discuss in its proper place.

136. Roslynn D. Haynes, *H.G. Wells: Discoverer of the Future: The Influence of Science*

on His Thought (New York: New York University Press, 1980), p.37.

137. Stover asserts this point in thoroughly ringing language: For Wells, he claims, "Men are but avatars of impersonal forces in the progressive movement of history, making for a non-individualized future, to be made official in the dedicated nihilism of the organic state" (*op. cit.*, p. 26).

138. *Ibid.*, p. 92.

139. FM, p. 64.

140. H.G. Wells, *The World Set Free* (New York: E.P. Dutton, 1914), p.178.

141. H.G. Wells, *The Camford Visitation* (hereafter CV) (London, Methuen, 1937), p. 48.

142. WWH, p. 86.

143. From "The Rediscovery of the Unique," quoted in Mackenzie, *op. cit.*, p. 87.

144. H.G. Wells, *What Is Coming? A European Forecast* (New York: Macmillan, 1916), p. 1.

145. *World Encyclopedia*, pp. 11–12. The same essay appears in WB, pp. 3–35.

146. On this see, e.g., Peter Kemp's amusing survey of Wells's debt to biology: *H.G. Wells and the Culminating Ape* (New York: St. Martin's, 1996). The only annoying thing about this rather jolly compendium of passages from virtually the entire Wellsian corpus is the utter lack of footnotes; if a passage amuses or infuriates the reader, she or he will have to read the book in question through to locate its context.

147. *World Encyclopedia*, p. 10. To say the least.

148. Haynes, *op. cit.*, p. 38.

149. FM, p. 55.

150. Robert Heilbroner, *An Inquiry into the Human Prospect* (New York: W.W. Norton, 1974), pp. 110, 135.

Chapter 3

1. Hannah Arendt, *Between Past and Future: Eight Exercises in Political Thought* (Harmondsworth: Penguin, 1993), p. 93.

2. See, e.g., *Republic* 494a: Socrates and Adeimantus are discussing the place of philosophers within society as presently constituted:

"So philosophy is impossible among the common people."

"Quite impossible."

"And the common people must disapprove of philosophers."

"Inevitably."

3. Arendt, *op. cit.*, p 108.

4. *Ibid.*

5. H.G. Wells, *Guide to the New World: A Handbook of Constructive World Revolution* (London: Victor Gollancz, 1941), p. 140.

6. See, e.g., Rud Whitlow in The *Holy Terror*.

7. OC, p. 21.

8. WWC, pp. 668, 669.

9. *Ibid.*, p. 671.

10. MU, p. 128.

11. Sartre, *Life/Situations*, p. 13.

12. *Republic* 473c–e.

13. 485b.

14. 484c.

15. 487a.

16. 492e–493a. See also the aforementioned section on the reasons for the decline of the ideal state (546b–e).

17. 540d.

18. 540e–541a.

19. 541a.

20. 473a. He grows rather testy at this point, it must be admitted: "Then don't insist on my showing that every detail of our description can be realized in practice," he admonishes Glaucon, "but grant that we shall have met your demand that its realization should be possible if we are able to find the conditions under which a state can most closely approximate to it" (473a–b).

21. EA, p. 562.

22. H.G. Wells, *The Way the World Is Going: Guesses and Forecasts of the Years Ahead* (Garden City, NY: Doubleday, Doran, 1929), p.59.

23. Both quotes *ibid.*, p. 64.

24. *Ibid.*, p. 70.

25. *Ibid.*, pp. 72; 75–76.

26. MU, p. 258.

27. *Ibid.*, p. 262. Wells describes the Samurai as having begun "as a private aggressive cult [who] won their way to the rule of the world" (*ibid.*, p. 279). This is a lapse of imagination on his part, I think; there seems no intrinsic reason why such a process could not come about peacefully.

28. *Ibid.*, p. 271.

29. *Ibid.*, p. 274.

30. MU, p. 285.

Notes—Chapter 3

31. *Ibid.*, pp. 279–280.
32. *Ibid.*, p. 289.
33. *Ibid.*, p. 286.
34. *Ibid.*, p. 297. One wonders what effect this requirement would have on the self-willed semi-literacy of most of our contemporary politicians. Some clear and forceful specifications as to content would probably be required in their cases, if not actual lessons in what a book is and how to read it.
35. *Ibid.*, p. 302.
36. *Ibid.*, pp. 302–303.
37. *Ibid.*, p. 303.
38. OC, pp. viii–ix.
39. *Ibid.*, p. 33.
40. *Ibid.*, p. 34.
41. *Ibid.*, p. 32.
42. The descriptions are found *ibid.*, p. 61; the exclusion on p. 62.
43. *Ibid.*, p. 65.
44. See MU, p. 259.
45. Erich Fromm, *To Have or to Be?* (New York: Harper & Row, 1976), p. 75.
46. H.G. Wells, *A Year of Prophesying* (London: T. Fisher Unwin, 1924), p. 267.
47. OC, p. 124.
48. *Ibid.* The parallel with science, it should be remarked, is a parallel with the process of scientific understanding, which develops gradually in spite of the petty rivalries of occasional scientists or interference from governments, not with the growth of the data so accumulated. It is not what we know that is vital, although the growth of knowledge is important, but the open-ended method by which we come to know it.
49. Theodor Adorno, *Prisms* (Cambridge, MA: MIT Press, 1992), pp. 116–117.
50. More, *op. cit.*, p. 84. The treatment of precious metals (using them for the manufacture of chamber-pots and suchlike humble products) is well known. More's reasons for this are similar to those underlying the restrictions, to be discussed below, applied by Plato and Wells: the fetishization of precious objects, a result of "the idiotic concept of scarcity-value" (p. 86), leads to social inequities and problematic behaviors. More's citizens are completely incapable of understanding "why a totally useless substance like gold should now, all over the world, be considered far more important than human beings, who gave it such value as it has" (p. 89).

Interestingly enough, Wells comments disparagingly on this very point: "Like any Whig, More exalted reason above the imagination at every point, and so he fails to understand the magic prestige of gold…" (SFEA, p. 217). In a Wellsian utopia, gold and other precious metals would be controlled by the society, but would be at the disposal of artists, to be used to produce things of beauty for public ornamentation and use. (Note also the passing comment about imagination and reason.)

51. Negley and Patrick, *The Quest for Utopia*, p. 333.
52. Jack Vance, *Big Planet* (New York: Ace Books, 1957), pp. 94–95.
53. 416d-417a.
54. *Laws*, 739c.
55. NWO, pp. 138, 139.
56. H.G. Wells, *This Misery of Boots* (n.p.: Folcroft Library Editions, 1973), p. 40.
57. NWO, p. 140.
58. *Ibid.*, p. 142.
59. *Ibid.*, p. 143.
60. STC, p. 403.
61. *Ibid.*, pp. 409–410. In *New Worlds For Old*, Wells speculates on "two collateral methods of home-building in the future." One is traditional long-term housing, including farms and vineyards, which will remain essentially unchanged. The other is limited-term housing, the character of which will change drastically:

> Nowadays such people are housed in the exploits of the jerry builder — all England is unsightly with their meagre pretentious villas and miserable cottages and tenement houses. Such homes in the Socialist future will certainly be supplied by the local authority, but they will be fair, decent houses by good architects, fitted to be clean and lit, airy and convenient, the homes of civilized people, sightly things altogether in a generous and orderly world [p. 145].

In fact, here Wells himself may have been too reliant on organized construction. There have been experiments in certain European countries in which the residents of publicly funded housing have been able to design their own apartments, with only the exteriors designed by professional architects. The results have invariably been better for the residents, though more expensive for the governments, but the former consideration has always given way to the latter. This, Wells would say, clearly inverts the proper priorities.

62. WB, p. 121.
63. OH, p. 1167; see MU, p. 286.
64. STC, p. 391.
65. More, *op. cit.*, p. 89.
66. Which is not to say that no utopias have imbibed deeply at the capitalist spring; as we have seen, aspects of Wells's own work, to go no further, suffer under this influence. Yet these aspects are not fundamental to the project as a whole, and can be modified without thereby falsifying the entirety of the rest.
67. *Politics*, 1263a27–28. "Indeed, we see that there is much more quarreling among those who have all things in common, though there are not many of them when compared with the vast numbers who have private property" (1263b22–26). *Where* we see this is unclear.
68. 1263b11–13.
69. Friedrich A. Hayek, *The Road to Serfdom* (Chicago: University of Chicago Press, 1945), p. pp. 103–104.
70. *Ibid.*, pp. 110–111.
71. *Ibid.*, p. 85.
72. *Politics*, 1263a31–33. In fact, Aristotle is not entirely consistent on this topic. Although he rejects holding property in common, he wavers on the necessity of restricting its acquisition, and never arrives at what is to be considered an appropriate amount in itself, as opposed to an appropriate amount in relation to the number of children had by the property owner. He remarks that "the equalization of property is one of the things that tend to prevent the citizens from quarreling. Not that the gain in this direction is very great" (1267a37–38). But the remedy for this limited gain is "to train the nobler sort of natures not to desire more, and to prevent the lower from getting more; that is to say, they must be kept down, but not ill-treated" (1267b6–7). In other words, if the citizenry is both properly educated and controlled the question of property is lessened. This ends up following Plato's line.
73. There are also good reasons for supposing that Aristotle's own views on private property weaken the force of his challenge against Plato. I will not examine this question here, as it is too far afield from the topic at hand, but it should be noted. On this, see T.H. Irwin, "Aristotle's Defense of Private Property," in David Keyt and Fred D. Miller, Jr., eds., *A Companion to Aristotle's Politics* (Oxford: Blackwell, 1991), pp. 200–225. After careful textual considerations, Irwin reaches the conclusion that "on Aristotle's own terms we have reason to conclude that his defense of private property is seriously defective" (p. 224).
74. In fact, it seems likely that, as my comments below shall suggest, no defense of private property can rest on the idea of private property in itself, and that any defense which is not rested thereon is really a defense of something else altogether, of which private property is but a subset. As this point would need considerably more development than I can supply here, and as it is not directly relevant to the discussion at hand, I shall do no more than indicate it.
75. Hayek, *op. cit.*, p. 72.
76. *Ibid.*, p. 73. Exactly why laws which cannot be seen as benefiting anyone in particular are ever created in the first place is a question which Hayek does not address. The creation of laws for the sake of creating laws seems a pointless, if not socially harmful, exercise.
77. *Ibid.*, p. 75.
78. *Ibid.*, p. 76.
79. Cf., e.g., the very conservative former Prime Minister of Canada Arthur Meighen, who attacks socialism on these same grounds: "Force has to come if the higher incentives go.... Freedom of enterprise is the very essence of our system of reward. Freedom of enterprise and political freedom live together and never can live apart. They never have lived apart and never will" (*Unrevised and Unrepented: Debating Speeches and Others* [Toronto: Clarke, Irwin, 1949], p. 443). Milton Friedman says much the same thing is much the same way. Like Hayek, neither ever showed any significant interest in the fates of individuals under the systems which they advocated, and, in Meighen's case, briefly led.
80. I say "putatively independent individual" to avoid such problems as parents holding coercive power over their children. It is by no means entirely clear, though, that, consistent with Hayek's account, the actions of at least the majority of parents most of the time could not be condemned, as the justifications for those actions are seldom thought out care-

fully, and are almost invariably directed toward a specific individual.

81. Hayek, *op. cit.*, p. 79.

82. *Ibid.*, p. 80.

83. *Ibid.*

84. *Ibid.*, p. 81 (emphasis mine). Note the implication that it is only union pickets who are violent; history suggests rather the opposite. Hayek admits that these regulations may also have "short-run effects on particular people which may be clearly known," but he denies that these effects are of importance in deciding to implement the regulations (*ibid.*).

85. *Ibid.*, p. 86. This is, of course, to assume that the government is justified in going to war in the first place (since, if it were not, such would be the time when free and open criticism of the strongest order would be most needed).

86. Hayek nowhere discusses such things as the ability of a corporation to virtually destroy the social fabric of whole cities by shutting down plants, for example, in line with the corporation's economic policies (maximizing of profits). This is because the corporation is private, and therefore seen by him as good, whereas unions are not (on what grounds is unclear). One may question the relative amounts of damage done to social structure by the exercises of power by the two groups.

87. *Ibid.*, p. 204.

88. *Ibid.*, p. 205.

89. Quoted in Naomi Klein, *The Shock Doctrine: The Rise of Disaster Capitalism* (New York: Metropolitan Books/Henry Holt, 2007), p. 50.

90. Hayek, p. 204. How Hayek, presumably "one of us," comprehends this he does not make clear; it is also unclear whether or not he feels that the millions of slaves who helped the market grow (in various ways) in the southern United States prior to the Civil War were, in their submission, helping to achieve something which, had they only recognized the fact, would have justified their captivity and sale.

91. Hayek himself refers to "the impersonal and seemingly irrational forces of the market" (*ibid.*, p. 205).

92. NWO, p. 149.

93. *Ibid.*, p. 153.

94. *Ibid.*

95. James Bonar, *Philosophy and Political Economy in Some of Their Historical Relations* 1832; rpt. (London: George Allen & Unwin, 1967), p. 102.

96. This is not a particularly radical point; as T.H. Green, certainly no revolutionary figure, wrote, "All the notions that we can form of human excellences and virtues are in some way relative to present imperfections" (quoted in I.M. Greengarten, *Thomas Hill Green and the Development of Liberal-Democratic Thought* [Toronto: University of Toronto Press, 1981], p. 41). (From the *Prolegomena to Ethics*).

97. H.G. Wells, *The New America: The New World* (London: Cresset Press, 1935), pp. 82–83.

98. WWH, p. 418.

99. 423b–c.

100. 369d.

101. *Nichomachean Ethics*, 1170b30–1171a1.

102. Although, it should be noted, it is likely that neither Aristotle's or Plato's account includes the number of slaves that each probably took for granted. There are no slaves, save of a purely mechanical sort, in any of Wells's states.

103. More, *op. cit.*, pp. 69, 70; it should be noted also that the island was created through the digging out of a fifteen mile stretch of a peninsula, so as to isolate the utopians from their neighbors (the parallel, in distance, with the situation of England relative to the continent is obvious).

104. A figure derived from More's description of each town as consisting "of six thousand households, not counting the country ones," with each household containing not "less than ten or more than sixteen adults — as they can't very well fix a figure for children" (*ibid.*, p 79).

105. For Plato, see 373d–e:
"And the territory which was formerly enough to support us will now be too small."

"That is undeniable."

"If we are to have enough for pasture and for plough, we shall have to cut a slice off our neighbours' territory. And if they too are no longer confining themselves to necessities and have embarked on the pursuit of unlimited material possessions, they will want a slice of ours too."

"The consequence is inevitable."

"And that will lead to war, Glaucon, will it not?"
"It will."
As this condition leads also to the creation of the guardians, on whom so much else rests, it would appear that Plato saw war as an inevitable concomitant of even the best possible human city-state.

More likewise took war for granted: "If the natives won't do what they're told, they're expelled from the area marked out for annexation. If they try to resist, the Utopians declare war — for they consider war perfectly justifiable, when one country denies another its natural right to derive nourishment from any soil which the original owners are not using themselves, but are merely holding on to as a worthless piece of property" (*Utopia*, p. 80).

106. "Humanism" here is to be understood as the placing of the collective interests of humanity as a whole at the center of political purpose. This in no way precludes the existence of religious attitudes of one sort or another, but only any religion which devalues either the unity of human politics and the diversity of human individuals.

107. MU, p. 11.

108. *The Way to World Peace* (London: Ernest Benn, 1930), p. 7 (emphasis Wells's).

109. For various versions of the military path to utopia, see, e.g., *The War in the Air* (1908), *The World Set Free* (1914), *The Shape of Things to Come* (1933), and *The Holy Terror* (1939). It must be stressed that this is not a necessary path on Wells's account, but only a regrettably probable one.

110. MU, p. 12.

111. G.W.F. Hegel, *Hegel's Philosophy of Right*, trans. T.M. Knox (London: Oxford University Press, 1979), p. 209 (¶324).

112. *Ibid.*, pp. 295–296 (Addition 188).

113. Since one of the frequent effects of powerful literary works is to create feelings of compassion for non-existent individuals, an argument based in compassion can to some extent appeal to the individual's prior experience and attempt, by analogy, to move them away from support for, in this case, war. That such an outcome is at least possible is illustrated by, among other things, the effect of John Galsworthy's play *Justice*, "Winston Churchill was so much impressed by the play that he put into immediate effect certain measures for prison reform, including reducing the hours of solitary confinement" (Catherine Dupré, *John Galsworthy: A Biography* [New York: Coward, McCann & Geoghegan, 1976], pp. 153–154). An even greater impact was had by Harriet Beecher Stowe's *Uncle Tom's Cabin* (although part of that impact contributed to the United States's Civil War, which in itself was presumably not among her aims). Other examples, including some involving Wells's own works, could be given.

In this context, it is interesting also to note that the physicist Leo Szilard refused to publish certain of his results on atomic reactions because he remembered all too vividly the description of atomic warfare in Wells's 1914 novel *The World Set Free* (in which Wells in fact coined the term atomic bomb). Szilard, who read the book in 1932, found the parts of it concerned with atomic warfare "exceedingly vivid and realistic," although he was leery of its later utopian aspects. A year later he began to think seriously about the possibility of splitting an atom in such a way as to sustain a chain reaction. He describes the sequel:

In the spring of 1934 I had applied for a patent which described the laws governing such a chain reaction. This was the first time, I think, that the concept of critical mass was developed and that a chain reaction was seriously discussed. Knowing what this would mean — and I knew it because I had read H.G. Wells — I did not want this patent to become public.

Szilard commented in a contemporary letter, regarding the consequences of the use of atomic energy, that "the forecast of the writers may prove to be more accurate than the scientists" (Leo Szilard, *Leo Szilard: His Version of the Facts: Selected Recollections and Correspondence*, ed. Spencer R. Weart and Gertrud Weiss Szilard [Cambridge, MA: MIT Press, 1978], pp. 16, 18, 38).

A similar reaction to the same novel was had by the physicist Joseph Rotblat, who read it during the 1920s and still remembered its impact seventy years later (Joseph Rotblat, personal communication, March 30, 1998); Rotblat ranked Wells with Bertrand Russell and Albert Einstein as a figure of inspirational importance to his own career as a proponent of the peaceful use of science.

114. But note that if the response is given that wars are in fact truly *necessary* at a metaphysical level then both the objection from human suffering and the justification of war as an avoidance of stagnation lose any moral weight; what cannot be otherwise cannot be judged morally.

115. William James, *Essays on Faith and Morals* (New York: Meridian, 1962), pp. 316–317.

116. *Ibid.*, pp. 322–323. This was written in 1910, well before the horrors of modern technological warfare were much more than a fantasy.

117. *Ibid.*, p. 321.

118. Klein, op. cit., pp. 9–10.

119. *Ibid.*, p. 451.

120. Anton Rubinstein, *Autobiography*, trans. Aline Delano (St. Clair Shores, MI: Scholarly Press, 1970), pp. 76–77 (all ellipses Rubinstein's). Surely there is a prefiguration of Orson Welles's great, and chilling, speech about democracy in *The Third Man* here.

121. In Barry Feinberg and Ronald Kasrils, eds., *Dear Bertrand Russell: A selection of his correspondence with the general public 1950-1968* (London: George Allen and Unwin, 1969), p. 125.

122. H.G. Wells, *Imperialism and the Open Conspiracy* (London: Faber & Faber, 1929), p. 13.

123. This, it may be necessary to remark, applies to the earlier stages of the utopian process, in which a formal government still exists. In the later stages, the whole of the human race is the government.

124. H.G. Wells, *Mr. Britling Sees It Through* (New York: Macmillan, 1916), p. 68.

125. "Most utopian" meaning most utopian by the scale of the book at hand, a history of the world written in the early twenty-second century, not by the scale of all history.

126. *World Encyclopedia*, p. 17.

127. It may be necessary here to acknowledge that my examination of utopian ideals is concerned with the vast majority of utopian thinkers who have taken freedom of some sort, even if limited in extent, to be one of the elements of their vision. There are a few utopias (B.F. Skinner's *Walden Two*, e.g.) in which freedom is arguably a negative value. I do not believe that the validity of what I am arguing is affected by the existence of these utopian visions, but I should acknowledge that I am not taking them into account.

Chapter 4

1. MU, p. 32.
2. AF, pp. 45–46.
3. Simone De Beauvoir, *The Ethics of Ambiguity* (New York: Philosophical Library, 1948), p. 24.
4. *Ibid.*
5. *Die Dreigroschenoper.*
6. I say "or merely perceived" because scarcity consists both in factual relations (a limited supply of food which means that some will necessarily starve at this point, regardless of the reasons behind the limitation, e.g.) and in relations of desire without necessity (the moral savages who murder people for their designer shoes, which product is scarce for no reason other than decisions by others to render it so). Both experienced material scarcities may lead to morally judicable actions, but in one case the choice is to some degree forced by physiologically necessity in itself, while in the other the choice is forced only by social structures (which, however coercive, are grounded purely in social relations, not biological requirements common to all persons).

7. Jean-Paul Sartre, *Critique of Dialectical Reason*, trans. Alan Sheridan-Smith (London: Verso, 1982), p. 128. The discussion of scarcity in relation to human history and society, pages 122–139, is extremely suggestive and helpful. That Wells's conception of the importance of overcoming scarcity in the formation and structuring of human society is compatible with this is implicit in his discussion of "How Man Became an Economic Animal" in *The Work, Wealth, and Happiness of Mankind*, pp. 35–61.

8. Philosophers may object that this ignores deontological ethics altogether. But a deontological approach requires consideration of the consequences as well, with the difference that the consequences considered are the results of a potential universalization of the action under examination. This makes no difference here; if I ought not to lie because the universalization of lying would logically undercut the very purpose of lying, the point

remains that it is the imagined consequence of my action writ large which is the crux of its moral refutation. Of course, Wells's position, Sartre's position, and (if I may so immodestly add) my own position taken together include a stronger claim: since in fact no action is ever universalized, logical claims about what would happen if it were are of little point in discussing morality as lived. Only the universal claims of freedom, which appear as soon as moral claims appear, can sustain the weight needed here.

It is for this reason that some philosophers have denied the possibility of duty, at least as traditionally understood. Cf., e.g., G.E. Moore, *Principia Ethica*, § 91, where he argues that we can have a duty only to produce the best results. Knowledge of duty rests, therefore, upon the certainty that no other action is as good or better than the one contemplated. After indicating the vast scope of the knowledge necessary in order to know that our action is the best possible, Moore concludes that "we can never have any reason to suppose that an action is our duty: we can never be sure that any action will produce the greatest value possible" (Buffalo: Prometheus, 1988, p. 149).

9. Jean-Paul Sartre, *Existentialism and Humanism*, trans. Philip Mairet (London: Methuen, 1948), pp. 51–52.

10. SL, p. 1390.

11. *The History of Mr. Polly* (New York: Press of the Reader's Club, 1941), pp. 261–262.

12. *The Secret Places of the Heart* (New York: Macmillan, 1922), p. 12.

13. MU, pp. 299–300.

14. NWO, pp. 202–203.

15. Kateb, *Utopia and Its Enemies*, pp. 198, 199.

16. Alfred Borrello, *H.G. Wells: Author in Agony* (Carbondale: Southern Illinois University Press, 1973), p. 87. Borrello, who implicitly claims that he, unlike Wells, has seen humanity correctly, later adds to the charges the claim that Wells, "in his failure to come directly to grip with the root cause of humanity's difficulties [that is, the irremediably flawed essence of being human], he supplied answers that were and are too simple to believe and to idealistic to be completely achieved. As a result, he committed the unpardonable aesthetic sin of misreading human nature.... He reduced human nature to rigid, immutable, and predictable patterns" (*ibid.*, p. 120). By now the error in the latter charge should need no further refutation.

(It may be supererogatory to point out the use of the masculine pronoun in both Kateb and Borrello, but there is an ambiguity present in their claims as expressed which is not present for the denier of human nature. Many claims have been advanced regarding the essential difference, in significant psychological ways, of men and women; in such claims, women are usually held to be inherently less destructive. Where an essential claim of the sort made by Kateb and Borrello is concerned, such further essential claims need to be distinguished and demonstrated false, since otherwise one may sensibly argue that the answer to their problem is simple: let the women run utopia. On this see, e.g., Carol Gilligan's *In a Different Voice: Psychological Theory and Women's Development* or Ashley Montagu's *The Natural Superiority of Women*. There are, of course, many similar texts, serious in varying degrees; their very existence poses a problem for the theorist of a unitary human nature.)

17. Bruno Bettelheim, *The Children of the Dream* (London: Macmillan, 1969), p. 175. This is not, of course, meant to suggest that Wells advocated anything quite like kibbutzim as the means to his world peace (although certain vaguely detailed elements in his discussions might well overlap with the idea). He would probably agree with Bettelheim's assessment of the applicability of the kibbutz structure to life on a world scale: "even the most cursory inspection convinces one that kibbutz society could not survive economically without drawing on the highly developed technology of surrounding Israel" (*ibid.*, p. 283). The effects of communal education and living reach far beyond interpersonal violence during childhood. Bettelheim indicates many other differences between kibbutz-raised adults and others; the range and scope of these effects is impressive and thought-provoking.

18. Please note that I am not here arguing either that there is a genetic flaw which leads human beings ineluctably into violent or destructive behavior or that society should embark upon a program of genetic engineer-

ing to eradicate the presumed flaw. I am merely pointing out that the essentialist who predicates such a flaw has not yet completed their argument against attempts to at least ameliorate its effects.

Nonetheless, that Wells was aware of the evolutionary heritage against which we would have to fight is amply clear. See, e.g., *The Croquet Player*, a fable concerned entirely with the topic.

19. One can, of course, adopt a full blown philosophical dualism here, but one is still left with the problem that all dualists have faced without being able to provide a completely satisfactory answer: how do the two utterly different substances manage to interact at all? On the other hand, a deterministic monism such as Spinoza's solves the problem at the cost of getting rid of political freedom and genuine morality altogether. A monism which retains freedom must give up the supernatural, since otherwise it is postulating the idea that the single substance both is and is not capable of being understood naturally.

20. See his *Man and the State* (Chicago: University of Chicago Press, 1956), pp. 189, 216. Maritain, as a Catholic, most probably accepted (and certainly did not deny) the doctrine of original sin, yet did not see it as vitiating any hope for a peaceful world state.

21. H.G. Wells, *The Croquet Player* (New York: Viking Press, 1937), pp. 89 *et seq.*

22. FHS, p. 288.

23. Fromm, *To Have or to Be?*, p. 6.

24. *Ibid.*, p. 81.

25. *Ibid.*, p. 78.

26. D, pp. 249, 257.

27. D, p. 73.

28. Christopher Caudwell, *The Concept of Freedom* (London: Lawrence & Wishart, 1977), p. 123.

29. Christopher Caudwell, *Studies in a Dying Culture* (New York: Dodd Mead, 1948), p. 87.

30. SL, p. 1393 (emphases mine).

31. This is in fact a problem for Marxist determinism of any stripe; if individual consciousness is wholly shaped by class situation, there is neither need nor room for revolutionary agitation. One does not agitate for what must come of its own accord and on its own schedule; it would be like agitating for an avalanche to hasten its pace as it rolls down a mountainside. If, on the other hand, agitation is potentially effective, then class consciousness and economic determinism are clearly not both sufficient and necessary causes for the revolution. Traditional Marxism is in fact every bit as teleological and reliant upon a unitary consciousness as the systems it seeks to replace, a fact which helps explain the tensions between conventional Marxism and feminist or race-based social analyses and movements.

32. FM p. 45. Wells here echoes the magnificent summation of the state of lawless nature given by Thomas Hobbes in *Leviathan*:

> In such condition, there is no place for Industry; because the fruit thereof is uncertain: and consequently no Culture of the Earth; no Navigation, nor use of the commodities that may be imported by Sea; no commodoius building; no Instruments of moving, and removing such things as require much force; no Knowledge of the face of the Earth; no account of Time; no Arts; no Letters; no Society; and which is worst of all, continuall feare, and danger of violent death; And the life of man. solitary, poore, nasty, brutish, and short [Thomas Hobbes, *Leviathan* (Harmondsworth: Penguin, 1980), p. 186 (Part I, Chapter XIII)].

The relevance of this description to the lawless areas of Africa or the drug dealer infested sections of Mexican and American cities requires little comment. Wells fully understood that laws are necessary, along with the means to enforce them; the question, as always, is which portion, and what percentage, of the populace will genuinely benefit from the laws and their enforcement.

33. MLG, p. 252; the principles are articulated and discussed on pp. 252–256.

34. MLG, p. 74. In the aforementioned critique of Wells by Leon Stover, *Men Like Gods* is not discussed; had Stover taken this book, or *The Open Conspiracy*, into consideration, his discussion of the role of the state in Wells would necessarily have been quite different.

35. Morton, *op. cit.*, p.189.

36. Bernard Bosanquet, *The Value and Destiny of the Individual* (London: Macmillan, 1923), p. 50.

37. H.G. Wells, *The First Men in the Moon*

(London: W. Collins Sons, n.d.), pp. 227–228. Morton's quotation of it, from an unspecified edition of 1901, is found in his book, pp. 189–190.

38. Morton, *op. cit.*, p. 190.
39. All quotations from *First Men in the Moon*, p. 232.
40. *Ibid.*, p. 234.
41. MU, p. 370.
42. MU, p. 226. Why utopia has a restorative effect on hair growth is never explained.
43. WWH, p. 275. Wells modifies here ideas taken from William James and Joseph Popper-Lynkeus; See also WWH, p. 689.
44. More, *op. cit.*, p. 76.
45. *Ibid.*, p. 77.
46. Oddly enough Wells rarely mentions, let alone explores, universal health care as a concomitant to his ideas concerning income. Here we see an example of reality superseding utopia. Widespread recognition that unexpected health care costs are every bit as devastating as loss of income to individual freedom and ability to make plans has resulted in the creation of various health coverage plans for the citizenry of at least the more democratic nations, something not foreseen by Wells at all.
47. STC, pp. 395–396.
48. *Ibid.*, p. 410.
49. Almost certainly Wells here means public architecture, through which the aspirations and attitudes of a particularly society are encapsulated and given solid form. In a later stage of utopia, of course, the distinction between public architecture and private (houses, etc.) will vanish, since the aesthetic imagination of architects will be at all levels a reflection of the aspirations of humanity.
50. All quotes from WWH, p. 784. Cf. also the comments, already quoted from *A Year of Prophesying*, on the attempts of many city dwellers to create some sense of beauty through small gardens and the like.
51. OH, p. 1164.
52. Eva Figes, *Tragedy and Social Evolution* (New York: Persea Books, 1990), p. 145. Cf. the views of Plato in *Republic*.
53. STC, p. 361.
54. EA, p. 422.
55. Sartre, *Life/Situations*, pp. 11, 13.
56. MLG, p. 256.
57. *Ibid.*, p. 404.
58. *Republic* 462b.
59. 457c–d.
60. 464a.
61. 464e.
62. 459d–e.
63. 458d.
64. 461b.
65. MLG, p. 78.
66. *Ibid.*, p. 80. Wells's admittedly imperfect and fumbling attempts to realize this ideal brought more censure on his head than any other aspect of his life. Many anti-Wellsians have used his life as a basis for rejecting his ideas, which at least has the advantage of not requiring any serious consideration of the latter.
67. D, p. 73.
68. AF, p. 180.

Chapter 5

1. *Republic* 386b.
2. 486b.
3. *Phaedo* 63b–c. Compare this to works such as John Fiske's *Outlines of Cosmic Philosophy* (1874, but based on lectures dating back as far as 1869). Fiske, at one time quite widely read and respected, based his work as much on Spencer as on Darwin, but his name remained associated with the attempt to render Darwinism palatable to the spiritual. His motives were straightforwardly expressed: "While Knowledge grows and old beliefs fall away and creed succeeds to creed," he wrote,

> nevertheless that Faith which makes the innermost essence of religion is indestructible. Were it not for the steadfast conviction that this is so, what could sustain us in dealing with questions so mighty and so awful that one is sometimes fain to shrink from facing their full import, lest the mind be overwhelmed and forever paralyzed by the sense of its nothingness? [*ibid.*, 13th edition (Boston: Houghton, Mifflin), 1892, Vol. 1, p. xii].

Such blatant attempts to sugarcoat the overwhelming message of suffering and death found in organic evolution tend to be derided today, yet they differ little from Socrates's calm assurances, save in their origin. Fiske, in fact, is an often thoughtful and thought-provoking writer.

4. 64a. Not, however, suicide, on the grounds that we are the possessions of the gods, who would be angry should we act to end our own lives.

5. See, on this, e.g., T.M. Robinson, *Plato's Psychology* (Toronto: University of Toronto Press, 1970), *passim*; he distinguishes at least five different senses of "soul" in the *Phaedo* alone.

6. *Utopia*, p. 91.

7. Miguel de Unamuno, *Tragic Sense of Life* (New York: Dover, 1954), p. 40.

8. *Ibid.*, p. 45.

9. Martin Heidegger, *Being and Time*, trans. John Macquarrie and Edward Robinson (New York: Harper & Row, 1962), p. 294 (emphasis Heidegger's).

10. *Ibid.*, p. 310.

11. *Ibid.*, p. 307.

12. FLT, p. 110.

13. MLG, p. 268; D, pp. 60–61.

14. WWC, p. 782.

15. H.G. Wells, *Select Conversations with an Uncle (Now Extinct)* (London: University of North London Press, 1992), p. 23.

16. 42/44, p. 171.

17. H.G. Wells, *The Conquest of Time* (Amherst, MA: Prometheus, 1995), p. 31.

18. One thinks here of the witty yet serious opening of G.K. Chesterton's autobiography: "Bowing down in blind credulity, as is my custom, before mere authority and the tradition of the elders, superstitiously swallowing a story I could not test at the time by experient or private judgment, I am firmly of the opinion that I was born on the 29th of May, 1874..." (*The Autobiography of G.K. Chesterton* [New York: Sheed and Ward, 1936], p. 1).

19. For an example of such a person, and of the peculiar consequences of a mental construction of the self, see Oliver Sacks, "A Matter of Identity," chapter 12 (pp. 108–115) in *The Man Who Mistook His Wife For a Hat* (n.p.: HarperPerennial, 1990). "Mr. Thompson" lives in a continual present, remembering "nothing for more than a few seconds." His solution, though, is a poignant shadow of precisely the idea under discussion here; "Abysses of amnesia continually opened beneath him, but he would bridge them, nimbly, by fluent confabulations and fictions of all kinds" (p. 109). As Sacks remarks later in the book, this sort of activity is fundamentally human; "It is this narrative or symbolic power which gives *a sense of the world*—a concrete reality in the imaginative form of symbol and story—when abstract thought can provide nothing at all" (p. 184).

20. AD, p. 283. (Ellipses, for once, not Wells's.)

21. H.G. Wells, *God the Invisible King* (New York: Macmillan, 1917), pp. 70–71.

22. H.G. Wells, *Boon, The Mind of the Race, The Wild Asses of the Devil, and The Last Trump: Being a First Selection from the Literary Remains of George Boon, Appropriate to the Times. Prepared for publication by Reginald Bliss, with an Ambiguous Introduction by H.G. Wells* (New York: George H. Doran, 1915), pp. 47–48. This is one of Wells's multi-leveled books; despite the various names, the whole thing is by him.

23. Pierre Teilhard de Chardin, *The Making of a Mind: Letters from a Soldier-Priest 1914-1919* (London: Collins, 1965), pp. 277, 280 (emphasis his). Teilhard is not the only theologically-oriented thinker influenced by Wells's religious conceptions; another was Charles Hartshorne, a major figure in process theology. Years after first reading *Mr. Britling Sees It Through*, Hartshorne acknowledged the impact of its conception of a limited god; Wells, Hartshorne said, "expresses this new faith with astonishing for me then—and indeed even now if I reread it—convincing eloquence. Rarely indeed has any novelist so explicitly and powerfully argued for a definite theological view" (Lewis Edwin Hahn, ed., *The Philosophy of Charles Hartshorne* [Evanston, IL: Library of Living Philosophers, 1991], p. 16). Hartshorne goes on to say that Wells's later abandonment of this position confirmed his own similar conclusions. Wells would presumably regard this as evidence of his having misled an intelligent reader. How much Hartshorne's later philosophical development owes to Wells's evolutionary utopianism is uncertain, but there are distinct parallels.

24. H.G. Wells, *The New Machiavelli* (London: John Lane/Bodley Head, 1911), pp. 321–322 (ellipses mine).

25. Anselm Feuerbach, *Thoughts on Death and Immortality* (Berkeley: University of California Press, 1980), p. 121.

26. *Ibid.*, p. 122.

27. H.G. Wells, *H.G. Wells in Love: Postscript to An Experiment in Autobiography*, ed. G.P. Wells (Boston: Little, Brown, 1984), pp. 53–54.

28. *Mind at the End of Its Tether* (New York: Didier, 1946), p. 18.

29. *You Can't Be Too Careful*, p. 298.

30. Jean-Paul Sartre, trans. Bernard Frechtman, *The Words* (New York: George Braziller, 1964), pp. 249–250.

31. CV, pp. 65–66.

32. Reprinted in *Early Writings, op. cit.*, p. 169.

33. H.G. Wells, *The Undying Fire* (New York: Macmillan, 1919), p. 160.

34. WWH, p. 894.

35. *Ibid*.

36. Lukács, *The Theory of the Novel*, p. 115.

37. Oscar Wilde, *The Soul of Man Under Socialism and Other Essays* (New York: Harper and Row, 1970), p. 246.

38. Ludwig Wittgenstein, *Tractatus Logico-Philosophicus*, trans. D.F Pears and B.F. McGuinness (London: Routledge & Kegan Paul, 1978), 6.4311.

39. WWH, p. 895.

40. For some of the bizarre concepts which extend the domain of life beyond the death of our universe, see Paul Davies, *The Last Three Minutes: Conjectures About the Ultimate Fate of the Universe* (New York: Basic Books, 1994). A sample: "In the very far future, when our own universe is becoming uninhabitable or approaching a big crunch, our descendants may decide to get out for good by initiating the budding process [of a new universe] and then scrambling through the umbilical wormhole into the universe next door before it pinches off—the ultimate in emigration" (pp. 137–138). Although I have deliberately chosen a rather exotic hypothesis, Davies's book is not short on them, all of which he is very careful to qualify heavily. Nonetheless, the imagination will find much to play with in this book, even with due regard for Davies's warnings.

41. MLG, p. 215. Here, and indeed throughout Well's utopianism, there appears to be a connection with the thought of Ernst Bloch, who, in his major work, described hope as "a place in the world which is as inhabited as the best civilized land and as unexplored as the Antarctic." Certainly such Blochian claims as the following are redolent of Wells's position, though not his language: "Expectation, hope, intention towards possibility that has still not become: this is not only a basic feature of human consciousness, but, concretely corrected and grasped, a basic determination within objective reality as a whole" (*The Principle of Hope* [London: Basil Blackwell, 1986], pp. 6, 7) The connection, though, is dissolved by Bloch's commitment to his own version of teleological Marxism, which I will not attempt to develop here. Bloch considered Wells to be the "first champion" of the "bourgeois-democratic future," but saw no virtue in this. Such a future "does not wear such a war-like death-mask as fascism. Instead it wears moral make-up, and feigns human rights as if the capitalist whore could become a virgin again" (p. 584). Specifically, Bloch dismisses Wells as incoherent:

> Half a dozen dream-trains, time-machines, and Mr Britlings who write until daybreak were dispatched into the future by Wells and brought back snapshots. And it is characteristic here that hardly one of these snapshots shows related landscapes ... [p. 617].

Bloch's criticism in fact singles out the very thing which makes Wellsian evolutionary utopianism anti-teleological in its means as well as its aims, and which makes hope something which must cease only with the cessation of self-consciousness, rather than with the attainment of a final state of being. Nonetheless, there *is* a fruitful link to be made here; but it would require a pruning of Bloch's prior ideological commitments.

42. Romolo Runcini, "H.G. Wells and Futurity," in Patrick Parrinder and Christopher Rolfe, eds., *H.G. Wells Under Revision: Proceedings of the International H.G. Wells Symposium London, July 1986*, pp. 153–161, p. 161.

43. WWH, p. 895.

Bibliography

Adorno, Theodor. *Prisms*. Cambridge: MIT Press, 1992.
Arendt, Hannah. *Between Past and Future: Eight Exercises in Political Thought*. Harmondsworth: Penguin, 1993.
_____. *The Human Condition*. Chicago: University of Chicago Press, 1998.
Aristotle. *The Complete Works of Aristotle: The Revised Oxford Translation*. Various translators. Princeton, NJ: Princeton University Press, 1984.
Ayer, A.J. *The Meaning of Life*. New York: Charles Scribner's Sons, 1990.
Beauvoir, Simone De. *The Ethics of Ambiguity*. New York: Philosophical Library, 1948.
Berkeley, George. *A Treatise Concerning the Principles of Human Knowledge*. In *The Empiricists*. Garden City, NY: Dolphin, n.d.
Bettelheim, Bruno. *The Children of the Dream*. London: Macmillan, 1969.
Black, Max. *The Labyrinth of Language*. New York: Mentor, 1968.
Bloch, Ernst. *The Principle of Hope*. London: Basil Blackwell, 1986.
Bonar, James. *Philosophy and Political Economy in Some of Their Historical Relations*. London: George Allen & Unwin, 1967.
Borrello, Alfred. *H.G. Wells: Author in Agony*. Carbondale: Southern Illinois University Press, 1973.
Bosanquet, Bernard. *The Value and Destiny of the Individual*. London: Macmillan, 1923.
Buber, Martin. *Paths in Utopia*. New York: Collier, 1988.
Busch, Justin E.A. "Utopia and Death: An Essay in Meaning." *The Undying Fire: The Journal of the H.G. Wells Society, the Americas*, #1 (2002) (This was drawn from the material found in Chapter Five).
Caudwell, Christopher. *The Concept of Freedom*. London: Lawrence & Wishart, 1977.
_____. *Studies in a Dying Culture*. New York: Dodd Mead, 1948.
Caws, Peter. *Sartre*. London: Routledge & Kegan Paul, 1979.
Chesterton, G.K. *The Autobiography of G.K. Chesterton*. New York: Sheed and Ward, 1936.
Crossman, R.H.S. "Plato and the Perfect State." In Thomas Landon Thorson, ed., *Plato: Totalitarian or Democrat?* Englewood Cliffs, NJ: Prentice-Hall, 1963. pp. 15–40.
Dahrendorf, Ralf. "Out of Utopia: Toward a Reorientation of Sociological Analysis." In Kateb, George, ed., *Utopia*. New York: Atherton Press, 1971. pp. 103–126.
Davies, Paul. *The Last Three Minutes: Conjectures About the Ultimate Fate of the Universe*. New York: Basic Books, 1994.
Draper, Michael. *H.G. Wells*. New York: St. Martin's, 1988.
Dupré, Catherine. *John Galsworthy: A Biography*. New York: Coward, McCann & Geoghegan, 1976.
Feinberg, Barry, and Ronald Kasrils, eds. *Dear Bertrand Russell: A Selection of His Correspondence with the General Public 1950–1968*. London: George Allen and Unwin, 1969.
Feuerbach, Anselm. *Thoughts on Death and Immortality*. Berkeley: University of California Press, 1980.
Figes, Eva. *Tragedy and Social Evolution*. New York: Persea Books, 1990.

Findley, Timothy. *Headhunter*. Toronto: Harper, 1997.

Fiske, John. *Outlines of Cosmic Philosophy*. Boston: Houghton, Mifflin, 1892.

Flew, Antony. "Introduction." *A Dictionary of Philosophy*. London: Pan, 1984. pp. vii-xi.

Fromm, Erich. *To Have or to Be?* New York: Continuum, 1997.

Gass, William. *Fiction and the Figures of Life*. New York: Vintage, 1972.

Goethe, Wolfgang. *Faust*. Translated by W.H. Van Der Smissen. London: Dent, 1926; Translated by George Madison Priest. New York: Covici-Friede, 1932.

Greengarten, I.M. *Thomas Hill Green and the Development of Liberal-Democratic Thought*. Toronto: University of Toronto Press, 1981.

Grierson, John. *Grierson on Documentary*. Ed. Forsyth Hardy. London: Collins, 1946.

Hahn, Lewis Edwin, ed. *The Philosophy of Charles Hartshorne*. Evanston, IL: Library of Living Philosophers, 1991.

Hayek, Friedrich. *The Road to Serfdom*. Chicago: University of Chicago Press, 1945.

Haynes, Roslynn D. *H.G. Wells: Discoverer of the Future: The Influence of Science on His Thought*. New York: New York University Press, 1980.

Hegel, G.W.F. *Hegel's Philosophy of Right*. Translated by T.M. Knox. London: Oxford University Press, 1979.

Heidegger, Martin. *Being and Time*. Translated by John Macquarrie and Edward Robinson. New York: Harper and Row, 1962.

Heilbroner, Robert. *An Inquiry into the Human Prospect*. New York: W.W. Norton, 1974.

Hobbes, Thomas. *Leviathan*. Harmondsworth: Penguin, 1980

James, William. *Essays on Faith and Morals*. New York: Meridian, 1962.

Johnson, A.H. *Whitehead's Theory of Reality*. New York: Dover, 1962.

Kant, Immanuel. *Perpetual Peace and Other Essays*. Translated by Ted Humphrey. Indianapolis: Hackett, 1988.

Kemp, Peter. *H.G. Wells and the Culminating Ape*. New York : St. Martin's Press, 1996.

Keyt, David, and Fred D. Miller, Jr., eds. *A Companion to Aristotle's* Politics. Oxford: Blackwell, 1991.

Klein, Naomi. *The Shock Doctrine: The Rise of Disaster Capitalism*. New York: Metropolitan/Henry Holt, 2007.

Kostelanetz, Richard, ed. *Esthetics Contemporary*. Buffalo, NY: Prometheus, 1989.

Lukács, Georg. *The Theory of the Novel*. Translated by Anna Bostock. Cambridge: MIT Press, 1990.

Mackenzie, Norman, and Jeanne Mackenzie. *H.G. Wells: A Biography*. New York: Simon and Schuster, 1973.

Mannheim, Karl. *Ideology and Utopia*. New York: Harvest, n.d.

Manuel, Frank, ed. *Utopias and Utopian Thought: A Timely Appraisal*. Boston: Beacon Press, 1971.

Manuel, Frank E., and Fritzie P. Manuel. *Utopian Thought in the Western World*. Oxford: Basil Blackwell, 1979.

Marcuse, Herbert. *The Aesthetics Dimension: Toward a Critique of Marxist Aesthetics*. Boston: Beacon Press, 1978.

Maritain, Jacques. *Man and the State*. Chicago: University of Chicago Press, 1956.

McCabe, Joseph. *H.G. Wells and His Creed: An Examination of the Chief Constructive Proposals in Literature*. Girard, KS: Haldeman-Julius, 1944 (Little Blue Book No. 1806)

Meighen, Arthur. *Unrevised and Unrepented: Debating Speeches and Others*. Toronto: Clarke, Irwin, and Co., 1949.

Moore, G.E. *Principia Ethica*. Buffalo, NY: Prometheus, 1988.

More, Thomas. *Utopia*. Translated by Paul Turner. Harmondsworth: Penguin, 1972.

Morgan, Robin. *The Anatomy of Freedom: Feminism, Physics, and Global Politics*. Garden City, NY: Anchor Press/Doubleday, 1982.

Morton, A.L. *The English Utopia*. London: Lawrence & Wishart, 1952.

Murray, Brian. *H.G. Wells*. New York: Continuum, 1990.

Negley, Glenn, and J. Max Patrick. *The Quest for Utopia*. New York: Henry Schuman, 1952.

Nussbaum, Martha. *Love's Knowledge: Essays on Philosophy and Literature*. New York: Oxford University Press, 1992.

Parrinder, Patrick, ed. *H. G. Wells: The Critical Heritage*. London: Routledge and Kegan Paul, 1972.

_____ and Rolfe, Christopher, eds. *H. G.*

Wells Under Revision: Proceedings of the International H.G. Wells Symposium, London, July 1986. Selinsgrove, PA: Susquehanna University Press, 1990.

Pieper, Joseph. *Leisure: The Basis of Culture.* New York: Mentor, 1963.

Plato. *The Collected Dialogues of Plato, Including the Letters.* Ed. Edith Hamilton and Huntington Cairns. Princeton, NJ: Princeton University Press, 1989. (Bollingen Series LXXI)

_____. *The Republic.* Translated by Desmond Lee. Harmondsworth: Penguin, 1967.

Robinson. T.M. *Plato's Psychology.* Toronto: University of Toronto Press, 1970.

Rubinstein, Anton. *Autobiography.* Translated by Aline Delano. St. Clair Shores, MI: Scholarly Press, 1970.

Russell, Bertrand. *Fact and Fiction.* London: George Allen and Unwin, 1961.

_____. *The Principles of Mathematics.* London: George Allen and Unwin, 1948.

Sacks, Oliver. *The Man Who Mistook His Wife for a Hat and Other Clinical Tales.* New York: Harper, 1990.

Santayana, George. *Interpretations of Poetry and Religion.* New York: Harper and Bros., 1957.

_____. *Three Philosophical Poets: Lucretius, Dante, Goethe.* Cambridge, MA: Harvard University Press, 1945.

Sartre, Jean-Paul. *Critique of Dialectical Reason.* Translated by Alan Sheridan-Smith. London: Verso, 1982.

_____. *Existentialism and Humanism.* Translated by Philip Mairet. London: Methuen, 1948.

_____. *The Family Idiot.* Vol. 1. Translated by Carol Cosman. Chicago: University of Chicago Press, 1981.

_____. *Life/Situations.* New York: Pantheon, 1977.

_____. *The Words.* Translated by Bernard Frechtman. New York: George Braziller, 1964.

Schilpp, Paul A., ed. *The Philosophy of Bertrand Russell.* Evanston, IL: Library of Living Philosophers, 1946.

_____, *The Philosophy of C.D. Broad.* New York: Library of Living Philosophers, 1959, pp. 43, 46

_____. *The Philosophy of George Santayana.* New York: Library of Living Philosophers, 1951.

Sterne, Laurence. *The Life and Opinions of Tristram Shandy, Gentleman.* N.p.: Books, Inc., 1942.

Stover, Leon. *The Prophetic Soul: A Reading of H.G. Wells's* Things to Come. Jefferson, NC: McFarland, 1987.

Szilard, Leo. *Leo Szilard: His Version of the Facts: Selected Recollections and Correspondence.* Ed. Spencer R. Weart and Gertrude Weiss Szilard. Cambridge, MA: MIT Press, 1978.

Teilhard de Chardin, Pierre. *The Making of a Mind: Letters from a Soldier-Priest 1914–1918.* London: Collins, 1965.

Tenner, Edward. "The Life of Chairs: How *Homo sapiens* became *Homo sedens*—and at what cost." *Harvard Magazine*, January-February 1997, Vol. 99, #3, pp. 46–53.

Turner, Mark. *The Literary Mind: The Origins of Thought and Language.* New York: Oxford University Press, 1998.

Unamuno, Miguel de. *Tragic Sense of Life.* New York: Dover, 1954.

Urban, Wilbur Marshall. *Language and Reality: The Philosophy of Language and the Principles of Symbolism.* London: George Allen and Unwin, 1951.

Vance, Jack. *Big Planet.* New York: Ace, 1957.

Wagar, W. Warren. *H.G. Wells and the World State.* New Haven: Yale University Press, 1961.

_____. *H.G. Wells: Traversing Time.* Middletown, CT: Wesleyan University Press, 2004.

Wells, H.G. *All Aboard for Ararat.* London: Secker and Warburg, 1940.

_____. *The Anatomy of Frustration: A Modern Synthesis.* New York: Macmillan, 1936.

_____. *Apropos of Dolores.* New York: Scribner's, 1938.

_____. *Babes in the Darkling Wood.* New York: Alliance, 1940.

_____. *Boon, The Mind of the Race, The Wild Asses of the Devil, and The Last Trump: Being a First Selection from the Literary Remains of George Boon, Appropriate to the Times. Prepared for publication by Reginald Bliss, with an Ambiguous Introduction by H.G. Wells.* New York: George H. Doran, 1915.

_____. *The Camford Visitation.* London: Methuen, 1937.

_____. *The Conquest of Time.* Amherst, MA: Prometheus, 1995.

_____. *Crux Ansata.* New York: Agora, 1944.

———. *The Discovery of the Future*. London: Jonathan Cape, 1925.
———. *The Dream*. New York: Macmillan, 1924.
———. *Early Writings in Science and Science Fiction*. Eds. Robert M. Philmus and David Y. Hughes. Berkeley: University of California Press, 1975.
———. *Experiment in Autobiography*. New York: Macmillan, 1934.
———. *The Fate of Homo Sapiens: An unemotional Statement of the Things that are happening to him now, and of the immediate Possibilities confronting him*. London: Secker and Warburg, 1939.
———. *The Fate of Man: An unemotional Statement of the Things that are happening to him now, and of the immediate Possibilities confronting him*. New York: Alliance, 1939.
———. *The First Men in the Moon*. London: W. Collins Sons, n.d.
———. *The Food of the Gods*. New York: Charles Scribner's Sons, 1924.
———. *'42 to '44: A Contemporary Memoir Upon Human Behaviour During the Crisis of World Revolution*. London: Secker and Warburg, 1944.
———. *God the Invisible King*. New York: Macmillan, 1917.
———. *Guide to the New World: A Handbook of Constructive World Revolution*. London: Victor Gollancz, 1941.
———. *The Happy Turning: A Dream of Life*. London: Heinemann, 1945.
———. *H.G. Wells in Love: Postscript to an Experiment in Autobiography*. Edited by G.P. Wells. Boston: Little, Brown, 1984.
———. *H.G. Wells's Literary Criticism*. Eds. Patrick Parrinder and Robert M. Philmus. Sussex: Harvester, 1980.
———. *The History of Mr. Polly*. New York: Press of the Reader's Club, 1941.
———. *Imperialism and the Open Conspiracy*. London: Faber & Faber, 1929.
———. *Joan and Peter*. New York: Macmillan, 1918.
———. *The King Who Was a King: An Unconventional Novel*. Garden City, NY: Doubleday, Doran, 1929.
———. *The Man with a Nose and the Other Uncollected Short Stories of H.G. Wells*. London: Athlone Press, 1984.
———. *Men Like Gods*. London: Cassell, 1923.
———. *Mind at the End of Its Tether*. New York: Didier, 1946.
———. *A Modern Utopia*. Lincoln: University of Nebraska Press, 1967.
———. *Mr. Britling Sees It Through*. New York: Macmillan, 1916.
———. *The New America: The New World*. London: Cresset Press, 1935.
———. *New Worlds for Old*. New York: Macmillan, 1908.
———. *The Open Conspiracy*. Garden City, NY: Doubleday, Doran, 1928.
———. *The Outline of History*. Garden City, NY: Garden City Publishing Co., 1931.
———. *Phoenix: How to Rebuild the World: A Summary of the Inescapable Conditions of World Reorganization*. Girard, KS: Haldeman-Julius, 1942.
———. *The Salvaging of Civilization*. New York: Macmillan, 1921.
———. *The Secret Places of the Heart*. New York: Macmillan, 1922.
———. *Select Conversations with an Uncle (Now Extinct)*. London: University of North London Press, 1992.
———. *The Shape of Things to Come*. New York: Macmillan, 1934.
———. *Social Forces in England and America*. New York: Harper & Bros., 1914.
———. *Star-Begotten: A Biological Fantasia*. New York: Viking, 1937.
———. *The Story of a Great Schoolmater*. New York: Macmillan, 1924
———. *This Misery of Boots*. n.p., Folcroft Library Editions, 1973.
———. *The Time Machine*. Everyman's edition. London: J.M. Dent, 1961.
———. *Travels of a Republican Radical in Search of Hot Water*. Harmondsworth: Penguin, 1939.
———. *The Undying Fire*. New York: Macmillan, 1919.
———. *The War of the Worlds*. New York: Harper and Bros., 1900.
———. *Washington and the Riddle of Peace*. New York: Macmillan, 1922.
———. *The Way the World Is Going: Guesses and Forecasts of the Years Ahead*. Garden City, NY: Doubleday, Doran, 1929.
———. *The Way to World Peace*. London: Ernest Benn, 1930.
———. *What Is Coming? A European Forecast*. New York: Macmillan, 1916.

_____. *The Work, Wealth and Happiness of Mankind*. Garden City, NY: Doubleday, Doran, 1931.

_____. *World Brain*. Garden City, NY: Doubleday, Doran, 1938.

_____. *World Encyclopedia*. n.p., Folcroft Library Editions, 1973.

_____. *The World of William Clissold*. New York: George H. Doran, 1926.

_____. *The World Set Free*. New York: E.P. Dutton, 1914.

_____. *A Year of Prophesying*. London: T. Fisher Unwin, 1924.

_____. *You Can't Be Too Careful*. New York: G.P. Putnam's Sons, 1942.

_____, Julian Huxley, and G.P. Wells. *The Science of Life*. New York: Literary Guild, 1934.

Wilde, Oscar. *The Soul of Man Under Socialism and Other Essays*. New York: Harper and Row, 1970.

Wittgenstein, Ludwig. *The Blue and Brown Books*. New York: Harper, 1965.

_____. *Tractatus Logico-Philosophicus*. Translated by D.F. Pears and B.F. McGuinness. London: Routledge and Kegan Paul, 1978.

Wykes, Alan. *H.G. Wells in the Cinema*. London: Jupiter, 1977.

Index

Titles with no author attributed are by Wells.

academic personality type 82
Adorno, Theodor 107
All Aboard for Ararat 69
The Anatomy of Frustration 153, 159
Anticipations 36
anti-semitism, Wells's purported 69–72, 74–75
anti-utopia defined 3
Apropos of Dolores 17, 51, 58
Arendt, Hannah 47, 48, 92–93, 96
arguments, persuasiveness of 165
Aristotle 111, 112–113, 120, 186n72, 186n73, 187n102
arrogance of reformers decried by Wells 32
art 49, 60–61, 149
atheism 66, 181n75
atomic bomb 188n113
authority 92–97
autobiography 151
Ayer, A.J. 42, 43

Bacon, Francis 45, 171
Baier, Annette 181n75
Bauman, Zygmunt 10
Beauvoir, Simone de 131
Bester, Alfred 34
Bettelheim, Bruno 138, 190n17
Big Planet (Jack Vance) 107
bigotry 27
biography, limitations of for utopian purposes 54
Black, Max 23
Bloch, Ernst 194n41
Bonar, James 118
Borden, Lizzie 176n20

Borges, Jorge Luis 173n5
Borrello, Alfred 137, 190n16
Bosanquet, Bernard 146
Brave New World (Aldous Huxley) 34, 65, 106
Brecht, Berthold 132
Broad, C.D. 183n128
Buber, Martin 179n38

The Camford Visitation 168
Campanella, Tommaso 36, 171
capital punishment 33, 35, 177n54
Caudwell, Christopher 142–143
Caws, Peter 46
chairs, problem of defining 23
Cherryh, C.J. 15
Chesterton, G.K. 37–38, 193n18
City of the Sun (Tommaso Campanella) 36, 107
classification 21, 23, 29–32, 34; *see also* human types
comedy 150
communication technologies, significance of advances in 127, 151
compassion 44–45, 64, 123
Comte, Auguste 67–68
consciousness 24, 25, 26
"The Contemporary Novel" 53, 60
Cornwell, John 182n90
Cratylus (Plato) 174–175n29
creativity unleashed in utopian society 149
crime 33, 34, 35
critics, superior, Wells's reply to 51
The Croquet Player 140, 191n18
Crux Ansata 70–71, 182n90

201

Dahrendorf, Ralf 5
Darwinian evolutionary science 1, 3, 13
Davies, Paul 194n40
Dawkins, Richard 173n8
death 9, Chapter 5 *passim*
death penalty *see* capital punishment
democracy 99, 183n128
The Demolished Man (Alfred Bester) 34
Dennett, Daniel 173n8, 180n49
deontological ethics 189–190n8
differences between men and women, essential 190n16
The Dream 25, 153, 159
dualism 191n19
dystopia defined 3

ecology 109–110
economics as religion 116
education 68, 75–90 *passim*, 138–144; chief elements of 75; formal 76–80; objections to Wells's views on 88–90
Eisenhower, Dwight D. 124
Eliot, T.S. 181n72
ellipses as used by Wells 61–62
emotivism 43, 45
eugenics 36–40, 177n58
evolution, implication of for utopian thought 13–14
extinction 167–168; *see also* death

Fact and Fiction (Bertrand Russell) 176n33
The Family Idiot (Jean-Paul Sartre) 178n2
family structure 151–152; *see also* sexual relations
Feuerbach, Anselm 163–164
fiction, importance of 8, Chapter 2 *passim*, 150
Figes, Eva 150, 182n112
film and utopia 54–56, 179n44
Findley, Timothy 46
Fiske, John 173n3, 192n3
Flew, Antony 178n7
The Food of the Gods 42
footnotes, significance of 7, 174n14
forms, Platonic 21–22, 24
'42 to '44 60, 177n54
freedom 48, 49, 104–105, 106–107, Chapter 4 *passim*, 189n127
Fromm, Erich 104, 141–142
Frye, Northrop 48

Galsworthy, John 188n113
Gass, William H. 48
God, the Invisible King 162

Goethe, Johann Wolfgang von 180n54
Gould, Stephen Jay 173n8
Green, T.H. 187n96
Grierson, John 179n44
guaranteed annual income 148

hair growth, restorative effect of utopia on 192n42
Haldeman, H.R. 183n124
happiness 169
Hartshorne, Charles 193n23
Hayek, F.A. 112, 113–118, 119, 128–129, 186–187n80, 187n84, 187n86, 187n91; defends injustice 114, 187n90; refuted by love 153–154
health in utopia 147, 192n46
Hegel, G.W.F. 122
Heidegger, Martin 157–158, 171
Heilbroner, Robert 89
Heraclitus 12
H.G. Wells and the Culminating Ape (Peter Kemp) 184n146
H.G. Wells: Traversing Time (W. Warren Wagar) 183n126
The History of Mr. Polly 135–136
history, teaching of 78–79
Hobbes, Thomas 191n32
Holmes, Sherlock 178n1
The Holy Terror 144
home-building in utopia 185n61
human nature 9, 26, 49–50, 105, 136–137, 139, 140
human types 29–30, 40; Base 40; Dull 31–32; Kinetic 31; Poietic 30–31
humanism 67, 121, 188n106
Hume, David 65
Huxley, Aldous 34, 180n70
Huxley, T.H. 1, 13

imagination 42–47, 50, 81, 165–166, 185n50
individuals and individuality 4, 19, 21, 24, 25, 26, 57, 82, 95, 130, 135–136, 147
Irwin, T.H. 186n73

James, Henry 59
James, William 123–124
Johnson, Lyndon 94
Judaism 69–70, 71–72
Jung, C.G. 143
justice 33
Justice (John Glasworthy), influence on Winston Churchill 188n113

Kant, Immanuel 63
Kateb, George 137
Kemp, Peter 184n146
kibbutzes 138–139, 190n17
Klein, Naomi 124, 125
Knight, Frank 116
Kostelanetz, Richard 45
Kumar, Krishan 10

labor requirements in utopian societies 148
law 143, 186n76, 191n32
Laws (Plato) 182n107
leaders 94, 99
Leaves of Grass (Walt Whitman) 167
Lenin, Vladimir 94
Leviathan (Thomas Hobbes) 191n32
liberalism, classical 72–73
liberty 143
love 62, 153–155, 164; as repudiation of free market ideology 153; *see also* sexual relations
"Lover-Shadow" 164
Lukács, Georg 52–53, 169

"Man of the Year Million" (Frederik Pohl) 20
Mankind in the Making 32
Mannheim, Karl 56
Manuel, Frank and Fritzie 173n5
Marcuse, Herbert 47, 56, 59
Maritain, Jacques 140, 191n20
Marxism; Karl Marx 68, 143, 145–146, 181n85, 191n31
meaning 169–170, 172
Meighen, Arthur 186n79
Men Like Gods 20, 128, 144, 158–159, 191n32
Mencken, H.L. 83
"Mind of the Race" 162
Mr. Britling Sees It Through 66, 127
"A Misunderstood Artist" 48–49
A Modern Utopia 5, 10, 13–14, 77, 81, 110, 128, 140, 180n70, 184n27
Monty Python and the Holy Grail 181n88
Moore, G.E. 190n8
moral purpose of utopianizing 6
morality and freedom 130–132
More, Thomas 111, 121, 148, 157, 171, 188n105
Morgan, Robin 58
Morton, A.L. 145–146, 180n68
Mumford, Lewis 10
myths, Platonic 73, 93–94

New Worlds for Old 181n85, 185n61
Newbolt, Henry 10

Nixon, Richard 183n124
novel defined 52
Nozick, Robert 107
Nussbaum, Martha 16, 57, 180n54

oligarchical ruling class, concerns about 88–89
"On Extinction" 168
Open Conspiracy 102–104, 106
original sin 137, 139, 140, 150, 191n20
Orwell, George 10, 124, 180n68
The Outline of History 11
Outlines of Cosmic Philosophy (John Fiske) 192n3

personality 25, 159–163
Phaedo (Plato) 156
philosophy, limits of 8, 42, 44–46, 52, 113, 163, 178n7, 178n12
Phoenix 177n58
Piercy, Marge 20
Pius XII 71, 182n90
Plato 5, 11, 12, 21–23, 24, 36, 44, 73, 79–80, 83, 90, 93, 96, 97–99, 104, 107–108, 111, 120, 152, 154, 156, 159, 165, 171, 174–175n29, 175n1, 175n4, 182n107, 183n114, 183n128, 185n50, 187n102, 192n52
pluralism opposed to revelation 73
Pohl, Frederik 20
political coercion 145
Politics (Aristotle) 186n67, 186n72
Popper, Karl 63–64
power 97–104, 125
Principia Ethica (G.E. Moore) 190n8
Principle of Hope (Ernst Bloch) 194n41
Principles of Mathematics (Bertrand Russell) 176n33
prisons 33
Pritchett, V.S. 174n28
private property 107–120, 186n67, 186n72, 186n73, 186n74
The Prophetic Soul (Leon Stover) 84–85

questions, necessity of in educative process 80

relativism 14–15
religion 62, 66–75, 136, 181n72
Republic (Plato) 11, 63, 107–108, 152–153, 154, 156, 175n35, 175n1, 182n111, 182–183n113, 184n2, 184n20, 187–188n105, 192n52
The Research Magnificent 159
revelation, opposed to pluralism 73

Der Ring des Nibelungen (Richard Wagner) 135
Robinson, T.M. 193n5
Roman Catholicism 70–71
Rotblat, Joseph 188n113
Rubinstein, Anton 126
Rule of Law 113–115, 119
ruling class: Platonic 98–99; Wellsian 100–102
Runcini, Romolo 171
Russell, Bertrand 126, 176n33, 178n4, 178n12

Sacks, Oliver 193n19
Sagan, Carl 173n8
Samurai (Wellsian leaders in *A Modern Utopia*) 100–102
Santayana, George 50, 62, 178n12
Sartre, Jean-Paul 52, 96, 131, 133, 135, 150–151, 167, 178n2
scarcity 132–133, 134, 189n6, 189n7
Schopenhauer, Arthur 66, 174n32
science 84–90, 185n48
The Science of Life 143
Secret Places of the Heart 136
self-definition 25–28
sexual relations 152–153; *see also* love
The Shape of Things to Come 35, 51, 78, 128, 144
The Shock Doctrine (Naomi Klein) 124–125
short story defined 179n29
Simpson, O.J. 176n20
Skinner, B.F. 189n127
slaves, slavery 187n90, 187n102
social divisions: Platonic 22–23; Wellsian 29–33, 40–41
socialism 53, 108–109, 136–137
Solzhenitsyn, Aleksandr 180n68
soul, Platonic 22, 156, 193n5
specialization 145–146
Star Begotten 32
Star Trek (television series) 55, 180–181n71
Sterne, Laurence 61
Stover, Leon 84–85, 184n137, 191n34
Stowe, Harriet Beecher 188n113
suicide 192–193n4
Szilard, Leo 188n113

Teilhard de Chardin, Pierre 162
theism, Wells's misguided foray into 66
Theory of the Novel (Georg Lukács) 52
Things to Come 55, 124
Thoughts on Death and Immortality (Anselm Feuerbach) 163–164

The Time Machine 1–2, 159
tragedy 149–150
Tragic Sense of Life (Miguel de Unamuno) 157
transition to utopia 96–97
travel 149
Tristram Shandy (Laurence Sterne) 61
Turner, Mark 57

Unamuno, Miguel de 157, 158
Uncle Tom's Cabin (Harriet Beecher Stowe) 188n113
The Undying Fire 168
unhappiness 76
universe, life extending beyond end of 194n40
Urban, Wilbur Marshall 51, 58, 180n54
utopia: appropriate dimensions of 120–121; defined 3; difficulty of making attractive 16; visions 169, 171
Utopia (Thomas More) 5, 107, 121, 157, 185n20, 187n103, 187n104, 188n105

vagueness 17, 176n33
Vance, Jack 107

Wagar, W. Warren 10, 84, 85, 183n126
Wagner, Richard 135
war 87, 121, 122–125, 187–188n105
The War in the Air vi
War of the Worlds 32
Wells, H.G.: aims as an author 60; disavows being a philosopher 90; historical significance of 10; influence of Plato upon 11–12; moral sympathies of 134
What Is Coming? 175n8
When the Sleeper Wakes 122
Whitehead, Alfred North 46
Whitman, Walt 167
Wilde, Oscar 169
Wittgenstein, Ludwig 170
Woman on the Edge of Time (Marge Piercy) 20
The World of William Clissold 12, 82, 95
The World Set Free 86, 159, 188n113
world-state, necessity of 121–129
Wykes, Alan 54

xenophobic racial classifications 27

You Can't Be Too Careful vi, 165–166, 168–169

zoological parks in utopia 110